Contemporary Social Issues

Series Editor: George Ritzer, University of Maryland

Between Politics and Reason
The Drug Legalization Debate

Erich Goode

State University of New York, Stony Brook

D0089342

St. Martin's Press
New York

To Nachman

Editor-in-chief: Steve Debow
Manager, publishing services: Emily Berleth
Senior editor, publishing services: Doug Bell
Project management: Richard Steins
Production supervisor: Joe Ford
Cover design: Patricia McFadden
Cover photo: UNIPHOTO / Bob Llewellyn
Composition: Ewing Systems

Library of Congress Catalog Card Number: 95-73187
Copyright © 1997 by St. Martin's Press, Inc.

Manufactured in the United States of America.
1 0 9 8 7
f e d c b a

For information, write:
St. Martin's Press, Inc.
175 Fifth Avenue
New York, NY 10010

ISBN: 0-312-13297-2 (softcover)
ISBN: 0-312-16383-5 (hardcover)

Contents

Foreword

As we move toward the close of the twentieth century, we confront a seemingly endless array of pressing social issues: crime, urban decay, inequality, ecological threats, rampant consumerism, war, AIDS, inadequate health care, national and personal debt, and many more. Although such problems are regularly dealt with in newspapers, magazines, and trade books and on radio and television, such popular treatment has severe limitations. By examining these issues systematically through the lens of sociology, we can gain greater insight into them and be better able to deal with them. It is to this end that St. Martin's Press has created this series on contemporary social issues.

Each book in the series casts a new and distinctive light on a familiar social issue, while challenging the conventional view, which may obscure as much as it clarifies. Phenomena that seem disparate and unrelated are shown to have many commonalities and to reflect a major, but largely unrecognized, trend within the larger society. Or a systematic comparative investigation demonstrates the existence of social causes or consequences that are overlooked by other types of analysis. In uncovering such realities the books in this series are much more than intellectual exercises; they have powerful practical implications for our lives and for the structure of society.

At another level, this series fills a void in book publishing. There is certainly no shortage of academic titles, but those books tend to be introductory texts for undergraduates or advanced monographs for professional scholars. Missing are broadly accessible, issue-oriented books appropriate for all students (and for general readers). The books in this series occupy that niche somewhere between popular trade books and monographs. Like trade books, they deal with important and interesting social issues, are well written, and are as jargon free as possible. However, they are more rigorous than trade books in meeting academic standards for writing and research. Although they are not textbooks, they often explore topics covered in basic textbooks and therefore are easily integrated into the curriculum of sociology and other disciplines.

Each of the books in the St. Martin's series "Contemporary Social Issues" is a new and distinctive piece of work. I believe that students, serious general readers, and professors will all find the books to be informative, interesting, thought provoking, and exciting.

George Ritzer

Preface

First, there were the atrocity tales. Federal agents assault the San Diego home of Donald Carlson, a 45-year-old executive for a Fortune 500 computer company, using "flash-bang" grenades and automatic weapons; Carlson is hit three times and winds up in a hospital in critical condition. He was not a drug dealer, of course, but a completely innocent victim. His name was supplied to the police almost at random by a police informant seeking leniency for his arrest (Levine, 1996). The name of a parking lot attendant, Miguel, is given to the Drug Enforcement Administration by Tony, an often-arrested drug dealer. Together with federal agents, Tony entraps his friend in a bogus operation that literally involves the exchange of no drugs—indeed, not even any *mention* of drugs. The dealer walks away scott-free, with $300,000 for his troubles, while Miguel is arrested, ultimately managing to plea-bargain his way down to a four-year prison sentence (Levine, 1996). A 13-member SWAT team breaks down the door of the domicile of a 75-year-old retired Methodist minister, Accelyne Williams, who is chased around the apartment and handcuffed. Rev. Williams suffers a heart attack and dies. It turns out the police had the wrong address (Anonymous, 1996). Kemba Smith, a college student, becomes romantically involved with a drug dealer; she is sucked into some of his operations. Today, Kemba sits in the Federal Corrections Institution for Women in Danbury, Conn., serving out a 24-year sentence; ineligible for parole, she will not breathe the air of freedom until 2016, five presidential elections from her sentencing (Stuart, 1996).

Taken by themselves, these tales are frightening enough. But then there are the statistics, the overall picture. In 1970, there were roughly 200,000 prisoners behind bars in the United States; today, there are over a million, with another half a million in local and county jails. In 1950, 30 percent of all inmates in the United States were Black; in 1970, it was 40 percent. Today, it is a majority, over 50 percent, and growing. Between 1980 and the mid-1990s, the number of *new* commitments per year to state prisons on drug violations jumped well over 10 times—over 1,000 percent—from 8,800 to more than 100,000. In contrast, the increase for violent offenses during that period was only a shade over 50 percent. Today, there are more inmates incarcerated in state prisons for drug violations than for violent offenses. In 1980, drug violators made up 25 percent of all federal prisons; today, it is a clear majority, over 60 percent.

A federally mandated sentence for the possession of 500 grams of *powdered* cocaine is five years imprisonment; possessing only *five* grams of crack draws the same five-year sentence. In federal court, while only 27 percent of powdered cocaine defendants are Black, 88 percent of crack cocaine defendants are African-American (Lindesmith Center, 1996).

Since 1981, with the administration of President Ronald Reagan, the United States has been waging a "War on Drugs." In many ways, this war has been harmful. One of its by-products has been the call for an *end* to the war. The issue has been hotly debated for more than a decade and a half, since this war was launched. Emphatic, righteous voices have chimed in on both sides. Today, what was regarded as an almost "unspeakable" proposal, the legalization of the currently illegal drugs, is seriously advanced in major newspapers and magazines across the country by serious, credible figures. Are we now facing a "new crisis of legitimacy" in the criminal justice system, brought on by a growing public awareness of penal institutions that are almost literally bursting at the seams with new prisoners and of a criminal justice system that administers grotesquely racially biased sentences (Duster, 1995)? Do these new and troubling developments cry out for drug legalization? Many observers believe so.

This small book will attempt to answer such questions. In investigating the drug legalization issue, I remain convinced of several basic propositions. For starters, yes, the current war on drugs has been harmful; yes, changes need to be made. To determine a wise and sane drug policy, we need relevant evidence, facts, information. But ultimately, our decision as to what works best will be based mainly on ideological, not factual, issues. Facts are relevant here; they certainly rule out manifestly loony proposals. But at bottom, we'll choose one over another because it is more likely to yield the results we like. Even if we all were to agree on what the facts are, we won't agree on weighing certain values over others. Thus, investigating questions of value and ideology are central in any consideration of drug legalization.

In the end, I am forced to remain a staunch proponent of a *harm reduction* policy. While the current system desperately needs fixing, I strongly believe that outright legalization would be a catastrophe. (In any case, there is quite literally no chance of implementing such a proposal any time soon; at the present time, discussing it remains little more than an interesting intellectual exercise.) Moreover, as I explain, different observers *mean* very different things when they use the term "legalization." Some imagine that the Netherlands, or the United Kingdom (or Canada, I have been told, or Sweden!), pursues a policy of legalization. Far from it! Hence, I've found it necessary to spell out just what different observers *mean* when they so glibly discuss what they imagine to be "legalization." I heartily endorse some of their proposals; some others would produce results that even those who propose them would have to agree are worse than our current conditions. Still, let's be clear on this: Many observers on both sides of the debate use the issue of harm versus harm reduction as window dressing. For them, the main issue is the triumph of one ideology or worldview over another. The victims be damned! In the face of such arguments, I cannot help but be a staunch pragmatist and utilitarian.

Let us explore, then, you and I, the world of drugs and drug use, drug abuse and drug control, drug criminalization and drug legalization, to determine what we should do about these pressing, disturbing issues. The answers are far from obvious, despite what many combatants in this debate claim; all too often, they attribute their opponents' views to stupidity or villainy. In my view, the issues are complex and are filled with painful dilemmas. We are inevitably forced to accept the least bad of an array of very bad options, a single mix of results that range from poisonous to somewhat less poisonous. And those of us who do nothing will be forced, willy-nilly, to take a stand one way or another, since, if we do nothing, someone else will do it for us. We need to be armed with facts, a clarity of vision, a logical frame of mind, courage, and an awareness of how these issues fit in with the big picture. I hope that this book provides some of these things, and enables the reader to draw his or her own conclusions concerning some of the more urgent questions of our day.

ACKNOWLEDGMENTS

I have adapted a very few sentences, paragraphs, and pages from the fourth edition of my book *Drugs in American Society* (New York: McGraw-Hill, 1993); they are sprinkled throughout this volume. Permission to use this material is gratefully acknowledged. I would like to thank a number of friends and colleagues who have helped me in one way or another in writing this book: Ethan Nadelmann, Barbara Weinstein, Josephine Cannizzo, William J. Goode, and Nachman Ben-Yehuda. The idea for the book was more George Ritzer's than my own. Scholars and researchers too numerous to mention shared necessary information with me. My students asked many questions that clarified my thinking about key issues. Perhaps most of all, I'm grateful to work in an area that offers interesting issues, lively debates, and intelligent researchers and authors. I would also like to thank the reviewers who offered constructive suggestions for the final draft of the manuscript: John F. Galliher, University of Missouri, Columbia; Marvin Krohn, State University of New York, Albany; and Peter J. Venturelli, Valparaiso University.

About the Author

Erich Goode is professor of sociology at the State University of New York at Stony Brook. He is the author, coauthor, editor, and coeditor of a number of books on drug use and deviance, including *The Marijuana Smokers* (Basic Books, 1970); *Drugs in American Society,* 4th edition (McGraw-Hill, 1993); *Deviant Behavior,* 5th edition (Prentice-Hall, 1997); and, with Nachman Ben-Yehuda, *Moral Panics* (Blackwell, 1994).

1

Introduction

In a predawn raid, a dozen Miami police officers crowd around the front door of a house in a poor, dilapidated neighborhood; three officers station themselves on the back porch. Announcing their presence, they break down the door and storm the house, awakening two startled occupants. The pair is led away, dazed, in handcuffs, to a nearby police van. In a modest working-class Los Angeles community, a former heroin addict enters a small, unobtrusive clinic. She signs a form and is handed a small paper cup containing an orange liquid, and she drinks it down. After exchanging pleasantries with the receptionist, she leaves the clinic and walks outside. In an affluent Long Island suburb, a police officer stops a car with a defective taillight. Peering inside, he sees two teenagers squirming nervously on the front seat. A distinctive, unmistakable odor fills the car. Without asking permission, he searches the glove compartment and finds two marijuana cigarettes. He gives them a lecture, drives them home, and informs their parents about the incident. In Amsterdam, an 18-year-old walks into a "hash" shop and looks around. She sees a dozen teenagers getting high and chatting amiably. She walks to the counter, purchases a small packet of hashish, and puts it into her pocket; nodding to an acquaintance, she leaves.

In Iran, a drug dealer is executed. In Colombia, a judge who has sentenced drug dealers to long terms is assassinated by a drug henchman. In Central Asia, an official is handed an envelope filled with American dollars; a caravan of opium passes through his jurisdiction, unimpeded. In a state capitol, the legislature votes to increase the penalty for the sale of 650 grams of cocaine to life imprisonment. The American military invades Panama, engages in a small war, captures its leader, arrests him, and brings him to trial in the United States; he is convicted of drug selling and sentenced to a long prison term. A U.S. senator calls for an expansion of methadone treatment programs; another calls for cutbacks for treatment programs, harsher penalties, and less judicial discretion for cases involving drug possession and sale. The mayor of Baltimore calls

1

for the legalization of all psychoactive drugs. The San Francisco city council bans smoking in all its public restaurants. A newborn baby tests positive for the presence of cocaine; its mother is arrested for "delivering a controlled substance to a minor," and the baby is placed in a foster home. In Malaysia, an American is apprehended with a substantial quantity of marijuana; over the objections of the president of the United States, he is hanged.

It has become something of a cliché among many observers that our current punitive policy of arrest and imprisonment for drug offenders "hasn't worked." Drug abuse is a medical matter, not a criminal matter, we are told—or, alternatively, that it is "none of the government's business." The United States is excoriated as a nation whose politicians are engaged in "pushing wars on drugs and locking people up" (Molotch, 1994, p.221), as if that were a self-evidently unjust and counterproductive policy. But if "locking people up" were so self-evidently ineffective, why is this not blatantly obvious to all who would examine the evidence? Are some of us *incapable* of seeing the truth because of our biases and prejudices? Or is it, perhaps, the fact that some of us *profit* from this ineffective, unjust policy, and we aren't willing to admit its failure? Does our failed policy serve certain *functions* for portions of the population—say, political, economic, ideological, moral, or religious functions—that some of us are reluctant to give up? For instance, do some of us have a need to punish transgressors—in this case, drug offenders, those who have crossed a moral boundary and violated the norms of our society? Or does drug control carve out a domain or an empire for the powers that be that a radically different policy would deprive them of? Do drug offenders serve as a handy scapegoat for the major social problems we can't solve? Or is it possible that the punitive policy doesn't work quite so badly as some critics charge? Or, perhaps, do some of us support a failed drug policy because, although we *know* our current system of drug control is working badly, we fear what may replace it?

The question of drug policy has become one of the burning issues of our day. What do we do about drugs? And what do we do about *which* drugs? What should our drug laws look like? *Should* the possession and sale of drugs be against the law? And should we imprison all drug violators? Or is treatment for all addicts and abusers a wiser policy? Should anyone above a certain age be permitted to purchase drugs legally in commercial and state-controlled establishments much the way we can now purchase alcoholic beverages? Should all drugs be administered by medical prescription? What is our drug policy to be? Should we continue to criminalize? Or legalize?

Last semester, I put questions on what the drug laws ought to be to the 200 students enrolled in my "Alcoholism and Drug Abuse" course.

Just over half the members of the class (51 percent) said that the *possession,* and four out of 10 (39 percent) said that the *sale,* of marijuana should be legalized. But between 80 and 90 percent said that both the possession and the sale of the harder drugs—amphetamine, LSD, cocaine, and heroin—should remain a crime.

In this book, I intend to examine several variations on the legalization proposal and the debate they have stirred up. In so doing, I will also contrast the current system of control with these proposals, as well as consider alternatives to both outright legalization and our current more-or-less punitive or punishment-oriented system.

Most people have an opinion about what is the wisest legal policy to pursue on drug control. And yet, not everyone has access to the relevant facts. True, no conceivable quantity of facts could possibly settle the question in everyone's mind. At the same time, facts are *relevant* to the case; we have no right to close our mind off to information that bears on the question of drug legalization versus criminalization. And while a simple accumulation of the facts will not definitively decide how most of us feel on the issue, the facts should *rule out* some of the less realistic policies. Still, when all is said and done, for many of us, the question of drug policy boils down to what *symbolic message* one or another policy conveys. Regardless of whether it reduces crime or not, does endorsing methadone maintenance clinics for all addicts who wish to enroll tell you the society is too "soft" on drugs? Do needle exchange programs seem to encourage drug use? Regardless of whether it reduces drug abuse or not, does permitting the police to break down doors and roust residents on mere suspicion strike you as unjust? Does it strike you as too much like a military dictatorship? Does the term "legalization" sound like an endorsement of drug use to you? Does locking up street junkies sound harsh and inhumane? The balancing act between ideology and fact will continue to dog us throughout any exploration of the issue of drug policy.

And yet, we must decide—someone *will* decide—what drug policy we will have. Drug suspects will be arrested—or they will not. Drug laws will be passed—or defeated. Needles will be exchanged with government support and approval—or they will not. Methadone clinics will continue to function, increase in number—or be closed down. Drug education programs will be funded—or zeroed out. Decisions like these will be made at the federal, state, and local levels all around the country—and throughout the world as well, for we now live in a "global village," an international community, all of whose lives are affected by what happens continents away. And regardless of what we think, others are making, and will continue to make, decisions concerning what to do about drugs. Do we really want to remain aloof from the issue? Can we afford to?

The issue of whether or not to legalize the production, sale, and possession of the currently illegal drugs has become one of the more hotly debated topics within the larger question of drug policy. It may have cooled off a bit since the early 1990s, but it remains a fiercely contested bone of contention. At present, the likelihood that any major jurisdiction of the United States will sanction full legalization for any of the presently illegal drugs is next to nil. Some observers claim that this makes the question of legalization a trivial, marginal issue. Not so. Legalization is not an all-or-nothing proposition; there are different *degrees* and *aspects* of legalization. Its proponents have offered certain specific reforms that do have some hope of implementation. Our present system of attempting to control drug abuse through the criminal law is vulnerable to criticism; it isn't working well, it costs a great deal of money, it has harmful side effects, and it is badly in need of repair. It is possible that some of the criticisms offered by the legalizers will be adopted—in a watered-down version—by advocates of more-mainstream positions. It could be that bits and pieces of the proposals offered by the legalizers will eventually be approved in one or another jurisdiction. It is possible that the legalizers are laying the foundation for a climate of opinion that will bear legislative fruit sometime in the twenty-first century. In any case, the legalization debate has enriched the discourse on the topic of drug policy and reform. And, to a sociologist, the debate itself is also fascinating for what the advocates of both sides are saying and for what that reveals about both their location in the society and, more generally, the nature of the society in which we live.

UNANTICIPATED CONSEQUENCES

In considering the feasibility of one proposal on public policy versus another, it is absolutely crucial to pay attention to the sociological concept of *unanticipated consequences*. As Robert Merton reminds us, we must distinguish between the *conscious motivations* for social behavior and *objective* or *concrete consequences* (1957, pp.60–61). Legislators, experts, reformers, and the general public can have the most noble and idealistic intentions imaginable for supporting and enacting a given policy, but *ideals* are not the same thing as *results*. All too often, a convergence of real-life forces works to undo what planners and reformers had in mind. We cannot anticipate exactly how a policy will unfold when it is put into practice; often, it has the opposite consequences from those that were intended. When American and Peruvian officials attempted to eradicate cocaine from the highlands of Peru, could they have anticipated that this would assist a terrorist organization, *Sendero Luminoso*, which was aimed at bringing down the Peruvian state and fomenting a world-wide Maoist revolution, by creating a "power vacuum" in the region (Gonzales, 1992)? In the 1970s and 1980s, when the United States backed Afghan rebels in their fight against the then–Soviet Union, could they have known that this would help finance a terrorist organization involved in illegal opium production and dedicated to the destruction of the United States (Weaver, 1995; Weiner, 1994)?

Once we become aware of the yawning gulf between intention and consequence, we begin to ask questions we didn't think about before. Does the punishment of convicted criminals rehabilitate them—or intensify their commitment to crime? Does criminalizing drugs discourage people from using them—or increase their price and make them profitable to sell? Would reform of the present drug laws have the consequences we intend? Or will unanticipated consequences rear its ugly head here, too? Will needle exchanges inadvertently stimulate use? Will legalization announce to the members of the society that it is acceptable to use drugs? Will taxes on cigarettes encourage smuggling and illegal sale? We can't assume we know the answers in advance; these are empirical questions which demand evidence. The point is, drug policies shouldn't just look good on paper—shouldn't, that is, simply *sound good* or *make sense* to intelligent observers. A lot of policies that "sound good" or "make sense" turn out to be disastrous when put into effect. When we keep the notion of unanticipated consequences in mind, we will be forever inoculated from a foolish optimism that will dupe us into thinking we have the perfect solution to America's drug problem. While the concept of unanticipated consequences has often been applied to the ironic and undesired impact of drug criminalization (Reinarman, 1994; Steinberg, 1994), far less often has such systematic discussion been devoted to how it would play out under legalization.

IDEOLOGY AND MORALITY

As more than one observer has pointed out (Grasmick et al., 1992; MacCoun, 1993, p.508;), much of the American public's support for retribution against or punishment of the criminal (the drug offender included) *transcends* the rational or deterrent effect. That is, regardless of whether or not a given law and its enforcement discourage crime, *the very fact* that a punishment is called for is extremely important for a substantial proportion of Americans. As I said earlier, the law has a strong *symbolic* function. For instance, most Americans cast their support for the death penalty in *deterrence* terms—that is, they claim it discourages murder. But most who support it are actually impervious to evidence which shows that execution does *not* deter murder more effectively than life imprisonment does. This is because the retributive or revenge function of punishing the offender is far more important to them than the deterrence function (MacCoun, 1993, p.508). It is almost certain that the same prevails for drug offenses. Regardless of its utilitarian effect, the legalization of the currently illegal drugs "would send a message"—a *symbolic* message—that many Americans find completely unacceptable. Somehow, many observers reason, it *legitimates* drug abuse. To the extent that this is so, much of the evidence that supports or undermines the legalization position is beside the point. Still, such empirical evidence has a *rhetorical* function—it is wielded as a weapon in the debate. And *some* observers are convinced by it, one way or another. (I know I have been.) While evidence may not be decisive for many—perhaps most—observers of the drug scene, it cannot be ignored, either.

The nonempirical or symbolic factor operates in both directions, of course. The legalizers, too, raise some issues that are largely beyond the reach of empirical documentation. As a number of observers have remarked (Kleiman and Saiger, 1990, pp.532–533; Moore, 1990a, p.15), advocates of legalization are making two very different arguments—the first, *utilitarian* or *consequentialist,* and the second, *moral.* The *utilitarian* side of the argument says that legalization will improve the society in a direct, concrete, real-world fashion by reducing some of the pathologies associated with drug abuse: drug-related violence, medical illness and death, moneymaking crimes, bloated criminal justice budgets, overcrowded prisons, and so on. Although we cannot directly or definitively prove or disprove this aspect of the argument with evidence, there is abundant evidence to *address* it. But on the other hand, the *moral* side of the argument is quite beyond the reach of empirical evidence. It says that enforcing a law against the possession and sale of illegal substances, which may be less harmful than substances that are legal, is inherently unjust—*regardless* of its practical or utilitarian consequences. And, they say, society *has no right* to pass or enforce laws against behavior that is harmful to no one except the individual who engages in it (McWilliams, 1993; Szasz, 1992). Such laws are, *by their very nature,* unjust and unfair; they do not deserve to exist. Legalization promotes the good society, its advocates would say, because it would represent the repeal of a law that is *inherently* in violation of a major feature of the good society. There is no empirical or factual evidence that could possibly be gathered that would test or even address this aspect of the legalization argument; one is free to accept or ignore it according to one's personal taste.

The moral argument is not insignificant. However, this book is a *sociological* essay on the legalization debate; hence, the practical, utilitarian, or consequentialist argument will be weighed more heavily than the moral argument. Given what we know about drug use in America at the present time, what is likely to happen if the presently illegal drugs were to be legalized? What are the costs of legalization likely to be, compared with the costs we now suffer with the current system? What alternatives to legalization do we have at our disposal?

Nonempirical ideological and moral values operate at a second level as well. Not only do different drug policies represent or symbolize different values to different observers; in addition, as we'll see, different policies produce a different and unique package of consequences. And choosing among those consequences entails choosing one value over another, not applying some objective scientific or medical measuring rod. Says Mark Kleiman, during Prohibition, hundreds of Americans died in gangland "beer wars," and 8,400 died of cirrhosis of the liver; after the repeal of Prohibition, the "beer wars" were gone, along with their murders, but 2,500 more Americans died of cirrhosis of the liver during a comparable period of time. Asks Kleiman: "Was that an improvement?" (1992b, p.17). He implies that the answer to this question is far from obvious. If cocaine were to be legalized, warfare among rival drug gangs would probably end. "But how many more would die from taking cocaine?" he asks (p.17). How do we measure one harm against another? What if a change in the drug laws results in fewer deaths and more addicts? Less crime and more drug use? What if our policy helps one social category but harms another? Too often, observers assume that their solution to the existing problems will produce nothing but positive results. But how do they juggle a mixture of positive and negative results? These questions are neither trivial nor facetious, nor is the answer to them self-evident. Again, choosing one value over another never represents a simple application of a scientific or medical principle. Morality and ideology always play a central role in matters of legal and public policy.

DRUG LAWS: AN INTRODUCTION

Humans have been ingesting psychoactive or psychotropic—*mind-influencing* or *mind-altering*—substances for well over 10,000 years, but not until the last few hundred have people attempted to control the distribution of such substances through the criminal law. Not all these attempts have been successful; it is entirely possible that there have been at least as many failures as successes.

> In the 1600s, after Europeans brought tobacco products back from the Western Hemisphere, rulers from England to Japan banned the sale and consumption of tobacco. These efforts failed everywhere and were quickly abandoned (Blum, 1969).

Between 1841 and 1855, in North America, 13 of the United States and two provinces of Canada banned the sale of alcoholic beverages; in less than a decade, the legislatures of these jurisdictions repealed their laws, modified them to allow liquor sales, or permitted them to languish unenforced (Lender and Martin, 1987).

In 1875, a city ordinance was passed in San Francisco forbidding opium smoking; within a half-dozen years, similar laws were enacted from coast to coast.

In December 1914, the Harrison Act required all persons who produced or sold cocaine and opium products (heroin and morphine included) to register with the government and keep records of the manufacture and sale of these drugs.

In 1920, national alcohol prohibition became the law of the land in the United States; in 1933, widely regarded as a disastrous failure, it was repealed.

During the 1920s, Canada passed a series of anti-opium laws which seemed to target specifically Chinese immigrants.

During the 1920s, half the states of the United States had passed a law outlawing the possession and sale of marijuana; by 1937, every state in the Union had passed such a law, and during that year, a federal law, the Marihuana Tax Act, was enacted.

In the 1980s, two conservative American presidents, Ronald Reagan and George Bush, waged a "War on Drugs." Congress passed a series of harsh penalties for a wide range of drug violations. This figurative war even became a literal one: The military was enlisted, for surveillance, apprehension, and search-and-destroy missions. By the late 1980s, it was clear that this war had failed; heroin and cocaine were cheaper, purer, and more abundant than ever, and, according to several key indicators, abuse of these two dangerous drugs had actually increased during this period.

Long before any drug policy is put in place, its merits and demerits are debated—in the media; by intellectuals and academics; by the medical fraternity and scientific researchers; by officials, politicians, and agents of social control; and by the general public.

On the one hand, there are a number of questions for which the disciplines that study drug use have a fairly reliable and valid answer. For instance, pharmacology, the field that studies drug effects, has learned a great deal about how drugs get users high—they know, that is, about the various drugs' *mechanism of action* (Goldstein, 1994). For each drug currently in use, we can predict the short-term and long-term effects that are likely to take place and at which dosage levels these effects occur.

Epidemiologists, medical scientists who study the distribution of diseases (including, by extension, drug abuse and addiction) in the population, have shown which drugs users are more likely to become dependent on, and for which drugs that potential is low. They have also found out that some drugs carry a higher than average risk of death by overdose and that, for others, that likelihood is relatively low. Sociologists and other social scientists have determined what percentage of the population, as well as which categories in the population, are more likely to use which drugs, and which ones use them less.

On the other hand, the answers to some other issues are not nearly so clear-cut; they remain controversial. The question of drug policy is one of these controversial issues. How do we deal with or control substances that affect the mind? The possession and sale of which substances should be controlled by the criminal law? Should the public be permitted legal access to certain psychoactive drugs? Do the drug laws do more harm than good? How do we measure the effectiveness of one policy against another? What should the government do about use, possession, and sale of substances that affect the mind? Change the present drug laws? Make the penalties for violations harsher or more lenient? Leave the laws on the books as they are? Enforce them more vigorously—or less? Use more judicial discretion in sentencing—or less?

Over the last decade, the legalization of the currently illegal drugs has been seriously proposed by a wide range of observers, commentators, and critics. The details vary from one specific proposal to another, and we'll look at several momentarily. One expert has referred to legalization as "a frustratingly vague and often confused term which means very different things to different interpreters" (Currie, 1993, p.164). Still, the broad outlines of all legalization proposals are essentially the same: the removal of one or more criminal penalties from the possession and sale of one or more currently illegal psychoactive substances. In turn, such proposals have been met with a range of responses from observers in different quarters.

DEFINITIONS: WHAT IS A DRUG?

Even before we tackle the issue of drug *policy,* it might be a good idea to address the question of *what a drug is* in the first place. There are many ways to define drugs—at the very least, as medical substances, as illegal or controlled substances, as publicly defined substances, as substances taken for a certain effect. Some definitions even rely on a *subjective* criterion: A drug is what the members of a society say or *think* it is. There is no single definition that is definitive or correct for all contexts. At the same time, some definitions are a great deal more useful for certain purposes than others. And some definitions actually prevent us from reaching a sound understanding of drug use and what the most productive policy toward drugs might be.

The first distinction we should make is between definitions of drugs that are based on the *legal status* of a substance and those based on *psychoactivity*. Some definitions rely on whether substances are *legal* or *illegal*. In contrast, a definition based on *psychoactivity* refers to the fact that some substances influence the workings of the mind. Let's look at these two definitions of drugs, one based on legal status and one based on psychoactivity, in a bit of detail.

LEGALISM

Once again, a *legalistic* definition holds that drugs are defined by the law. For instance, it is the policy of the federal government that *the drug problem* is made up only of the *illegal* drugs. The consumption of alcohol and cigarettes may be a problem in themselves, but since alcohol and cigarettes are not illegal, to the legalistic definition, *they are not drugs;* therefore, the problems caused by them are not part of "the drug problem." By wrapping a definition of a drug up in its legal status, one is judging alcoholism and the addiction to tobacco cigarettes to be *irrelevant* to the drug problem—*beside the point*. The legalist seems to be saying that the drug problem is defined by a violation of the law, *not* by harm to the society. In effect, according to the legalistic definition, the user of an *illegal* drug is seen as engaging in "a species of treason" (Zimring and Hawkins, 1992, p.9); he or she becomes "a declared enemy of the state" (p.9). What seems to concern the legalist "is the threat that illegal drugs represent to the established order and political authority structure. In this view, it is the consumption of the prohibited substance rather than any secondary consequences that might ensue that is the heart of the matter. The taking of drugs prohibited by the government is an act of rebellion, of defiance of lawful authority, that threatens the social fabric" (p.9).

The legalistic approach—which focuses on *illegal* but ignores *legal* psychoactive substances as drugs—provides the foundation-stone for the campaign funded by the Partnership for a Drug-Free America, which accepts millions of dollars from legal drug manufacturers but overlooks the harm caused by alcohol, tobacco, and pills (Cotts, 1992). It was behind the then–First Lady Nancy Reagan's 1986 statement that "Drug use is a repudiation of everything that America is," and her 1988 declaration that the casual drug user is an "accomplice to murder." Like the Partnership for a Drug-Free America, Nancy Reagan does not regard the *legal* psychoactive substances as drugs at all, in spite of their impact on the mind and the harm their use causes. The legalistic definition is behind the federal government's policy statement, the *National Drug Control Strategy* (issued in 1989), which it regards as the nation's blueprint for controlling drug abuse. In it, we are told that "drugs represent the gravest present threat to our national well-being," that "there is no such thing as innocent drug use," that "more police" and "more prisons" are needed in the War on Drugs—but, again, alcohol and tobacco are excluded. (Indeed, the concept "drug" is not defined anywhere in this crucial document's 150 pages!)

The legalistic definition is based on a *double standard* from the point of pharmacology, the study of drug effects; it is a definition that is based on *ideology* and *morality,* not on the effects of drugs themselves. By excluding the legal substances from a definition of drugs, the legalist emphasizes that what matters in the issue of drug control is not what a drug does to the body or mind but how a drug is classified by the law. Says Mark Kleiman, any drug policy that omits alcohol and tobacco from consideration "is about as useful as a . . . naval strategy" that omits the Atlantic and the Pacific oceans (1992b, p.7). I agree. I believe that the legalistic definition of drugs represents a barrier to our understanding of the drug legalization debate. In effect, the legalistic definition *closes off* the debate on legalization. If the currently illegal drugs were legalized, would that mean that, overnight—according to this definition—they would magically *cease to be* drugs? This is what the legalization definition would be forced to say. In contrast, many observers feel, it is more useful to think of the legal status and psychoactive properties of substances as distinct qualities that overlap but are not dependent on one another.

PSYCHOACTIVITY

One of the most commonly promulgated definitions of what a drug is— and the one I've used from the very beginning of this discussion—is: *any and all substances that influence or alter the workings of the human mind.* What I have been referring to as "drugs" are *psychoactive* (or psychotropic) substances, that is, substances that influence mood, emotion, feeling, sensation, perception, and thinking. This does *not* mean that substances that are not psychoactive are not drugs in some *other* essential or concrete way. In fact, definitions are neither wrong nor right in some abstract, objective sense; a "correct" definition is one that is both widely adopted and useful. When I say that we will agree that psychoactivity defines what drugs are, I mean that *this* definition is the one that is most relevant for an understanding of what the most viable and workable drug policy is. Other definitions may be perfectly valid in *other* contexts. Thus, penicillin and antibiotics, which are not psychoactive but are used in medical therapy, will not be discussed as drugs in this discussion, but alcohol and tobacco will be. According to the definition of psychoactivity, any substance that influences the workings of the human mind in a significant way must be considered a drug; anything that does not should *not* be considered a drug and, hence, will *not* enter into our discussion at all, except, perhaps, by way of comparison.

Of course, psychoactivity is a matter of degree. Some drugs influence the mind in significant and profound ways, while others are far milder. Coffee is an extremely *mild* psychoactive agent; LSD is an extremely potent one. In addition, some substances generate a psychic or emotional state that causes a dependency that is very hard to break; here, cigarettes provide an excellent example. In contrast, other substances are given up extremely readily. Our interest here will be focused on the substances that cause significant transformations of the mind that, in turn, produce behavior that some of the members of the society wish to control. The psychoactivity of drugs is important to us because it is often at the root of social policy: Because some of us get high or become dependent on such substances, others want to step in and prevent our use of them. It is from this starting point that our story unfolds.

Thus, alcohol can produce an intoxication at moderate doses; hence, it is a drug. Tobacco produces a dependency; hence, it is a drug. (The same is true of alcohol.) In addition, tobacco produces a sensation of well-being which one drug expert has dubbed "a low-key high" (Goldstein, 1994, p.111). Users take marijuana, cocaine, and heroin to get high; hence, they are drugs. Psychoactivity influences use and abuse in crucial ways; and how drugs are used and abused, in turn, influences why they are, whether they can be, and whether they should be, legally controlled. But let's be clear about this: The distinction between legal and illegal drugs is an *artificial* or humanly fabricated distinction. The *law* does not decide what effects drugs have, or what their dangers are (although the law may *influence* how and under what circumstances drugs are taken and, therefore, can influence how harmful they become). There is absolutely *no* natural or pharmacological distinction between alcohol and nicotine on the one hand and the illegal drugs, viewed as a whole. All influence the workings of the mind, all can produce a dependency or addiction, and all can be dangerous. Thinking that alcohol and tobacco are not illegal and, therefore, are not drugs implies that they are perfectly safe, while only the illegal "drugs" are dangerous (Goldstein, 1994, p.2); this is a monumental fallacy. It is entirely possible, for instance, that public policy has been too *lenient* toward the legal drugs and too *harsh* toward those that are illegal. These are issues that need to be explored here.

2

Drug Use in America:
An Overview

How will we know a wise and workable drug policy when we see one? How do we know that legalization will be better—or worse—than our current policy? To know what is likely to happen when and if the currently illegal drugs are legalized, it is necessary to know something about the extent of the use of the relevant drugs. How harmful are they? To know this, we have to have a picture of how frequently they are used, and by how many people. How many users will the change in legal policy affect? Again, to answer this question, we have to have an overview of the extent of drug use in America. Will legalization result in a change in patterns and frequencies of drug use? To address this question, we need baseline comparisons against which to compare what the new use rates and frequencies could be. Specifically, we have to know about the extent or *prevalence* of the use of the most commonly taken drugs, their changes over time, and crucial *correlates* or *accompaniments* of the various levels of use. Then, perhaps, we can address the question of whether our current policy is making these things worse or keeping them under control. The drug legalization debate is practically meaningless without a fairly accurate snapshot portrait of current patterns of use.

STUDYING DRUG USE

How many experimenters, users, abusers, and addicts of each drug are there in the United States—and how do we know? To answer these questions, it is necessary to stress two points. First of all, when estimating drug use in the general population, or major segments of it, we need *systematic* information. That means that it is not permissible to rely exclusively on examples, cases, anecdotes, or small, unrepresentative samples; examples are illustrative, not definitive. We need a *cross-sectional* view:

evidence that is drawn from and which reflects the society as a whole, that gives us a picture of what Americans *generally* are doing. And second, to have confidence in the data we do have, we need a *triangulation* of sources. As a general rule, the greater the number of *independent* sources of information that reach the same conclusion, the more confidence we can have in that conclusion. This is what we mean by triangulation: getting a factual fix on reality by using several separate and disparate sources of information. To the extent that several independent data sources say the same thing, we can say that their conclusions are more likely to be true or valid.

The data we have on *legal* drugs is a bit different from the information that comes to us on *illegal* drugs. In principle at least, the sale of all legal products is recorded for tax purposes; we know how many bottles of alcoholic beverages and cartons of cigarettes are sold each year in the United States; we also know how many prescriptions are written annually for each pharmaceutical drug. It is true that a certain proportion of these legal drugs are purchased by private parties abroad and brought back to the United States; hence, they are not included in the sales total, even though they may be consumed here. Quantities of some legal drugs—for instance, bottles of alcohol purchased as a gift for someone else—may be placed on a shelf and never consumed; and some of what was consumed one year was purchased during the previous year. But nearly all experts agree that taking these unrecorded sources of legal drugs into account does not add up to a major change in the picture; basically, we can take the *sales* of legal drugs in a given year as synonymous with the *use* of these drugs. Thus, if want to know about the level of alcohol, tobacco, and prescription drug consumption in the United States, and whether they have increased or decreased over time, we need only look at the sales figures for these three legal products. However, in order to get a closer look at legal drug consumption—for instance, what *segments* or *categories* in the population use these legal drugs—we must rely on surveys. Do men drink more than women? Which racial and ethnic categories smoke tobacco cigarettes the most? The least? Which age categories are most likely to use which prescription drugs? Again, surveys help us answer questions such as these.

For a picture of the extent and frequency of *illegal* drug use and who uses which drugs, experts have to rely mainly or exclusively on surveys. Common sense tells us that most people lie about their participation in illegal or criminal activities, but, in fact, common sense is at least partly wrong. The fact is, if respondents are assured of *confidentiality*, that is, that their names will not be used, that they cannot be tracked down after the survey, and that they will not get into any trouble as a result of telling researchers the truth, most give fairly honest answers—to the best of their ability. Some will lie, of course, and some do not give accurate answers because of problems in recall and interpretation, but most answers will be reasonably honest and accurate. How do we know? Here is where triangulation comes in. We compare the answers respondents give in surveys with independent and fairly "hard" information, such as hospital or medical records, arrest or prison records, and blood or other objective tests; most of the time, the two sources of data correspond *fairly* well, although far from perfectly (Chaiken and Chaiken, 1982; Hindelang, Hirschi, and Weis, 1981; Johnson et al., 1985, p.23). To put the matter another way, the discrepancies tend to be only moderate rather than huge. The figures we get in such surveys are close enough to be useful.

Most researchers feel that the problem of *sampling* the population is somewhat more serious than the problem of getting truthful answers. Sampling difficulties come into play in an especially problematic way when we study illegal behavior, because the segments of the population that are *least* likely to be included in a researcher's sample and be surveyed because they are difficult to locate are also *most* likely to engage in the behavior in which we are interested. For instance, the *homeless* do not appear in a household survey because they do not live in a household; the same is true of jail and prison *inmates* (in the United States today, nearly 1.5 million on any given day). In addition, high school *dropouts* do not appear in surveys on the illegal activities of high school students. It is almost certain that the homeless, the incarcerated, and dropouts are more likely to use, or to have used, psychoactive drugs, than Americans who live in households, are not incarcerated, and/or are attending or have completed high school. Sampling problems usually represent a more formidable challenge to the researcher than problems of responder truthfulness—but they can be overcome. In addition to the problem of getting a sample that looks like or "represents" the population as a whole, researchers face the problem of interviewer refusal; even where researchers are very clever and persistent, some 20 percent or so of the sample refuses to be interviewed. Are those who refuse distinctly different in important ways from people who agree to be interviewed? At times, refusals may bias our results, although usually not fatally.

The federal government sponsors two surveys of drug use which are based on very large, nationally representative samples. One is conducted every year; high school seniors, secondary school, and college students and noncollege young adults are surveyed about their legal (alcohol and tobacco) and illegal drug use, attitudes toward drug use and drug legalization, whether they think that drug use is harmful, and their perceived availability of illegal drugs. Roughly 15,000 to 20,000 respondents are contacted in each category, that is, high school seniors, secondary school students, and young adults, either noncollege or in college. This survey is known as the

"Monitoring the Future" study. (It used to be referred to as the "High School Senior Study," since, originally, it focused its drug questions exclusively on high school seniors.) Another federally sponsored survey asks questions of the residents of households a nationally representative sample of households; it is called the *National Household Survey on Drug Abuse*. Its sample is quite large; it is made up of roughly 30,000 persons age 12 and older who are members of the selected households.

One crucial warning is in order. Looking at the number of users of the various psychoactive drugs and their frequency of use is one crucial piece of the drug puzzle. It's possible, however, that there is a much more important piece of the puzzle: *society's addicts*. It can be argued that the occasional or less-than-weekly drug user rarely poses a comparably serious threat of harm to the society. It is entirely possible that the public health issue, as well as the issue of any and all potential dangers that drug use poses to the society, *is more or less entirely confined to the heavy or chronic user*. The less-than-weekly user of even heroin and cocaine is much less likely to rob to support a drug habit; die of an overdose; contract a serious, life-threatening, drug-induced disease; or kill someone in connection with drug use. It could be that the harms we associate with drug use and abuse are mostly confined to that segment of users we refer to as the behaviorally dependent—in a word, to "addicts." And yet, as we know, addicts tend to be far more difficult to locate and study by means of a survey than occasional users. We'll look at society's addicts and drug abusers more or less throughout this book. The fact is, however, we need to look at both the full range of use—from the experimenter to the addict—*as well as* focus more intensely on the upper end of use: the heavy, chronic, repetitive addict who takes drugs to the point of self-harm and creates major problems for the society. Both are relevant to the question of legalization, but what happens at the upper end of the use spectrum is especially important: The addict is capable of creating far more problems for the rest of us than legal policy can either alleviate or worsen. For this reason, we need to pay special attention to the relatively atypical heavy user. And this denizen is very unlikely to be captured by the conventional sample survey; we need to study him or her through more imaginative research methods. At the same time, we cannot ignore the more typical and common casual user, either. Knowing what the *average* or *typical* levels of use are is an important piece of information; among other things, it provides us with a basis of comparison with the abuser. Hence, use in general is a good place to start. What do our surveys tell us about drug use in the population?

ALCOHOL

Alcohol is the drug that is consumed by the greatest number of users—and by a considerable margin. Roughly two-thirds of the American population age 12 and older (in 1994, this figure was 67 percent) say that they have used alcohol once or more in the past year; 54 percent did so in the past month; and in 1993, just over one in five (21.5 percent) say that they drank once a week or more during the past year (HHS, 1994a, p.119; 1995a, p.85). The "Monitoring the Future" study of secondary, high school, and college students and young adults also shows high levels of alcohol use. Nearly half of *eighth*-graders (47 percent for 1994) had consumed alcohol in the past year, and nearly a fifth (18 percent) admitted having being drunk at least once during that period of time. Half of high school seniors (50 percent) said that they had drunk alcohol in the past *month;* over seven out of 10 college students (72 percent) and non-college young adults (70 percent) had done so (Johnston, O'Malley, and Bachman, 1994, pp.85, 162; 1995, p.43).

Sales of alcohol average out to roughly 2.3 gallons of absolute alcohol per person for the population age 18 or older per year, or just under one ounce per person per day (Williams, Clem, and Dufor, 1994, p.15). This means that the American population as a whole consumes about 60 to 70 billion "doses" of alcohol per year. (Keep in mind that distilled beverages are 40 to 50 percent alcohol, wine is 12 percent, and beer is about 4 percent; thus, how much alcohol is consumed in a given quantity of a beverage has to be calculated from its potency.) However, there is great variation from one person to another in the amount of alcohol consumed. There is a kind of *polarization* in use: While one-third of the American population is made up of abstainers, and over half are moderate or "social" drinkers, that very small one-tenth of the population which is made up of the heaviest drinkers imbibes more than *half* the total alcohol consumed. Thus, the category "drinker" or alcohol "user" represents an extremely mixed bag. It should be emphasized that the concept "alcoholic" is extremely controversial; different experts define it radically differently, and the field cannot agree on how many alcoholics there are in the population (Hilton, 1989). However, taking as our handy working definition of addiction the use of a psychoactive substance on a *frequent, repetitive,* and *compulsive* basis to the point of physical or psychological dependence, one researcher estimated that there are betv 10 and 15 million alcohol addicts in the United States today (Gol? 1994, pp.7, 263).

TOBACCO

Far fewer Americans smoke tobacco cigarettes than drink alcohol; slightly more than a quarter of the adult respondents questioned in recent surveys (28.6 percent) smoked a cigarette in the past month (HHS, 1995a, p.89). However, while fewer people smoke than drink, cigarettes are used *vastly* more often than alcohol. Though three-quarters of the American population abstain completely from cigarettes, those who *do* smoke consume far, far more "doses" of their drug than drinkers consume of theirs. A typical drinker will have one or two drinks during an evening of drinking, and will do so once a week or once or twice a month, whereas a typical smoker will smoke 20, 30, or more cigarettes a day. During the early 1990s, roughly 500 billion cigarettes (or "doses") were purchased in the United States each year, nearly *eight times* as many as drinks of alcoholic beverages. (Is it a bit arbitrary to refer to one cigarette as equivalent to a one-ounce drink of alcohol? Sure it is, but what "dose" of tobacco *would* be equivalent?) Thus, while alcohol is the drug that is taken by the *greatest number of people*, during a given stretch of time, tobacco is the drug that is used the *greatest number of times*. If drug dependence (or "addiction"), as with alcohol, is measured by repetitive and compulsive use of a psychoactive substance (Goldstein, 1994, p.3), there are far more persons dependent on or addicted to tobacco—roughly 50 million in the United States (p.263)—than *all other drugs combined!* Let's put it another way: *While most drinkers use alcohol in moderation, almost all smokers are addicted to tobacco.*

PRESCRIPTION DRUGS

Since the sale of the prescription drugs, like the sale of alcohol and tobacco products, is legal, it is tabulated fairly accurately. In the United States each year, roughly two billion prescriptions, each authorizing the purchase of 30 or so doses (tablets, capsules, or "pills"), are written. A minority of all prescription drugs, roughly one out of seven, are psychoactive, even by an extremely broad definition; the rest work more or less exclusively on the body and do not affect the mind. Eliminating the nonpsychoactive drugs from the total, we see that roughly eight or nine billion doses of psychoactive prescription drugs are administered in the United States each year, or less than one tablet or capsule of a psychoactive prescription drug per adult American per week. This sum is a bit more than one-tenth the total for alcohol, and between 1 and 2 percent of that for cigarettes (again, taking each cigarette, each one-ounce alcoholic drink, and one tablet or capsule as a "dose"). Even so, the sale of prescription drugs represents a substantial, even huge—more than $40 billion a year—industry in America (Ray and Ksir, 1997). And certainly in terms of absolute numbers, many Americans take many doses of prescription drugs. Nonetheless, relative to these two other legal drugs—alcohol and tobacco—prescription drugs do not make up a hugely prodigious source or category of psychoactive drug use. (Of course, some drugs that are dispensed via prescription are *also* manufactured illegally, but, in this case, we would be discussing illegal, not prescription, drug use.) With respect to number of users and total volume of use, the use of psychoactive pharmaceuticals is much more comparable to the use of some of the more popular illegal drugs than to legal use.

Moreover, for most psychoactive prescription drugs, use in the United States is declining over time. There are exceptions, of course. For instance, the sales of Prozac, introduced in 1987, increased five times from its first full year of sale to its third; in 1994, Prozac was the nation's ninth most frequently prescribed pharmaceutical and its most popular antidepressant, by far. But for the vast majority of the psychoactive drugs that were widely prescribed in the 1960s and 1970s—especially those whose use leaked out into the illegal, recreational arena—sales have plummeted. The number of prescriptions written in the 1990s for barbiturates is *one-twentieth* of that written in the 1960s; for the amphetamines, it is less than one-tenth. In the early to mid-1970s, Valium was the nation's number one prescription drug. Today, it posts sales less than one-quarter of its peak; in 1994, Valium ranked 145th in sales among all prescription drugs. (IMS America, of Ambler, Pennsylvania, tabulates the sales of prescription drugs each year. In addition, in the April issue of the journal *Pharmacy Times,* the nation's 200 top-selling prescription drugs are ranked; these 200 drugs make up slightly more than half of all prescription drug sales.) Some prescription drugs that were extremely popular 20 years ago are no longer being prescribed at all, such as methaqualone (Quaalude) and Benzedrine, an amphetamine. (Consider this, however: While certain prescription drugs have declined sharply in popularity, with some, substitutes that did not exist a generation ago are now being sold. Tabulating sales over time for an entire drug type is not a simple proposition.) A generation or more ago, prescription use represented a far more substantial source of all psychoactive drug use; today, although it cannot be dismissed as inconsequential, prescription drug use does not rival that of our two legal drugs, alcohol and tobacco.

CONTINUANCE RATES

An extremely important measure of drug use is something known as the *continuance* rate. This is the "loyalty" of users to each drug: Of all the people who have *ever* taken a given drug, even once, what percentage is *still* using it? What percentage "sticks with" a given drug? For some drugs, the "continuance" rate is high, while for other drugs, most of the people who have used it once or more have given it up or use it extremely infrequently. Of all drugs, the "continuance" rate for alcohol is the highest; roughly six out of 10 people who have ever taken at least one drink of alcohol in their lifetime are still using it, that is, have taken a drink in the past month. Put another way, only four out of 10 of all the people who have taken at least one alcoholic drink were abstainers from alcohol during the past month. With cigarettes, in contrast, the "continuance" rate is roughly four out of 10: Over six out of 10 of all persons who have smoked at least one cigarette are no longer smoking (HHS, 1995a, p.91). The issue of the continuance rates of different drugs is so important that we'll encounter it several more times down the road.

ILLEGAL DRUGS

Illegal drugs are used far, far less often by far, far fewer people than our two legal drugs. Roughly one-third of the American population age 12 and older (31 percent) say that they used marijuana at least once during their lifetime; fewer than one in 10 (8.5 percent) say that they did so during the past year, however; and only one out of 20 (4.8 percent) says that he or she did so in the past month (HHS, 1995a, p.23). The "Monitoring the Future" study shows essentially the same picture: While marijuana is, by far, the most widely used *illegal* drug, its use is far lower than that of alcohol or even tobacco. Just over one in eight (13 percent) claimed to have used marijuana in the past year; one in 13 (7.8 percent) used it in the past month. These figures increase as the person grows older: Three high school seniors in 10 (31 percent), and a bit more than one out of four college students (28 percent) and noncollege young adults (25 percent), used marijuana in the past year; and between one-fifth and one-seventh (19, 14, and 13 percent, respectively) did so in the past month (Johnston, O'Malley, and Bachman, 1994, p.6; 1995, p.59).

Although these figures are much smaller than those for alcohol, the percentages for the illegal drugs *other than* marijuana are, in turn, much smaller than those for marijuana. For instance, cocaine, the second most popular illegal drug in the general population, is used by roughly one-fifth as many Americans as marijuana. Fewer than 2 percent of Americans age 12 and older (1.7 percent, to be exact) say that they have used cocaine even once in the past year; less than 1 percent (0.7 percent) say that they did so a dozen times or more (HHS, 1995a, p.31). In the "Monitoring the Future" study, 2 percent of eighth-graders, 3 percent of high school seniors, 3 percent of college students, and 5 percent of noncollege young adults used cocaine at least once during the past year; the comparable figures for use in the past month was 1 percent across the board (Johnston, O'Malley, and Bachman, 1994, pp.84, 85; 1995, pp.60, 62).

In addition, only about 1 percent or less of the National Household Survey said that they used one or more hallucinogens, such as LSD (1.3 percent); a stimulant, such as amphetamine (0.7 percent); a sedative, such as a barbiturate (0.4 percent); a tranquilizer, such as Valium (1.1 percent); or an analgesic, such as Darvon (2 percent) nonmedically at least once in the past year (HHS, 1995a, pp.49, 61, 67, 73, 79). The annual figures for eighth-graders to college students and young adults which are generated by the "Monitoring the Future" study are several times the national totals. For instance, 3 percent of high school seniors and 6 percent of college students say that they took a hallucinogen during the past year; for the stimulants, the comparable figures are 4 percent for both groups (Johnston, O'Malley, and Bachman, 1994, p.161; 1995, p.62). Heroin is perhaps the *least* often used of the well-known illegal drugs. These surveys specifically ask about "nonmedical" drug use. When prescription drugs such as amphetamine or barbiturates are used for recreational purposes, of course, they are *illegal;* in addition, most recreational use of such drugs stems from illicit or illegal manufacture as well. However, let's keep in mind the three warnings I issued earlier about relying on surveys to estimate illicit drug use in the population: One, some respondents (a minority) lie, forget, or even exaggerate; two, some of the target population (a minority) refuse to participate in the study; and three, some categories (such as the homeless, the institutionalized, and school dropouts) do not appear at all in most surveys like this—and, chances are, they are *more* likely to use drugs, and more likely to do so *heavily,* than the sample we draw and interview.

In addition to vastly lower levels of use for the illegal drugs than for the legal, it is also true that the *continuance* rates of the illegal drugs are far lower. Persons who try or experiment with the illegal drugs are much more likely to give them up or use them extremely infrequently than is true of the legal drugs. Remember that about 60 percent of all persons who have ever imbibed an alcoholic beverage in their lifetime are still drinking, that is, they drank at least once within the past month; fewer than four out of 10 of all persons who have ever had at least one puff of a cigarette are still smoking. For marijuana, the comparable figure is 15 percent; for cocaine it is 7 percent; and for hallucinogens such as LSD, it is less than 6 percent (HHS, 1995a, pp.25, 31, 47). As a general rule, the continuance rates for illegal drugs are significantly lower than they are for legal drugs. This is true in the United States, and it is true in the Netherlands as well (Sandwijk, Cohen, and Musterd, 1991, p.25).

Even though most experts regard these survey data on casual or recreational illegal drug use as fairly accurate and reliable, our estimates of heavy, chronic users are far less reliable. In fact, we have to rely on what is referred to as "guesstimates," based on information sources such as hospital admissions, admissions to drug treatment programs, surveys of street-corner addict populations, anthropological-style observation, and so on. A commonly cited figure for the number of heroin or opiate addicts in the United States is between 500,000 and one million (Goldstein, 1994, p.241); for persons using cocaine weekly or more, it is between two and three million (Kleiman, 1992b, p.288). It should be pointed out, however, that there are different definitions of what defines someone as dependent or addicted; they are not always in complete agreement with one another. Most experts see the use of marijuana and the hallucinogens as less of a public health problem than the use of heroin, cocaine, and amphetamine. For all practical purposes, alcohol, cocaine, heroin, and nicotine constitute the bulk of the public health issue when it comes to psychoactive drugs.

3

Drug Abuse: Definitions, Indicators, and Causes

Clearly, "use" is not the same thing as "abuse." It is one thing to describe patterns, frequencies, and incidences of drug use in the general population; it is quite another to examine the phenomenon of drug *abuse*. Most users are experimental or moderate in their consumption of psychoactive substances; are casual users "abusing" drugs when they "use" them? When I mentioned the issue of drug dependence or addiction, I implied the crucial role that frequency of use plays in abuse. Clearly, addiction or heavy, compulsive use and "abuse" overlap heavily. We'll see their relationship in more detail momentarily. How, in any case, do we know "abuse" when we encounter it? Two definitions of drug "abuse" are widely used. The first is the *legalistic* definition of abuse; it dovetails exactly with the legalistic definition of drugs, which I discussed in the previous chapter. According to the legalistic definition, drug "abuse" is any and all *illegal* or *illicit* use of a psychoactive substance. The only legitimate use of a "drug," this definition holds, is for medical purposes. (Alcohol and tobacco, according to the legalistic definition, not being "drugs," are exempt from this rule.) Hence, drug abuse is *any* nonmedical drug use, that is, *drug use outside a medical context.* The second definition may be referred to as a *harm-based* definition of abuse; it defines abuse by the concrete harm or damage that drugs do and users cause to themselves and others as a consequence of their use. Let's put some flesh on the bones of these definitions.

THE LEGALISTIC DEFINITION OF DRUG ABUSE

The *legalistic* definition of abuse argues that drug "abuse" is defined by the law: It is any and all *illegal* drug use (Abadinsky, 1989, p.5), that is,

23

any and all use of a "drug" outside a medical context. One puff of a marijuana cigarette, by definition, constitutes abuse, because it is illegal; alcoholism to the point of illness and death to oneself, and pain and suffering to others, is *not* drug abuse, because alcohol is not illegal and, therefore, not a drug. Does the legalistic definition make much sense? Not to me. In studying drug use, is our central concern obedience to the law? It's not my central concern. It's difficult to imagine how such a definition of drug "abuse" can be defended. When we look at what impact legalization is likely to make, we're interested in the concrete results this policy would have. As with our definition of what a drug is in the first place, if we based our definition of drug abuse on the law, does that mean that if the law were changed, the use of the currently illegal drugs would no longer constitute abuse? The legalistic definition of abuse says next to nothing about what people are actually *doing* with their lives when they take drugs. What does referring to a certain instance of drug use as "abuse" add to our understanding of the drug phenomenon, above and beyond saying that it is illegal? Absolutely nothing; they are simply two words for the same thing. Paying attention to such a fanciful definition does help us understand what some participants in the drug controversy *believe*, but it is of no use whatsoever as a basis for helping us reach a reasonable and workable drug policy.

A HARM-BASED DEFINITION
OF DRUG ABUSE

In contrast, a definition of drug abuse that is based on harm seems far more useful to me. After all, the term "abuse" conveys an impression that a given person's consumption of a psychoactive substance is harmful; it implies a kind of medical, psychological, or social pathology, a sickness in need of treatment or a solution of some kind. To separate a definition of drug "abuse" from harm, damage, threat, or danger seems extremely unrealistic. Thus, according to this definition, drug abuse is defined by "deleterious effects on the user's life or the lives of others around [him or her]—effects which are a result of drug use" (White, 1991, p.7). However, let's keep in mind that if we base our definition of drug abuse on harm, clearly, we have to agree about what constitutes harm in the first place. And, of course, we have to untangle the question of whether it was the consumption of one or more psychoactive substances that actually *caused* the harm and not some other factor. Nonetheless, after these and other qualifications are registered, harm still seems to be the most reasonable basis for a definition of abuse that researchers have come up with. One qualification has to be registered, however: Drugs can be harmful in different ways. One drug can be harmful in a specific way, while another drug is not—although it is harmful in a very different way. Nicotine, smoked in tobacco cigarettes, is medically harmful when used over the long run; on the other hand, it does not result in discoordination—and, hence, it does not cause accidents which injure or kill. Marijuana does not result in death by overdose, but some experts believe it is a "gateway" drug, or a facilitator or introduction to more dangerous drugs. Heroin does not cause brain or other organ damage, but a user can die of an overdose after administering it. And so on. Still, *all* forms of widely agreed-upon harm are relevant to the picture, and abuse is measured by harm, whatever the source.

All drug experts will agree that we'll never find a perfect measure or indicator of *all* the harm that drug use causes. A teenager gets drunk, drives a car, has an accident, and her injuries paralyze her for life; a 60-year-old man, after decades of smoking, develops lung cancer; two crack dealers engage in a gunfight on the street over a business deal gone bad and accidentally kill an innocent bystander; an addict injects four times her customary dosage of heroin into a vein and dies of an overdose. All of us would agree that these cases represent drug-induced harm. At the same time, how do we find a measure or indicator that tallies these and all other such episodes of harm? The fact is, we can't. There are simply too many different ways that drug abuse can be harmful for us to be able to reduce their variability to a single measure or indicator. The best we can do is to find a small number of measures or indicators and use them as representative of, if not the whole picture, then at least a major portion of it. There is much more to drug-induced harm than these limited indicators, but they also can't be dismissed as unimportant. Each drug can be harmful in its own way, and the intelligent observer looks at several of the most important of these drug-induced harms.

DAWN

A federal agency that is usually referred to by its acronym, *DAWN* (the Drug Abuse Warning Network), collects data on two kinds of drug-induced harm. The first is *emergency room episodes*. The second is *medical examiner reports*. By looking at these two measures, we have some idea of *which* drugs are most likely to be abused, *changes* in drug abuse patterns over time, and which *areas of the country* are most subject to drug abuse. But one absolutely crucial limitation of these figures should be stressed: DAWN only examines *acute* untoward drug-related events, that is, only those that take place within a single episode of use, and only those that are specifically medically related. The agency does not gather data on the *chronic* harms that drugs cause, that is, those that take place gradually, over a long period of use, and it does not gather data on specifically nonmedical events, that is, those that are not caused *directly* by drugs, such as violence or accident. Thus, DAWN does not tabulate statistics on lung cancer, cirrhosis of the liver, murder, automobile fatalities, and so on. If it's drug-related, acute, and medical, DAWN tabulates it. (For two comments on DAWN's limitations and flaws, see Caulkins, Ebener, and McCaffrey, 1995; and Ungerleider et al., 1980).

Emergency room episodes include incidents such as drug-induced suicide attempts, nonlethal drug overdoses, painful or life-threatening withdrawal episodes, and unexpected and undesired drug reactions by users that resulted in a trip to a short-stay hospital, clinic, or emergency room. DAWN estimates that some 466,900 drug-caused emergency room episodes took place in 1993 in the contiguous United States (that is, excluding Alaska and Hawaii). In 1992, two or more drugs were responsible for these episodes in over half (54 percent) of the cases. What are the "big three" drugs—those that are associated with the greatest number of trips to the emergency room, nationwide? They are *alcohol, cocaine,* and *heroin.* Alcohol (which is listed only if it is used in combination with another drug) was mentioned in a third of these cases (33 percent), cocaine in just over a quarter (28 percent), and heroin (or morphine) in roughly one in 10 (11 percent). Of course, a given drug that is *mentioned* may or may not have *caused* the episode, but a drug that appears often in emergency room episodes can be assumed to be frequently abused (HHS, 1994b, p.32; 1994d).

A second drug-related tally that is conducted by DAWN is *medical examiner reports.* These are reports turned in by county coroners on the number of drug-induced causes of death in a given year. Unlike the reports on emergency room episodes, which attempt to be complete for the contiguous United States, medical examiner reports represent only a sampling of drug-induced deaths; 145 facilities located in 43 metropolitan areas reported about 8,500 drug abuse-related deaths in 1993. Still, even with this sampling, again, we should be able to know which drugs are most likely to be related to harmful reactions, whether they are rising or falling over time, and which areas are hardest hit by drug abuse. In a quarter of the cases (23 percent), suicide was judged to have been the motive. Two-thirds of all cases (69 percent) were judged to have been drug-induced overdoses; for the remaining one-third (30 percent), drugs were deemed to have played a significant contributing role. In three-quarters of the reported cases (76 percent), two or more drugs were mentioned. Again, the "big three" among drugs in causing drug-induced or drug-related deaths were cocaine, alcohol, and heroin. Cocaine was the drug that was most often found in the body of the deceased, accounting for nearly half (46 percent) of all drug mentions; heroin (or morphine) appeared in nearly the same number (45 percent), and alcohol in combination with another drug (40 percent) also made its appearance with great frequency (HHS, 1995b, p.16).

DAWN's data are extremely important. They tell us that there are three drugs that stand head and shoulders above all other drugs and drug types in causing or contributing to both acute untoward emergency room episodes and death by overdose: *alcohol, cocaine, and heroin.* No other drug even comes close to these three. (And remember, since alcohol is tallied by DAWN only if it is used in combination with another drug, the number of alcohol-induced reactions, both lethal and nonlethal, is *far* higher than its figures indicate.) DAWN's data indicate that these drugs are abused extremely frequently in the United States. It is also important to look at *frequencies of use,* because this gives us some idea of the *likelihood* that harm will take place in a given episode of use. For instance, in the United States, heroin is used one-tenth as often as cocaine; the fact that it has similar rates of serious harm associated with use indicates that it is a far easier drug to abuse—in a word, a far more *dangerous* drug. Measures of abuse have to be compared with total incidences of use to permit us to understand the degree of *risk* associated with each drug.

TOBACCO

Again, DAWN tabulates only acute, medically related, drug-induced episodes of harm. Interestingly, the drug that produces the greatest number of deaths from *chronic* or *long-term* causes is not heroin or cocaine, and not even an illegal drug at all. This drug causes more deaths than all other drugs combined—alcohol, heroin, and cocaine included. The drug is tobacco, of course. Technically, tobacco is not a drug, but a plant product that *contains* a drug, nicotine; tobacco can be regarded as a vehicle for the *administration* of this drug. In 1991, the Centers for Disease Control estimated that tobacco smoking causes or significantly contributes to over 430,000 deaths in the United States annually. This includes over 110,000 deaths from lung cancer; 50,000 deaths from other cancers; 200,000 deaths from cardiovascular, mainly heart, diseases; and 80,000 deaths from respiratory diseases. Smokers have nearly three times the likelihood of dying before the age of 65 as nonsmokers do—28 percent versus 10 percent—and twice the likelihood of dying before 75—50 percent versus 25 percent. In fact, a smoker has a lower likelihood of reaching the age of 65 than a nonsmoker has of reaching the age of 75! Smoking only a half a pack of cigarettes a day increases one's chance of contracting lung cancer by four times; two-pack-a-day smokers increase their odds 23 times! The American Cancer Society estimates that smoking is responsible for 20 percent of deaths from all sources in the United States each year. It is possible that even *passive* or *second-hand* smoke kills more Americans than all illegal drugs combined—53,000 per year (Anonymous, 1991a, 1991b; HHS, 1987b). As we might expect, representatives of the tobacco industry deny that cigarettes cause any disease or premature death.

Clearly, then, when we discuss the harm that drugs cause, tobacco *towers* above all other drugs; it causes far more medical harm than all other drugs combined. It is in a league of its own. In this sense, most drug *abuse* is cigarette smoking. Clearly, a major reason for this is the fact that almost *all* cigarette smokers are addicts. If, for instance, most drinkers of alcohol were to imbibe at alcoholic levels, alcohol would cause far more death and disease than it does. Of course, remember that tobacco does not harm users in a single episode of use; smokers do not die of a tobacco "overdose." Instead, they die slowly, over a period of years, even decades, when they are middle-aged or even elderly. One drug expert refers to the use of tobacco cigarettes as "addictive suicide" (Goldstein, 1994, pp.101–117). Keep in mind, too, that tobacco manufacturers do not gun one another down in battles over drug "turf"; they do not have to—the product they sell is legal. And the use and sale of tobacco and alcohol does not demoralize entire communities the way the use and sale of crack cocaine and heroin do. Nonetheless, tobacco is a dangerous drug; its use is extremely costly to the society; it causes medical damage, and it kills. In a nutshell, its use constitutes drug *abuse*. It has been said that tobacco is a product that "when used as directed, causes illness and death" (Goldstein, 1994, p.102). Experts estimate that 20 percent of all premature deaths in the United States can be traced to the consumption of tobacco.

ALCOHOL

Alcohol, too, contributes its share to premature deaths in the United States. We've already seen from DAWN's data that alcohol is one of the "big three" drugs in making a contribution to lethal and nonlethal overdoses; it is in the same league in this respect with heroin and cocaine. But alcohol causes far more harm than simply acute medical emergencies, important as they are. A bit more than a third of the 45,000 or so automobile fatalities that take place in the United States are caused by a driver who is legally intoxicated. (This proportion has been dropping, however; in the 1970s, half of all fatal accidents were caused by drunk drivers.) Roughly half the victims of death by accident of all kinds are intoxicated; for boating accidents, this is 70 percent; for victims of a fire, 46 percent; and it is 33 percent for all victims of a fall; a third of all pedestrians killed by a passing car are intoxicated. Not all of these can be traced directly to alcohol intoxication, of course; at any given point in time, a certain proportion of persons going about their routine activities are intoxicated anyway, and most do not fall victim to accidents, lethal or otherwise. To know alcohol's contribution, we'd have to know whether the intoxication figures for accident victims are substantially *higher* than those that we'd observe for *all* persons engaging in the activities from which these accidents are drawn. Half the 20,000 to 25,000 or so criminal homicides are committed by an alcohol-intoxicated assailant, and over a third of homicide *victims*, likewise, are drunk at the time of their demise; a quarter of all suicides are under the influence at the time they killed themselves. Taken together, experts estimate, alcohol's contribution to accident, suicide, and homicide adds up to roughly 60,000 premature deaths in the United States each year (HHS, 1987a, 1990, 1993; Ravenholt, 1984).

Alcohol kills by causing medical damage, too. Of all chronic ailments, alcohol plays the most prominent role in causing cirrhosis of the liver, defined as a "diffuse scarring" of the liver. Almost all cirrhosis fatalities are caused by heavy alcohol consumption, although poor diet does exacerbate the condition. Cirrhosis of the liver claims roughly 25,000 American lives a year (although this figure has been declining since 1973); today, it is the ninth leading cause of death in the United States. Heavy alcohol consumption also contributes or is related to a variety of other illnesses as well. Medical experts refer to this phenomenon as "comorbidity"; rates of alcohol-related "comorbidity" for diseases of the pancreas is 20 percent; for late-stage tuberculosis, 13 percent; for hepatitis, it is 12 percent; and for liver cancer, 11 percent. Medical experts agree that the 3 percent of all deaths in the United States that are officially attributed to causes directly linked to alcohol consumption "represents a considerable underestimation" (HHS, 1990, p.22; 1993; Van Natta et al., 1984—85). In fact, the excessive use of alcohol "is associated with deleterious effects on virtually every part of the body" (HHS, 1990, p.20). Experts place the total number of deaths caused by the consumption of alcohol in the United States somewhere between 100,000 and 150,000. Worldwide, of course, the total is many times this figure.

IS DEPENDENCE ALWAYS ABUSE?

A number of drugs—alcohol, tobacco, heroin, and cocaine most notably—produce an addiction or dependence in large numbers of users. The question of whether dependence is *automatically* abuse, or harmful use, is not as easy to answer as it might seem at first blush. Clearly, the two overlap heavily: Most addiction is made up of abuse, and most abuse is addiction. But is dependence *by definition* abuse? Are the two linked not only empirically—that is, in concrete fact—but also definitionally and conceptually? Goldstein (1994, p.3) includes three elements in his definition of addiction: A drug must be used *repeatedly, compulsively,* and *self-destructively.* But do *all* addicts harm themselves with frequent and compulsive use? There are three separate issues on which the link between dependence and abuse hinge. One issue is the identity of the specific drug itself. The second issue is whether it is the current *legal structure* that causes the harm associated with dependence on drugs, or the intrinsic properties of drugs themselves. And the third is the moral question of whether addiction to a drug represents, *by its very nature,* harm to the addict—and, hence, a form of abuse.

No drug expert doubts that addiction to *certain* drugs entails self-harm—or at least a substantial *risk* of self-harm. *No* alcoholic escapes *some* medical harm after a period of such heavy use. No pack-or-more-a-day cigarette smoker is as healthy as he or she would be in the absence of smoking. (Not all smokers die of a tobacco-related disease, but all increase that risk, and, at the very least, the lungs of all of them are less efficient at taking in, utilizing, and expelling oxygen.) The crack-dependent, likewise, compromise every organ of their bodies. But this is not true of all drugs. The link between heavy marijuana use and damage to the human brain has not yet been established; it may not exist. (However, smoking marijuana does entail much the same—or more serious—pulmonary compromises as smoking tobacco cigarettes.) Ironically, it is the opiates, including heroin—perhaps the most feared and most strongly condemned street drug—that may be the *least* harmful for addicts. Medically, opiate addicts are not harmed by their use of the narcotic drugs. In fact, overdosing aside, narcotics such as heroin are remarkably *safe* drugs; they harm no organ or function of the body (Ball and Urbaitis, 1970; Isbell, 1966; Wikler, 1968). Hence, for *most* drugs, addiction *does* automatically lead to harm and therefore abuse—but this is *not* automatically true of some drugs, particularly heroin and the narcotics.

Doesn't this statement contradict what I said above on the huge contribution that heroin makes to the DAWN overdose statistics? Not entirely. *Empirically,* heroin use is *strongly* associated with a variety of medical harms, including death by overdose, AIDS, hepatitis, pneumonia, and so on. Roughly 2 percent of all heroin addicts die each year in the United States (and in the United Kingdom as well), most from overdoses—an extraordinarily high death rate, given their relative youth (Goldstein, 1994, p.241). But is this death rate a *primary* and *direct* effect of heroin itself? Or is it a *secondary* product of the way heroin is used and the legal structure in which use is implicated? Most experts agree that it is not heroin use per se that causes addiction-related death and disease—that is, it is not a *direct* product of the action of the drug itself but is a product of *who* uses it, *how* they use it, and the *way* it is used. Illegal, illicit street heroin is highly variable in potency (contributing to drug overdoses); it is used by addicts who exhibit little care for their health and often share contaminated needles; and it is used in a reckless, risk-taking fashion, often in conjunction with other drugs, alcohol included. Empirically, opiate addiction *almost always* entails harm and therefore abuse. Theoretically and in principle, however, it *could* entail use without abuse; under ideal circumstances, if standard doses were administered in a sterile setting and addicts took customary steps to protect their health, they would not get sick or die at a rate any different from the nonaddicted population as a whole. But addicts almost never use heroin under ideal circumstances. For all practical purposes, and under the current circumstances, *practically all narcotic addiction entails abuse.*

And lastly, does addiction to a drug, *by its very nature,* entail harm and therefore abuse? After all, hardly anyone would *choose* to be dependent on a drug. Independent of medical harms, is addiction *in itself* a form of harm? My view is, this is not a medical or empirical question, it is a moral or ideological question, a question of values. While we *can* demonstrate that a given drug effect can harm the functioning of an organ in an objective and concrete fashion, we *cannot* demonstrate that addiction, by itself, is, at least with a nontoxic drug, medically harmful. It is inconvenient, but not intrinsically harmful. Who would *want* to be "enslaved" to a drug? But, again, that is a question of values, not of medical harm. Let's simply say that the two dimensions of addiction and harm are *theoretically* separate, while, *in concrete reality,* they are closely intertwined. When we have our hands on an addict or a drug-dependent person, *for all practical purposes,* we have someone who is abusing that drug. For our purposes, the two dimensions are intricately intertwined.

For a moment, let's look at the opposite side of the coin: Are all drug abusers addicted, or dependent? Not necessarily. A certain proportion of users who are not physically or even psychologically dependent use the drug they take abusively, that is, in a fashion that is harmful to themselves. Alcohol causes brain damage at levels of use far below what would constitute an addiction; many nondependent drinkers kill themselves in automobile accidents as a result of being drunk just once in a while—or even once; heroin overdoses can occur even with occasional recreational use; and so on. Clearly, users do not *have* to be addicted or dependent to abuse a drug. Thus, let's be clear about this: *The heavier and more frequent the use, the greater the likelihood of harm.* Abuse is *more likely* to take place at the upper reaches of use levels. While more-occasional users are not *immune* from harming themselves and others, they are *less likely* to do so than frequent, compulsive users. While almost all addicts are abusers, a *minority* of occasional users are. When the frequency of drug use becomes much more than weekly—depending on the drug, of course—the likelihood that it constitutes abuse escalates correspondingly.

CONCLUSIONS ON ABUSE

Basing our definition of abuse on the harm caused by the consumption of psychoactive substances leads us to two important conclusions. First, drug abuse from all sources causes hundreds of thousands of premature deaths each year in the United States; on a worldwide basis, the figure is certainly in the millions. And second, the vast majority of these deaths are caused not by illegal drugs but by our two legal drugs, alcohol and tobacco. In fact, tobacco causes more deaths than all other psychoactive substances combined. As we'll see, these facts will have extremely important implications for the drug legalization debate. I'll be referring to them at the appropriate time. Of course, keep in mind that the medical harms caused directly by the excessive consumption of drugs represent only *one* of a *wide range* of possible drug-induced harms. In fact, drug abuse is a *multifaceted phenomenon;* it comes in many guises. Perhaps one of the most momentous of these facets is what the excessive use of certain psychoactive substances does to the social and economic structure of entire communities.

WHY DRUG ABUSE?

In the late 1970s, the National Institute on Drug Abuse (NIDA) commissioned statements from experts and researchers in the drug field which were intended to explain drug use and abuse. The resulting volume (Lettieri, Sayers, and Pearson, 1980) included some 40 more or less distinct theories or explanations of drug abuse—and this volume was far from complete. A substantial proportion of the theories included in the NIDA volume were *micro* in their approach; that is, they attempted to explain why certain individuals or categories of individuals try, use, and become involved with drugs. A number of these "micro" perspectives focused on the personality of the potential addict or abuser: He or she is inadequate and uses drugs as a means of escape or a "crutch." Micro perspectives, focusing as they do on the individual, are not necessarily wrong, but they do leave a major portion of the drug scene out of the picture. In contrast, a *macro* approach looks at the big picture—not at individuals or personalities but at major *structural* factors, such as the economy, the political situation, social inequality, racism, and the condition of cities, neighborhoods, and communities—a societywide condition of anomie or normlessless. Another important point: The theories in the NIDA volume focused on a variety of different *aspects* of drug use—some on addiction, some on use per se, and some on heavy, chronic use, or abuse. This latter distinction will become extremely important very shortly. An explanation that applies to experimentation, casual, or moderate use may not apply to heavy, chronic use, or abuse.

One theory or explanation the NIDA volume did *not* include makes use of a series of extremely crucial recent "macro" developments that help us understand drug abuse: the *conflict* theory or approach. Conflict theory applies more or less exclusively to the heavy, chronic, compulsive abuse of heroin and crack, and only extremely marginally to the use and abuse of tobacco and alcohol. This is the case because tobacco and alcohol are legal, while the aspects of drug abuse that conflict theory deals with focus largely on the legal picture and its consequences for certain neighborhoods and communities. This theory also applies only marginally to the heavy use of marijuana, partly because it attracts a different (although overlapping) circle of drug abusers than is true of heroin and crack cocaine, partly because it has different consequences for both the user and the community, and partly because the distribution system of marijuana is distinctly different. The conflict theory of drug abuse makes a great deal of sense and helps explain a major portion of the drug abuse picture. It is not a complete explanation of drug abuse—no theory can be that—but it is one that is tied in most closely with the question of legalization and other policy changes.

Conflict theory holds that the heavy, chronic abuse of crack and addiction to heroin are strongly related to social class, income, neighborhood, and power. A significantly higher proportion of lower- and working-class inner-city residents abuse the hard drugs than is true of more affluent members of the society; more important, this is the case because of the influence of a number of key *structural* conditions, conditions that have their origin in *economics* and *politics*. More specifically, several economic and political changes have taken place in the past generation that bear directly on differentials in drug abuse; they are discussed in dramatic detail in Elliott Currie's book, *Reckoning: Drugs, the Cities, and the American Future* (1993). Some version of this theory is endorsed by perhaps a majority of left-of-center African-American politicians and commentators, such as the Rev. Jesse Jackson and the Rev.

Al Sharpton. Sociologist Harry Gene Levine summarizes the perspective in his paper, "Just Say Poverty: What Causes Crack and Heroin Abuse" (1991). In my view, it is the most adequate and most comprehensive explanation for recent developments in the world of drug abuse. The connection that has *always* existed between income and neighborhood residence on the one hand and drug abuse and addiction on the other has become *exacerbated* by these recent developments.

First, over the past 20 years or so, the economic opportunities for the relatively unskilled, relatively uneducated sectors of the society are shrinking. In the 1970s, it was still possible for many, perhaps most, heads of households with considerably lower-than-average training, skills, and education to support a family by working at a job which paid them enough to hoist their income above the poverty level. This is much less true today. Far fewer family heads who lack training, skills, and education can earn enough to support a family and avoid slipping into poverty. Decent-paying manual-level jobs are disappearing. Increasingly, the jobs available to the unskilled and semi-skilled, the uneducated and semi-educated, are dead-end, minimum-wage, poverty-level jobs. In other words, the bottom third or so of the economy is becoming increasingly impoverished. One consequence of this development: the growing attractiveness of drug selling.

As a result, second, the poor are getting poorer; ironically, at the same time, the rich are also getting richer. This has not always been the case. In fact, between 1945 and 1973, the incomes of the highest and lowest income strata grew at roughly the same annual rate. However, since 1973, the income of the top fifth of the income ladder grew at a yearly rate of 1.3 percent, while that of the lowest stratum *decreased* at the rate of 0.78 percent a year (Cassidy, 1995). Additional factors such as taxes and entitlements (like welfare payments) do not alter this picture at all. Clearly, we are living in a society which is becoming increasingly *polarized* with respect to income. This development is not primarily a racial phenomenon. In fact, the income gap between Black and white households hasn't changed much in the past 20 or 25 years. What has changed is that, among *both* Blacks *and* whites, the poor are getting poorer, and the rich are getting richer. Among married couples, both of whom have jobs and work year-round, the Black-white income gap is actually diminishing; today, African-Americans in this category earn 90 to 95 percent of what whites in it earn. But among Blacks, there is a growing "underclass" whose members are sinking deeper and deeper into poverty. Ironically, at the same time that the Black middle class is growing, the size of the poverty-stricken Black inner-city "underclass" is also growing. Again, one consequence of the polarization of the class structure is the increased viability of selling drugs as a means of earning a living. Not only are the poor becoming poorer; in addition, the visibility of the display of affluence among the rich acts as a stimulus for some segments of the poor to attempt to acquire that level of affluence, or a semblance of it, through illicit or illegitimate means—again, a factor that increases the likelihood that some members of the poor will see drug dealing as an attractive and viable livelihood.

A third development is especially relevant to the issue of the distribution of illegal drugs: community disorganization and political decline. In large part as a consequence of the economic decline of the working class and the polarization of the economy as well as the "flight" of more-affluent members of the community, the neighborhoods in which poor, especially minority, residents live are becoming increasingly disorganized and politically impotent (Wilson, 1987, 1996). Consequently, they are less capable of mounting an effective assault against crime and drug dealing. The ties between such neighborhoods and the municipal power structure have become weaker, more tenuous, even conflictual. The leaders of such communities have become adversaries with City Hall rather than allies, and, over time, are less likely to be able to count on the mayor's office to deal with local problems. In short, as their economic base shrinks, poor, inner-city, minority neighborhoods become increasingly marginalized, disenfranchised, and politically impotent. As with the other two developments, this makes drug dealing in such communities attractive.

In these neighborhoods, criminals and drug dealers make incursions in a way that would not be possible in more-affluent, organized communities, communities with stronger ties to the loci of power. In cohesive, unified, and especially prosperous neighborhoods, buildings do not become abandoned and become the sites of "shooting galleries"; street corners do not become virtual open-air "markets" for drug dealing; the police do not *routinely* ignore citizens' complaints about drug dealing, accept bribes from dealers to look the other way, steal or sell drugs, or abuse citizens without fear of reprisal; and innocent bystanders do not become victims of drive-by gangland "turf" wars. In communities where organized crime becomes blatantly entrenched, it does so either because residents approve of or protect the criminals or because residents are too demoralized, fearful, or impotent to do anything about it. Where residents can and do mobilize the political influence to act against criminal activities, open, organized, and widespread drug dealing is unlikely; where communities have become demoralized, disorganized, and politically impotent, drug dealing of this sort is far more likely to thrive. And the fact is, many poor, inner-city minority communities have suffered a serious decline in economic fortune and political influence over the past generation or so. The result: Drug dealers have been able to take root and flourish (Hamid, 1990).

These three developments—the decay of much of the economic structure on which the lower sector of the working class rested, the growing economic polarization of the American class structure, and the political and physical decay of poorer, especially minority, inner-city communities—have contributed to a fourth development: a feeling of hopelessness, alienation, depression, and anomie among many inner-city residents. These conditions have made drug abuse especially attractive and appealing. For some, getting high—and getting high *frequently*—has become an oasis of excitement, pleasure, and fantasy in lives that otherwise feel impoverished and alienated. *Most* of the people living in deteriorated communities *resist* such an appeal; most do *not* abuse drugs. But *enough* succumb to drug abuse to make the lives of the majority unpredictable, insecure, and dangerous. A dangerous, violent counterculture or subculture of drug abuse flourishes in response to what some have come to see as the hopelessness and despair of the reality of everyday life for the underclass.

As I said, this theory is a *macro* perspective on drug abuse; it is based on the major structural factors, the big picture, the overarching conditions of the society and the community as a means of understanding the behavior of individuals on the "micro" level. Drug abuse is able to take root and flourish as a result of major structural conditions. Drug abuse is also effective in alleviating feelings of despair and anguish among certain individuals in a sector of the society; again, such feelings have been generated or exacerbated by these major structural conditions. Ultimately, of course, it is the individual who chooses to use, or chooses not to use, illegal drugs. But the factors that make these illegal drugs *available,* and their use *appealing,* are not merely individual in nature; they can be traced to much larger social, economic, and political forces.

A crucial assumption of the conflict approach to drug abuse is that there are two *overlapping but conceptually distinct* forms or types of drug use. The first, the vast majority of illegal drug use, is made up of "casual" or "recreational" drug use. It is engaged in by a broad spectrum of the class structure, but it is most characteristic of the middle class. This type is "controlled" drug use, drug use for the purpose of pleasure, drug use which takes place experimentally, or, if repeated, once a week, once or twice a month; it is drug use in conjunction with and in the service of other pleasurable activities. This type of drug use is caused by a variety of factors—unconventionality, a desire for adventure, curiosity for a "forbidden fruit," hedonism, willingness to take risks, sociability, and subcultural involvement (Goode, 1993, pp.64–86). Relatively few of these drug users become an objective or concrete problem to the society, except for the fact that they are often *targeted* as a problem.

The second type of drug use is "compulsive," chronic, or heavy drug use—drug use which may properly be referred to as *abuse,* drug use that often reaches the point of addiction or dependency and is *usually* accompanied by social and personal harm. A relatively *low* percentage of recreational drug *users* progress to becoming drug *abusers.* For all illegal drugs, there is a pyramid-shaped distribution of users, with many experimenters at the bottom, fewer occasional users in the middle, and a small number of heavy, chronic abusers at the pinnacle. This second type of drug use is motivated, as I said above, by despair, hopelessness, alienation, poverty, and community disorganization and disintegration. It is not merely a "problem" in that the society and the community *defines* it as such; it is also a problem *objectively.* Here, users are harming themselves and others—as well as the community as a whole. Use—whether directly or indirectly, whether a function of drug use per se or of secondary factors—results in medical complications, drug overdoses, crime, violence, imprisonment, or a trip to the city morgue. Experts argue that moving from use to abuse is *more likely* to take place among the impoverished than among the affluent (Currie, 1993; Johnson et al., 1990; Levine, 1991). And, while drug abuse is *facilitated* by the political and economic developments I discussed above, when abuse becomes widespread in a community, it contributes to *even greater* community disorganization. Thus do inner-city residents become trapped in a feedback loop: Powerlessness and community disorganization contribute to drug abuse and drug dealing in their communities which, in turn, entrench those communities in even greater powerlessness and disorganization.

Once again, *most* drug use—even involving heroin and crack cocaine—is experimental, or casual, self-limiting, more or less occasional and does *not* result in individual or community harm. However, a *minority* of users *cannot* control their drug use—and this is more likely to take place with heroin and crack; such users progress from experimentation to casual use to heavy, compulsive, chronic abuse. Such a progression to abuse is *more common* among the poverty-stricken, and more common in neighborhoods that lack a solid economic base, are socially disorganized, and politically disenfranchised. It is the economic and political conditions in which poor people live that make drug abuse more appealing to them, and drug sales more likely to gain a foothold in their communities. And poor residents of inner cities become doubly and triply victimized—first, by a decaying economic structure; second, by the declining political clout of their communities; and third, by the growing entrenchment of drug abusers and dealers. And there is a fourth victimization process as well: Conservative politicians and other power brokers *blame* the residents of poor communities for the drug abusers that victimize their neighborhoods, and they refuse to do much about the problem. Once again, the third process exacerbates the first two, creating a vicious spiral, while the fourth process, likewise, exacerbates all the others.

Let's be crystal clear about this point: Drug abuse is *not* unknown among members of the middle classes and among residents of affluent, politically well-connected communities. Significant proportions of *all* categories of the population fall victim to drug abuse. Moreover, as I said before, there is a large and growing African-American middle class, whose members do *not* face the economic problems the Black "underclass" struggles with every day. I'm making two very different points here. While *some* members of *all* economic classes abuse cocaine and heroin, the members of certain classes are *more likely* to do so. But my second point is far more important: Even if there were *no* class differences in drug abuse, the fact is, *heavy drug abuse has especially harmful consequences in poor, minority communities.* The class and even neighborhood differences in drug abuse *rates* are important, but secondary. The main point is that drug abuse more seriously disrupts the lives of people who lack the resources and wherewithal to fight back effectively than is true of the lives of those who possess these resources. Poor neighborhoods are especially *vulnerable* to intrusions by drug dealers and increases in drug abuse.

Poor and minority people and neighborhoods are *already* struggling with a multitude of problems they are trying to overcome; drug abuse is another major exacerbating difficulty. Members of more-affluent neighborhoods are more likely to have "connections," ties with City Hall and the State House, "clout," or political influence, money to tide them over, a bank account, mobility, autonomy, and so on—a variety of both individual and institutional resources to deal with problems they face. Hence, the drug abuse of some of their members is not as devastating as it is among the poor and the powerless. And the communities in which they live, likewise, get favored treatment from the powers that be; they are less likely to fall victim to the many social marauders and exploiters that prey on the powerless and the vulnerable. In contrast, poor, minority communities are shortchanged by local, state, and federal governments and bypassed by developers and entrepreneurs. Banks are reluctant to lend money to open businesses in such communities; stores that do open are undercapitalized and frequently fail; landlords abandon buildings, which then become sites of "shooting galleries." It is the *vulnerability* and relative *powerlessness* of such neighborhoods that makes them a target for organized and petty criminals, for drug dealers large and small, for corrupt officials and police officers; vulnerability and powerlessness enable drug abuse to flourish in such communities and wreak havoc with their residents' lives. In short, when we ask, "Why drug abuse?" our answer must inevitably be tied up in issues of economics and politics. What takes place at the individual and local (or "micro") level has roots in the institutional, the structural, or "macro" level.

4

Prohibition: The Punitive Model

The "legalistic" definition of drugs and drug abuse spelled out earlier translates fairly readily into one possible model of drug policy: the *prohibition* or "punitive" model. Nearly all observers who see drugs as defined by the fact that they are illegal, and who exclude legal substances from that definition, support drug prohibition; that is, they wish to keep the currently illegal drugs illegal. The word "prohibition" has both a *specific* and a *general* meaning. In its most specific meaning, "Prohibition" refers to the legal ban on the manufacture and sale of alcohol beverages which was in effect in the United States between 1920 and 1933; used in this way, the word is usually capitalized. In its more general sense, the word refers to banning *any* activity, service, or product through the criminal law. This may be referred to as a *punitive* approach, that is, a policy which calls for *punishing* persons who ignore the law and purvey or partake in the relevant activity, service, or product. Clearly, the word "prohibition" can refer to a ban on *any* psychoactive substance. With reference to drugs, a punitive policy would mean that, if a violation occurs, and someone who is engaged in a drug transaction, or who is in possession of a quantity of an illegal substance, is apprehended by the police, he or she may be arrested, prosecuted, convicted, and imprisoned. Under a punitive policy, drug possession and sale are *crimes,* much like rape, murder, and armed robbery; a criminal *penalty* is provided in the penal code for infractions. This penalty could entail a fine, a jail or prison sentence, or probation instead of imprisonment; in some jurisdictions (outside the United States), this may even entail execution. When laws are passed providing penalties for a given offense, this is referred to as *criminalization.* Prohibitionists want drug possession and sale to be criminalized—or even more harshly criminalized than they are— because, prohibitionists feel, use will decline as a result (or because they feel that such penalties symbolize society's opposition to such use). Since they support a "war" on drugs, advocates of the punitive policy may be referred to as "hawks," a term that is usually used to refer to the more warlike factions in a society. In contrast, legalizers may be referred to as "doves," since they oppose this "war" on drugs and believe we should "lay down our weapons" and "declare peace" (Reuter, 1992, p.16).

Of course, jurisdictions do vary in just *how* punitive their policies are. At least three factors define a jurisdiction's *degree* of punitiveness. First, the *penalties* provided by law will vary from one jurisdiction to another. The laws in some jurisdictions are extremely harsh, calling for capital punishment and life sentences for drug selling and possession; others are more lenient and call for fairly brief jail or prison time. Second, police *priorities* may or may not focus on drugs. Some jurisdictions devote a substantial proportion of their budget to drug violations; their police departments have specialized narcotics squads, and they purchase expensive equipment to aid in surveillance, engage in undercover drug operations, and seek out drug violators with a special vigilance. For the police in other jurisdictions, in contrast, drug enforcement represents a low priority; they will arrest suspects only when they stumble on violations by accident. And third, the *likelihood* of carrying out the sentence which is called for in the law may be either flexible or ironclad. In many jurisdictions, a variety of alternate penalties—such as house arrest, community service, probation, fines—are most often invoked. In others, a prison sentence is not subject to discretion—the felon *must* serve prison time. In addition, as we'll see, in many countries, states, or communities laws are on the books which call for substantial penalties, but violations of these laws are ignored, and the prescribed penalties are never meted out. Thus, although many jurisdictions have a punitive policy, in which the possession and sale of certain drugs is against the law, the variation in just *how* punitive law enforcement is, is enormous.

Let it be said that the more *extreme* versions of the punitive approach that are used elsewhere are not legally possible in a society such as the United States, which values civil liberties, the right of due process, and freedom from unreasonable punishment. For instance, very few commentators support the death penalty for drug violations. (A few do, and have so stated in public.) In 1949, when the Communist party seized power, there were tens of millions of opium addicts in China. Most observers agree that, within a decade, the problem had been all but eliminated. Of the many weapons in its arsenal, the Chinese government used public execution of drug traffickers as well as "reeducation" or resocialization camps for users and addicts. Today, as a result of more contact with its neighbors, the problem of drug abuse is making a comeback in China, many observers feel. While lecturing at Beijing's Medical University, Goldstein (1994, p.258) watched the television coverage of a public hanging of 52 alleged heroin dealers. With a crowd of thousands watching, the governor of the province declared: "This is how we deal with drug traffickers!" Such a draconian penalty is simply not a viable option in the United States. When I refer to the punitive policy toward drug possession and sale, therefore, I refer to longer and especially more-certain sentences for violators, as well as a relaxation of the rules of due process, largely governing search and seizure by the police. Execution is simply not in the cards here, thankfully.

The criminalization of psychoactive substances through the law, and the enforcement of that law, make up one of the more fascinating of all human activities. Of all psychoactive substances, only caffeine is not regulated anywhere by the criminal law (Goldstein and Kalant, 1990, p.1513). Drug laws and their enforcement are remarkably variable the world over. Alcohol is illegal in some jurisdictions (Iran and Saudi Arabia) and legal in most others; coca leaves containing cocaine are legally obtainable in Bolivia and Peru but not in the United States; though technically illegal, marijuana may be openly purchased in "hash" shops in Amsterdam, but not—openly, at least—in Toronto; heroin may be administered by physicians to addicts in Liverpool but not Los Angeles. The reasoning behind the passage and enforcement of drug laws is, presumably, that substance use has become a problem to the society and that it can and should be eliminated, or at least reduced, by arresting and imprisoning violators. The reasoning behind tolerating or *not* criminalizing the possession and/or sale of psychoactive substances is that drug use is not a major problem or that punishment would create more problems than it would solve. Which approach is correct? Can generalizations be made concerning the relative merits of criminalization versus the legalization of drugs? Or is the validity of statements about drugs and the law specific to the society, the jurisdiction, and the drug in question?

While lawmakers may have noble intentions in mind when drafting and enacting a piece of legislation, as Robert Burns, Scottish poet (1759–1796) reminds us, "The best laid schemes o' mice and men / Gang aft a-gley" (or, "often go astray"). As we've seen from the concept of unanticipated consequences, our efforts do *not* always achieve their desired goal, and a variety of unintended, unanticipated, and undesired consequences *often* result from even the loftiest of goals. In fact, some legislation *has* caused a great deal more harm than good, as we learn from the lesson of national alcohol prohibition (1920–1933). However, this should not condemn *all* legislation, for surely there are some laws which have had beneficial results. Hardly anyone would vote to repeal laws against serious crimes such as rape, robbery, and murder, simply because they fail to eliminate the behavior they crimi-

nalize, or because such criminalization may sometimes have unanticipated consequences.

Laws requiring motorists to stop when a school bus is loading and
unloading students, motorists to buckle up when the car is in motion,
and motorcyclists to wear protective helmets have been effective; by
"prohibiting" certain behaviors, they have saved countless lives. No one
would seriously propose that selling outright poisons as food or medicine to the public be made legal, or that tampering with food or medicine sold by others by introducing poisonous substances into them be
subject to no penalty whatsoever. Should potentially harmful substances
be sold as medicine? Should manufacturers be allowed to pollute the air,
the water, the earth? If restrictions apply to actions that harm others, do
the same restrictions apply to actions which harm only the individual
actor, for instance, the drug user? Should the drug seller be exempt from
the restrictions that apply to other types of harm? Yet, what happens in
a society when it attempts to control behavior through the criminal law?
Useful and intelligent answers to these questions are not easy to come
by. It should be clear that the issue of drug control and legislation is a
difficult and thorny issue, not one that can be solved with glib, simple,
pat formulas. Anyone claiming that a given proposal is self-evidently
true, and that opponents of that policy are villains or fools, cannot be
trusted.

TWO PUNITIVE ARGUMENTS

It should also be noted that there are two entirely different punitive
arguments; many observers confuse the two. Let's call them (1) the
"hard" or the "strict" and (2) the "soft" or the "moderate" versions. The
"strict" punitive version makes use of the logic of *absolute* deterrence,
while the "moderate" punitive version makes use of the logic of *relative*
deterrence.

The "hard" or "strict" punitive argument says that a given activity
can be *reduced* or *eliminated* by law enforcement. It argues that crime is
deterred or *discouraged* in some absolute or abstract sense by law enforcement. This is the rationale for the government's "war on drugs": Escalate
the number of arrests of users, addicts, dealers, and producers; hand
them longer prison sentences; fill the jails and prisons; and eventually
drug use will be "defeated." The advocates of the "hard" punitive argument quite literally suppose that drug use can be wiped out, or at least
drastically curtailed, by an escalation in arrests and sentencing; arrest
and imprison enough drug users and sellers, and use will drop to nearly
zero, or at least to tolerable, minimal levels.

In contrast, the "soft" or "moderate" punitive position does not see a defeat of or even a drastic reduction in drug use or abuse as feasible. This argument is quite different from the hard or strict criminalizer's position; in contrast, it says, *in the absence of law enforcement,* a given activity would be much more common than it is *with* law enforcement. It relies on a logic of *relative* deterrence because, it says, with law enforcement—as compared with *no* law enforcement—certain kinds of crime take place more often. If there were no laws or penalties against robbing or inflicting violence upon others, more people would engage in such behavior (not most people—*more* people). Law enforcement does not *reduce* the incidence of these acts so much as *contain* them. Same thing with drug use: Punishing the drug violator is not, and, under most circumstances, cannot be, a means of drastically reducing or eliminating drug use. But if there were no drug laws—and no *penalties* for the production, importation, possession and sale of the presently illegal substances—use would be considerably *higher* than it is now. Thus, the "soft" or "moderate" criminalizers do not see the inability of law enforcement to "stamp out" drug abuse as a failure of the punitive policy. "Stamping out" drug abuse is a futile and literally impossible task, and an absurd measure of the effectiveness of the laws against drugs. Legalizers who argue that "everyone knows" that the drug laws have "failed" (Best, 1990; Hyse, 1994; Yett, 1990), the moderate criminalizer argues, are basing their claim solely on the "hard" or "strict" punitive approach; it leaves the "soft" or "moderate" punitive argument completely untouched. In looking at the drug legalization debate, the differences between these two versions of the punitive argument should be kept in mind. It will assume central importance in several later discussions.

DRUG CONTROL: THE CURRENT SYSTEM

In the United States at the present time, a range of psychoactive substances are regulated by the criminal law; they are *controlled* substances. The Controlled Substances Act—also referred to as the Drug Control Act—provides for "schedules" or categories of drugs with varying controls and penalties for violations. To simplify a complex situation, three categories of psychoactive substances or drugs are controlled by the law.

The first category of drugs may be referred to as the *legal* drugs. They are not included in the Controlled Substances Act at all; in effect, the government does not consider them drugs in the first place. These psychoactive substances are available to anyone over a certain age. A variety of laws, rules, and regulations stipulate the conditions of their sale and consumption—where, when, and by whom they may be purchased and consumed. Violation of these laws may result in arrest and/or a criminal fine. Still, these substances may be acquired and consumed under most circumstances without violating the law. Alcoholic beverages and tobacco cigarettes provide examples of legal drugs. Their sale and use are controlled by law, but they are not mentioned anywhere in the Controlled Substances Act. In addition, some other substances, not strongly psychoactive, commonly referred to as drugs because they are used for medicinal and quasi-medicinal purposes, do not appear in the Controlled Substances Act either. These are the over-the-counter (OTC) drugs, such as aspirin, Tylenol (acetaminophen), No-Doz, Dexatrim, and Compoz. Controls on them are less stringent than they are for alcohol, but, like alcohol, they may be purchased legally by practically any adult, without a prescription. Since OTC drugs are not psychoactive and are not used recreationally, we will not consider them here.

The second category of substances is made up of the *prescription* drugs. These are the Schedule II to V drugs in the Controlled Substances Act. Thousands of drugs that are psychoactive are available by prescription, which are written by physicians for their patients' medical and psychiatric problems, illnesses, or maladies. These drugs are controlled more tightly than alcohol, tobacco, and OTC medicines, that is, those that are completely legal. These drugs are available *only* by prescription, and *only* within the context of medical and psychiatric therapy. The "schedules" define the degree of control over the dispensing of prescription drugs as well as spell out the penalties for violating the law. Schedule II drugs (such as cocaine, amphetamine, and short-acting barbiturates) are *tightly* controlled; Schedules III through V are *less* tightly controlled. Sale of any of these drugs for nonmedical purposes—for instance, to get high—can result in arrest and imprisonment. In addition to their legal prescribed use, as we saw, a number of prescription drugs mentioned in the Controlled Substances Act that are psychoactive are also widely used illegally, for the purpose of intoxication; some are manufactured illegally in clandestine labs rather than by legitimate pharmaceutical companies.

In addition to individual physicians' prescribing drugs for use by individual patients to treat specific ailments, prescription drugs are widely used for two other populations: first, the mentally disordered, both as inmates of mental hospitals and as outpatients; and second, narcotic addicts who are clients or patients of methadone maintenance programs.

In 1955, there were over half a million residents of publicly funded mental hospitals; today, there are roughly 80,000. Where did they all go? The far-smaller number of mental patients in residence today is not a result of a mentally healthier population; in fact, today, there are more than twice as many hospital admissions each year than there were 40 or 50 years ago. The decrease in patients in residence in mental hospitals is due to the fact that patients are staying in mental hospitals for a much shorter period of time—an average of two weeks as compared with six months. The fact is, since 1955, these patients have been administered *antipsychotic* drugs and are released either into the street or into the care of some sort of group home or small managed facility. Still, if we are thinking about whether the country's policy toward psychoactive drugs is punitive or based on some other philosophy, the fact that hundreds of thousands of mental patients, mostly schizophrenics, are administered drugs that are intended to treat their disorder must be considered.

In addition, nationally, there are about 100,000 outpatients of methadone maintenance programs. Methadone is a slow-acting narcotic whose effects are designed to block the effects of heroin. Taken orally, dissolved in a liquid, methadone does not produce an intoxication or high. Evaluations of methadone maintenance programs have shown that a substantial proportion of their clients, perhaps a third to 40 percent, cut down sharply on their use of illegal drugs, including heroin, and reduce their rate of crime. Methadone is not a panacea, or cure-all. It is not even effective for a majority of the program's clients. Still, a substantial minority are helped in a significant way, and the program seems to be cost effective (Hubbard et al., 1989). Again, methadone maintenance programs provide a partial exception to the rule that American society pursues mainly a punitive approach to drug use. As a general rule, "doves" advocate an expansion of methadone programs, while "hawks" either wish to hold the line on maintenance programs or call for a serious cutback on their funding.

The third category of drugs is made up of those whose possession and sale is *completely* illegal; they are not available even by prescription. The Controlled Substances Act regards these drugs as having "no medical utility" and a high potential for abuse; they are classified as Schedule I drugs. (The "no legitimate utility" is, of course, largely a legal fiction, since some medical experts regard marijuana and heroin, two Schedule I drugs, as being medically useful.) They cannot be purchased or obtained for any reason whatsoever (except under extremely rare experimental conditions); anyone who possesses, transfers, or sells them *automatically* violates the law, is subject to arrest, and, if convicted, may have to serve a jail or prison sentence and/or pay a criminal fine. Examples of the Schedule I drugs include marijuana, heroin, MDMA (or "ecstasy"), LSD, and PCP (or "angel dust"); they are *always* (or almost always) obtained illegally, and are widely used, illegally, for the purpose of intoxication.

For the completely *legal* drugs, the *use* of a given substance is not in question; possession and sale for the purpose of just about *any* and *all* use—including intoxication—are legal. The completely *illegal* drugs represent exactly the opposite side of the coin—possession and sale for almost *no* use whatsoever are legal. It doesn't much matter *why* one wishes to use heroin; even medical uses in the United States are against the law (again, excepting extremely rare experimental conditions). In sharp contrast to these two, for prescription drugs, the matter is quite different: It is the *use* of the drug (and how it is obtained) that defines its legal status. If used in a manner the government deems medically acceptable and obtained by means of a legal prescription, the possession and sale of prescription drugs are legal; if used for what are regarded as illicit or disapproved purposes (say, getting high), or obtained without benefit of a prescription, possession and sale are illegal. Notice, too, that, technically speaking, drug *use* is not a crime; it is *possession* and *sale* that are against the law. When observers refer to the illegal use of prescription drugs, this is shorthand for nonprescription possession and sale *for the purpose of* illicit use. For Schedule I drugs, likewise, although it is possession and sale that are *technically* illegal—and not use—it is ultimately the *use* of these substances that the law is presumably intended to control.

A small exception to the punitive policy toward Schedule I drugs is provided by the *partial decriminalization* of marijuana in nine states of the United States: California, Colorado, Maine, Minnesota, Mississippi, Nebraska, New York, North Carolina, and Ohio. (In 1989 and 1990, the electorate of two states, Oregon and Alaska, voted—at least partially—to *re*criminalize small-quantity marijuana possession.) In these partially *de*criminalized states, possession of a small quantity of marijuana (the amount varies from one state to another) is not a crime. If someone is apprehended with less than the stipulated amount, one cannot be arrested (although one's stash will be confiscated) or convicted and will not serve jail or prison time, and one has no criminal record. For such an offense, one will receive a citation much like a traffic ticket, and pay a small fine. The *sale* or *transfer* and the *cultivation* of marijuana, and the possession of *more* than the stipulated amount, remain on the books as crimes in these states; only the possession of small quantities is exempt. All the partial decriminalization statutes were enacted in the 1970s; since 1980, no state has decriminalized marijuana possession. As we'll see in Chapter 6, there is a world of difference between the *partial* decriminalization policy just described and one of *full* or *complete* decriminalization, which is, as yet, only pie in the sky.

In short, then, at present, the predominant legal stance in the United States is *punitive* toward a wide range of drugs. Many drugs are completely illegal; their possession and sale is controlled through the criminal law in every jurisdiction of America. These are the *prohibited* drugs. The punitive approach has been pursued more or less continuously in this country since the passage of the Harrison Act of 1914. Prior to that time, drugs such as heroin, morphine, cocaine, and marijuana were contained in a variety of medicines and could be purchased, without prescription, in a variety of retail outlets, including pharmacies and even grocery stores. Historians estimate that hundreds of thousands of persons, mainly women, became addicted before or just after the turn of the nineteenth century as a result of the indiscriminate use of these "patent medicines" which contained psychoactive drugs, mainly narcotics (Courtwright, 1982; Morgan, 1974; Musto, 1987). The Harrison Act outlawed the over-the-counter or off-the-shelf purchase of what it referred to as narcotics, which many of these patent medicines contained. (The act included narcotics or opiates such as opium, morphine, and heroin, as well as, oddly enough, cocaine—which is actually a stimulant.) With the passage of the Harrison Act, these so-called patent medicines could no longer be sold in the United States. However, hundreds of thousands of persons remained addicted to their ingredients and sought prescriptions to maintain their addiction.

The Harrison Act did not technically outlaw the possession and sale of narcotics as such; it required lawful manufacturers and dispensers of these drugs to be registered and taxed and keep records of their drug transactions. The act's language permitted the prescription and dispensing of narcotics by physicians to their patients for "legitimate medical purposes" and "in the course of legitimate practice." After 1914, many physicians continued to maintain their addict-patients on drugs by writing prescriptions for anyone who was addicted. However, in a series of rulings, the Supreme Court determined that medical maintenance was illegal (Inciardi, 1992, pp.15–16). Tens of thousands of physicians were arrested for writing prescriptions for addicts, and roughly 3,000 actually served jail or prison time. As a result, by the early 1920s, physicians had abandoned treating addicts; by the end of 1923, every narcotic addict in the United States was by definition a criminal. In addition to the penalization of narcotics (and cocaine) through the Harrison Act, although a number of states had already criminalized the possession and sale of marijuana earlier, by 1937, laws were in place which made it illegal to possess and sell marijuana in every state of the United States. Additionally, that year, a federal law, the Marihuana Tax Act, was enacted. The Harrison Act and the Marihuana Tax Act represent *punitive* policies toward the drug problem; whether through intent or practice, they prohibited and criminalized the use and sale of narcotics, cocaine, and marijuana.

In a nutshell, the punitive policy toward drug use is this: To solve the drug problem, its proponents argue, *arrest* sellers and users, *convict* them, prosecute them to the full extent of the law, and *incarcerate* them.

If any nonusers contemplate taking up the habit, the example of what happens to those who get caught should dissuade them from such foolish behavior. Of course, as I said earlier, there are variations on a punitive theme. Some advocates of criminalization approve of the current policy; others call for *even harsher* laws, longer and more-certain prison sentences, fewer alternatives to incarceration, less discretion by judges, even (rarely) execution of the most serious offenders. In testimony to the Senate Judiciary Committee, Darryl Gates, former chief of the Los Angeles Police Department testified that casual marijuana smokers "ought to be taken out and shot," because, he said, "we're in a war" (Beers, 1991, p.38). William Bennett, former federal drug "czar," speculated on a nationwide radio talk show that perhaps anyone who sells illegal drugs to a child should be *beheaded.* "Morally," he said, "I don't have any problem with that at all" (Lazare, 1990, p.25). Most criminalizers do not support such harsh penalties, of course, but they do endorse criminal penalties for most of the currently illegal drugs. In short, regardless of how severe or mild the penalties proposed, the criminal law, arrest, and incarceration—punishment—remain the cornerstones of the punitive approach to drug abuse. It is our current policy for many drugs, and it is a policy that most Americans support. Public opinion polls find that roughly 90 percent of all Americans believe that the possession and sale of hard drugs should remain illegal, and 75 percent support such a policy even for marijuana.

SUMMARY OF THE CURRENT SYSTEM

At present, then, the United States follows the *maintenance* model for 100,000 or so narcotic addicts who are enrolled in methadone programs; the *partial decriminalization* model for small-quantity marijuana possession in nine states; the *legalization* model for alcohol and tobacco cigarettes; the medical or *prescription* model for psychoactive pharmaceuticals such as Valium, Halcion, morphine, Prozac, Thorazine; and a *criminalization* or *punitive* model for its illegal drugs: marijuana (completely illegal in 41 states), crack, ecstasy, PCP, LSD, and heroin (completely illegal), and a variety of prescription drugs, such as barbiturates, amphetamine, and cocaine, which are completely illegal if used recreationally or without benefit of prescription. To put the matter another way: *All recreational drug use in America is prohibited unless otherwise exempted.* The exceptions are alcohol and cigarettes. Marijuana is a partial exemption in that, even in the decriminalized states, the user cannot possess above a given quantity and, even if he or she does possess less than that, may receive a fine similar to a traffic ticket. (The prescription drugs do not represent an exception to this rule, since, in principle, they are to be used *exclusively* for therapeutic, not recreational, purposes.) In effect, in the United States, the only significantly psychoactive drugs that users are completely free to take legally for pleasure (caffeine excepted) are alcohol and tobacco.

Of course, in addition to what the law says about drug possession and sale (the "de jure" reality), we must also consider the *actual enforcement practices* with respect to drugs (the "de facto" reality). For instance, in the states where marijuana possession is a crime, what is the statistical likelihood that someone who is apprehended will be arrested with two joints in his or her possession? It depends on the officer and the jurisdiction, of course, but arrest is a great deal less likely than it is when someone is caught with a kilogram of heroin, even though both substances may be technically equally illegal. The fact is, for crimes generally, a substantial proportion of suspects who are apprehended committing a crime are simply released without being arrested; moreover, only a small minority of first-time offenders convicted of even a serious crime or felony will actually be sent to prison (Walker, 1994, pp.41–43). The factor that influences the likelihood of arrest and conviction (aside from the quality of the evidence) is the seriousness of the offense. And many officers and departments do not consider small-quantity marijuana possession specifically, and small-quantity drug possession generally, serious enough to warrant arrest. (Still, according to the Federal Bureau of Investigation's figures, there were over 350,000 arrests for marijuana violations in the United States in 1994, over 80 percent of which were for the possession of a quantity of the substance rather than for distribution or sale.) It is important to know that actual enforcement practices may be quite different from what the law says.

ARE WE BECOMING INCREASINGLY PUNITIVE ON DRUG CONTROL?

What does our current trend on drug policy look like? Is our drug policy becoming more punitive—or less? As we moved from the 1980s to the 1990s, and as we move into the twenty-first century, are the suggestions of the legalizers taking hold? Who's winning—the "hawks" or the "doves"? The evidence is very strong that the punitive or punishment-oriented approach is winning out. We saw some of the figures in the Preface. This is part of a more general trend, nationwide, for all crimes; the country seems to be abandoning the treatment-oriented or rehabilitative approach and moving increasingly in the direction of incarceration as a solution to the crime problem. "Lock 'em up and throw away the key!" seems to be our contemporary watchword. Budgets are increased every year for the construction of new jails and prisons; even so, our jails and prisons continue to be filled to overcapacity. Between 1970 and 1995, the state and federal prison population increased from 200,000 to over one million, while the number of inmates per 100,000 in the general population more than tripled during this period, from 100 to over 300. There are two main reasons for this virtual *explosion* of incarcerated offenders. First, inmates, especially those convicted of violent offenses, are being kept in prison longer; that is, increasingly, they are serving out a longer portion of their sentences instead of being released early and placed on parole. For instance, in 1988, violent offenders served 43 percent of their sentence, whereas today, this figured climbed to 51 percent (Butterfield, 1995). Parole boards are becoming increasingly choosy about which prisoners they will release early. And second, while first-time drug offenders in the past were *very rarely* sent to prison (in the past, probation was a common sentence for a drug offender), today, increasingly, they are far more likely to be incarcerated. In 1980, only 8 percent of the population of state prison inmates were incarcerated for a drug offense; today, this is 26 percent; over a third of *new* admissions to prisons are drug offenders (Butterfield, 1995; Lindesmith Center, 1996). Hence, our hugely expanding prison population. American society is not committing more crime (in fact, the crime rate has been dropping since the 1980s), but our criminal justice system is clearly becoming more punitive, specifically toward violent offenders and drug offenders.

Reuter (1992, p.21) estimates that, in the early 1990s, nearly $30 billion was spent per year at all levels of government on drug control, more than a tripling over the past decade and a half. Of this total, roughly 75 percent was for enforcement of the drug laws; only 25 percent remained for treatment and education. But budgetary allocations represent only one measure of the growing strength of the punitive approach to drug control, says Reuter. The harshness or length of the sentences handed down, as well as those actually served, for drug offenses have increased significantly in the past decade and a half. According to the Federal Bureau of Investigation (FBI), in 1980, there were 581,000 drug arrests nationally; in 1994, there were 1,351,000. Between 1980 and the 1990s, the percent of drug arrests that resulted in conviction rose dramatically, and the percent of convictions resulting in a prison sentence, likewise, increased dramatically. On average, a drug violator *released* from federal prison in 1992 served a 33-month sentence; those sentenced in 1992 must serve a mandated minimum of 70 months (Lindesmith Center, 1996). In fact, the number of convicted drug felons going to prison increased by over 10 times during this period, and the the total number of prison years they received, likewise, increased by over 10 times

(Reuter, 1992, p.25). As of 1996, just under two-thirds of the nearly 100,000 inmates of federal prisons are serving time for drug violations. The conclusion is inescapable: The "hawks" are winning; the punitive approach to drug control has become more ascendant over time. There is no evidence to suggest that this will turn around any time soon; for the time being, the cry of reformers remains a voice in the wilderness.

5

Strange Bedfellows: Ideology, Politics, and the Drug Legalization Debate

So far, we've looked at the drug legalization debate mainly from an "objectivistic" perspective. That is, I've attempted to establish something of a factual or empirical foundation for the debate: What proportion of the population uses which drugs, with what frequency, and, to some extent, with what effect? However, as I said early on, this approach is misleading or at least incomplete for a very good reason: Approaches to drug legalization are powerfully influenced by the political and ideological position of the observers and analysts who adopt them. Consequently, at this point, before laying out the nuts-and-bolts proposals of each plan and evaluating each one, it might be interesting to explore in what ways the various positions on legalization versus criminalization rest on their moral, ideological, political, and philosophical foundations. For the moment, let's set aside the empirical adequacy of the various views on legalization and try to understand where the authors of several of the most prominent views on the question are "coming from" ideologically and politically. How does each argument fit into the larger value framework?

Let it be said at once that the political landscape is a maze of contradictions. Politics, we are told, "makes strange bedfellows." Perhaps nowhere is this more apparent than on the issue of drug legalization. Positions that are very close to one another in general may actually have drastically differing views on drug policy; likewise, positions that seem poles apart on most other issues may agree on the question of what to do about drugs. Here, a distinction between legalizers and prohibitionists may very well be fractured by crosscutting political views. In other words, seen politically, views toward legalization may be seen as the secondary manifestation of deeper and more compelling ideological commitments. To be more specific about it, most conservatives *oppose* a relaxation of the drug laws, but many *extreme* conservatives favor a program of complete decriminalization. Many radicals oppose certain forms of legalization as state control and, in that view, agree with many extreme conservatives, who propose something of a laissez-faire or "hands-off" policy. Black politicians, usually well at the liberal end of the political spectrum, are (with a few exceptions) *staunchly* opposed to drug legalization (Rangel, 1988, 1991a, 1991b). Technically, and looked at in either-or terms, legalizers and prohibitionists stand on opposite sides of the fence on the issue of legalization, but "progressive" legalizers and "progressive" prohibitionists share much more in common than the first does with the more extreme or "hard-core" legalizers and the latter does with the more extreme or "hard-core" criminalizers. Consequently, the usual political spectrum is not a very useful road map for finding out where someone stands on drug policy. Here are some of the more high-profile views on the drug legalization issue: *cultural conservatives, free-trade* or *free-market libertarians, radical constructionists, progressive legalizers*, and *progressive prohibitionists*.

CULTURAL CONSERVATIVES

Cultural conservatives believe in "old-fashioned" values; they feel that what's wrong with the country, drug abuse included, is that too many people have strayed too far from age-old custom and tradition. We should return to mainstream religion, the traditional family, conventional sexual practices, the "basics" in education, strong communities where neighbors care about one another, conformity to traditional values, moderation in our consumption of alcohol, and complete abstention from illegal psychoactive substances, and so on. What's bad about this country is too much freedom, rampant individuality, hedonism, selfishness, a lack of concern for our fellow human beings, Godlessness, lack of a communitarian spirit, a too-heavy reliance on the federal government to do things for us, not enough self-control—all leading to divorce, abortion, pornography, illegitimacy, crime, violence, and drug abuse. Cultural conservatives believe that everyone is responsible for his or her own actions, that all actions are an individual moral choice. No one has the right to hide behind social "factors" or "conditions" which, others claim, cause or influence people to do things. The cultural conservative would see the conflict theorist's statement that drug abuse is related to power, residence, and socioeconomic status as little more than an *excuse* for illegal and immoral behavior. To the cultural conservative, strengthening morality means *defeating* illegal and immoral behavior, including drug use; when morality fails to take hold, law enforcement must step in and take over. In fact, law enforcement is an *agent* of morality, since it *teaches* violators that they can't get away with breaking the law. Just as important, it is the job of law enforcement to ensure that *justice* is meted out, and justice is trampled on whenever the law is violated.

Cultural conservatives adopt the legalistic definitions of drugs and drug abuse which I spelled out much earlier; that is, a drug is an *illegal* psychoactive substance, and drug abuse is use of a drug *outside a medical context*. They draw a sharp distinction between alcohol on the one hand and all currently illegal drugs on the other; alcohol is not a drug, nor is alcoholism a type of drug abuse. For the cultural conservative, drug abuse is immoral, a repugnant vice. (As is alcohol—although it is not *drug* abuse.) By their very nature, drugs degrade human life. They should be outlawed because indulgence in them is a repudiation of the status quo—that is, tradition, conservative values, all that is good and true (Kleiman and Saiger, 1990, pp.535–536). Intoxication represents an unhealthy decadence; an expression of degeneracy; a quest for a spurious, insidious, ill-gotten, *illegitimate* pleasure. It is *incompatible* with a decent life; the two are contradictory. In *The Index of Leading Cultural Indicators,* a documentation of what's wrong with this country, William Bennett (1994), former federal drug "czar," quotes James Q. Wilson to the effect that: "Even now . . . , many educated people still discuss the drug problem in almost every way except the right way. They talk about the 'costs' of drug use and the 'socioeconomic factors' that shape that use. They rarely speak plainly—drug use is wrong because it is immoral and it is immoral because it enslaves the mind and destroys the soul. It is as if it were a mark of sophistication for us to shun the language of morality in discussing the problems of mankind" (p.42).

Interestingly, cultural conservatives believe that there is *too much* government spending and intervention in nearly all areas of life, but with some major exceptions—where there is *too little*. One exception is that far more money should be spent for a "more effective and tough-minded criminal justice system, including more prisons, judges, and prosecutors" (Bennett, 1994, p.11). Juveniles who commit violent crimes should be tried as adults; convicts should serve out at least half their sentences, and less parole should be granted; fewer cases should be dismissed on technicalities; less probation and fewer suspended sentences should be handed out; and so on. Cultural conservatives are *adamantly* opposed to the legalization of the currently illegal drugs. Bennett refers to arguments for legalization as "morally scandalous," "irresponsible nonsense" (Massing, 1990, p.30). Again, note that the ravages of the *legal* drugs do not enter into the cultural conservative's equation at all; says Wilson, while tobacco *shortens* human life, cocaine *debases* it (1990a, p.27). A clear-cut expression of the cultural conservative point of view on the drug question was vented by Senator Jesse Helms in 1995; in attempting to derail a bill designed to allocate more federal dollars to AIDS sufferers, Helms argued that, instead, we should *reduce* funding for AIDS, because those who contracted the disease did so as a result of their own "deliberate, disgusting, revolting conduct" (Seelye, 1995). He was, of course, referring mainly to homosexuals and drug addicts (and not to hemophiliacs, contaminated-blood transfusion victims, or children of infected mothers). The fact that Senator Helms is the tobacco industry's staunchest and most powerful ally—and that tobacco kills as a result of the "deliberate" actions of smokers—underscores the selective vision of the cultural conservative.

The answer to the drug problem for the cultural conservative, then, is a return to traditional values. Law enforcement is seen as an ally in this struggle. Victory cannot be achieved without government intervention, and that means, mainly, long sentences for violations and increased allocations for the police and for building jails and prisons. There should be "zero tolerance" for drug use—zero tolerance in the schools, the workplace, the government sector, on the highway, in the street, in public, even in the home—anywhere and everywhere intervention is feasible. If private parties can bring this about, so much the better, but the government must be enlisted in this fight because it has the resources, the power, and the influence to exert a major impact. Cultural conservatives believe in the feasibility of a "war on drugs"; Richard Nixon (1969–1974), Ronald Reagan (1981–1989), and George Bush (1989–1993), all conservative presidents, used the term often and were zealous generals in this "war." More specifically, cultural conservatives have a great deal of faith in a principle we encountered much earlier: *absolute deterrence.* That is, they do not believe simply that law enforcement is more likely to "contain" or keep a given activity at a lower level than no enforcement at all. Even further, they believe (or, at least, in their speeches, they state) that law enforcement, if not restrained by loopholes, technicalities, and restrictions, will actually reduce that activity, ideally, nearly to zero. In short, we *can* win the war on drugs, the cultural conservative asserts, if we have sufficient will, determination, and unity. Cultural conservatives are not particularly interested in calculating cost and benefit to minimize the harms that the current drug policy might inflict, nor in considering the impact of alternate drug policies, since that opens the door to thinking about some forms of legalization. What counts is crushing the monster of drug abuse. This is a kind of holy war, a struggle of good against evil, and winning it represents an end in itself. There can be no compromise with evil. It is simply *assumed* that harsher penalties translate into less drug use, but it is not especially important if they do not. What counts is being on the right side and being tough and uncompromising against the enemy.

Not all supporters of the present system of drug criminalization are cultural conservatives. Somewhere in between cultural conservatives and progressive prohibitionists (a denizen we'll encounter shortly) lies a position which, I suspect, may encompass a majority of the American population. Their position may be dubbed "meat-and-potatoes" or "garden-variety" criminalization. Its endorsers do not bring the heavy ideological and moral baggage to the drug legalization debate the cultural conservatives bring, but they are not as pragmatic or as "cost-benefit analysis" or "harm-reduction" oriented as the progressive legalizers, either. They are opposed to legalization because it just doesn't sound like a good idea. They are afraid of change, they don't want to seem to encourage the use of the illegal drugs by legalizing them, they think it would send the wrong message to potential users, and they don't think the government has any business dispensing heroin or cocaine. They think that drug violators should be arrested—especially dealers. They don't think that sending addicts to jail is a great idea, but they don't have a clear idea of what should be done to them. They favor treatment, but are skeptical about its efficacy. In short, they borrow elements of positions that stretch on either side of their own. They do not have a strong or clear-cut view on the question. Still, ultimately, it is their voice that will be listened to most in the debate, since their numbers are so great. On many issues, politicians have a way of listening to the majority, and the drug legalization debate is no exception to this rule.

FREE-MARKET LIBERTARIANS

Both cultural conservatives and free-market libertarians are at the right—or conservative—end of the political spectrum, but they disagree on almost everything pertaining to drug legalization. For one thing, while cultural conservatives believe that there are real differences between legal and illegal drugs, free-market libertarians believe that the legal-illegal distinction is artificial and should be dismantled. Technically, free-market libertarians are opposed to legalization, but for exactly the *opposite* reason as the cultural conservatives. While the cultural conservatives feel that legalization would represent a dangerous step toward *too little* government intervention and control, for the free-market libertarian, legalization would result in *too much* government intervention and control. The libertarian wants a laissez-faire or "hands-off" government policy—no government-administered methadone maintenance programs, no government "drugstores" or "supermarkets," no Alcohol Beverage Control package stores, no laws telling citizens what they can and can't do, no medical prescriptions for imaginary neuroses or mental illnesses; in short, no restrictions, controls, legislation, or regulations. No one should be *forced* to take drugs, and no one should be forced *not* to take drugs. One major exception, a condition for which a law is necessary, is made for underage users: An adult should not be allowed to sell drugs to a minor. Otherwise, more or less "anything goes." What free-market libertarians want is *complete decriminalization,* not state-controlled, state-supervised legalization (Friedman and Szasz, 1992; Szasz, 1992).

An important concept here is *caveat emptor*—"let the buyer beware." No seller should be held responsible for selling anything that might be potentially dangerous to any legally competent adult; free-market libertarians take the principle that we are all responsible for our own actions to a far greater extreme than do cultural conservatives. Just as we do not blame the seller of food for the obesity of a customer, we should not blame the "drug habits" of the addict on the drug dealer (Szasz, 1992, p.12). While falsely listing the contents of what one sells should not be permitted, *not disclosing* its contents is acceptable—even if it is dangerous and harmful—again, because the buyer should "beware" of what he or she purchases; and if the contents do harm people, well, after a while, sellers of such products will lose their customers. After all, forcing sellers to disclose the contents of what they sell represents too much government intervention (p.149).

Free-market libertarians argue that freedom from government constraint inevitably produces the greatest good for the greatest number of people. This sounds like a consequentialist or empirical argument—that is, that government nonintervention is good *because* it produces positive results. But more closely examined, it becomes clear that this is a moral and ideological argument, that libertarians are in favor of nonintervention as a good *in and of itself.* If, in a specific instance, a particular case of government intervention results in producing a result all would agree is good, the libertarian would nonetheless oppose it because, *by its very nature,* and *as a general principle,* government intervention is undesirable. In fact, in the introduction to his book, *Our Right to Drugs: The Case for a Free Market* (1992), Thomas Szasz, perhaps the most prominent free-market libertarian on the drug issue, states explicitly that his criticism of the war on drugs is not based on pharmacological or therapeutic arguments but on "political-philosophical considerations" (xvi). William Bennett's strong endorsement of 1960s civil rights legislation (1994, p.10) as laws that have had a positive consequence would be anathema to free-market libertarians, who believe any effort to legislate people's behavior is wrong—*the less government, the better* is their motto.

Thomas Szasz argues that government taxation is "legalized robbery" (p.7); politicians and other officials are "government parasites with a comfortable living" (p.7); a system of government-controlled medical licensing, he says, results in a "loss of personal freedom," whose results have been "undesirable" (p.7); the system whereby drugs are reviewed by the Food and Drug Administration to determine whether they are safe and effective is "therapeutic slavery" (pp.9–11); support for government funding for medical research is a product of "crowd madness," "dogma," a "pharmacological phobia and pharmacological hubris" (p.69); any effort to control drugs is "chemical socialism (or communism)" (p.96); drug legalizers, he says, are in fact "medicalizers and thus, de facto, paternalistic prohibitionists" (p.99). Once again, government intervention not only *does* harm—it *is* harm by its very nature. The government has no right to intervene in the lives of its citizens, nor should the government set up controls or regulations that attempt to protect citizens from their own behavior, nor should the government institute programs that are designed to do good of any kind. Left to their own devices, the people will get together and do what's best for themselves. If people make mistakes as a result of exercising their freedom, well, they'll learn from their mistakes. All citizens have the right to do and to purchase anything they wish, so long as this does not harm someone else; it's the government's job to stay out of the people's business, which is exercising our freedoms and maximizing our potential.

Some free-market libertarians would probably fall out with one another over whether there should be *any* restrictions on drug possession, sale, and use at all. For instance, most would support a law prohibiting an adult from selling or giving psychoactive substances to a minor, while a few would not. Some, such as Thomas Szasz, support the right of the government to prohibit smoking in a public building (1992, pp.161–162) and driving a car or flying an airplane under the influence (p.162), as well as permitting drug testing of employees who work at jobs where the public's safety is a consideration (p.62); some others would not. Still, the central point is that the free-market libertarians regard drugs as a form of property, and they feel that ownership of property is sacred, not to be tampered with by the government in any way. Only under extremely limited circumstances does the government have the right to step in and take away such a basic and fundamental right. Under most circumstances, they believe, where such restrictions are practically nonexistent, the public good will be maximized; where this is harmful to some people, nonetheless, the *general principle* of nonintervention must be preserved. There are very few instances, many free-market libertarians feel, where this principle is so blatantly violated as with the drug laws. And legalization is not much better, they believe; it simply results in even more state intervention.

To the free-market libertarian, as I said, the ideal solution is complete decriminalization of the currently illegal drugs. Free-market libertarians do not believe that decriminalization will eliminate either drug use or the medical harm that drug use causes. But they do believe that instilling a sense of personal responsibility in citizens for their own actions is more likely to result in their choosing the most reasonable path than if the government forces them to do something against their will or prevents them from doing what they might otherwise choose to do. Such paternalism breeds the very dependency that we (mistakenly) attribute to drugs (Szasz, 1992, p.149). Our aim should be not a "drug-free America" but an "America free of drug laws" (p.149). In the nineteenth century, there were no legal controls on drugs; in our century, we must "return to a free market in drugs. We need not reinvent the wheel to solve our drug problem. All we need to do is to stop acting like timid children, grow up, and stand on our own two feet" (p.163).

RADICAL CONSTRUCTIONISTS

To some degree, all sociologists are constructionists; all of us are interested in how interpretations of reality are constructed, what functions they serve, and how they grow out of broader political and ideological views. However, some sociologists seem to be arguing that facts in the material world count for very little in these social and cultural constructs, that almost any interpretation of reality can be dished up and accepted as true, no matter how much it may run counter to the facts, if it serves the interests of certain privileged segments of the society. I will refer to these observers as *radical constructionists*. Radical constructionists are not so much in favor of legalization as opposed to the war on drugs. They argue that, objectively speaking, there is no real drug crisis. The government has targeted drugs and drug users because they serve as a convenient scapegoat: Most are poor and powerless; many are members of racial and ethnic minorities; they do not have the resources with which to fight back; they are members of a despised, stigmatized deviant category; and they are inconvenient for the affluent segments of the society. Attention to the phony drug "crisis" serves the function of diverting attention away from the real problems of the day—problems which either cannot be solved within the existing institutional framework or which, if they were solved, would snatch privileges away from the affluent, the powerful, and the privileged.

Consider the drug "crisis" that gripped American society between 1986 and 1992. In a series of speeches between June and September 1986, President Ronald Reagan called for a "nationwide crusade against drugs."

Federal bills were passed in 1986, 1988, and 1992, increasing allocations for fighting the drug war several fold. The number of drug arrests which led to imprisonment, as we saw, shot up by some 10 times during the decade of the 1980s. Media attention to the drug problem increased by 20 times between the early to the late 1980s. Public opinion polls revealed that the proportion of Americans who regarded drug abuse as the "number one problem facing the country today" increased from the 2- to 3-percent range in the early to mid-1980s to 64 percent in September 1989. (After 1989, the percentage declined; it declined again after 1992.) There was no doubt that, in a *constructed* or *subjective* sense, there was a drug crisis in the late 1980s, into the early 1990s. Perhaps never before in the country's history had so many Americans felt so such intense concern about drug abuse (Goode, 1993, pp.48–53). Even more important, never before was law enforcement so vigorously involved in incarcerating drug violators.

But radical constructionists argue that this public concern, and the repression that accompanied it, were based on an exaggerated fear, not on any corresponding increase in objective harm caused by drug abuse. In fact, they argue, the use of illegal drugs actually *declined* in the 1980–1990 period, and by quite a bit (Reinarman and Levine, 1995, pp.156–165). Why an *increase* in concern over drugs at the very period when *rates of drug use* and, presumably, the magnitude of the drug problem, were decreasing? In fact, fear and concern over drugs in the late 1980s turned out to be a "panic," a "scare"—not a true crisis at all. Why? Why this exaggerated concern over illegal drug abuse—a declining problem objectively speaking? Why the sudden rush to imprison drug users, addicts, and dealers at a time when drug abuse posed little threat to American society? Why the intense, biased, hysterical, sensationalistic depiction of illegal drug use in the media?

The scare was generated, radical constructionists feel, for political, bureaucratic, and financial purposes. The rise of the New Right, and its need to protect the interests of the rich and the powerful, was behind the drug scare. Instead of focusing on the real problems—poverty, urban decay, unemployment, an unjust distribution of society's resources—these social problems were blamed on a "chemical bogyman," a "scapegoat," an "ideological fig leaf" (Reinarman and Levine, 1995, pp.169, 170). Poverty is blamed on character flaws in the poor; drug use is also a product of these selfsame character flaws, while, in turn, further contribute to poverty. If structural conditions and disastrous conservative policies were pinpointed as the causes of poverty, the affluent would have to relinquish some of their privileges. Thus, the drug scare of the late 1980s was "concocted by the press, politicians, and moral entrepreneurs to serve other agendas" (Reinarman and Levine, 1995, p.176). It appealed to "racism, bureaucratic self-interest, economics, and mongering by the media." In addition, "the issue of illicit drug use . . . focuses attention away from structural ills like economic inequality, injustice, and lack of meaningful roles for young people. A crusade against drug use allows conservative politicians to be law-and-order minded; it also permits them to give the appearance of caring about social ills without committing them to do or spend very much to help people" (Levine and Reinarman, 1988, p.255). The social construction of drug abuse as a major social problem in the late 1980s, radical constructionists argue, served a political agenda for the powers that be (including the media): to maintain the status quo and to profit from doing it. Notice that the radical constructionists do *not* deny that drug abuse is a problem for the society. But they *do* argue that it is a less serious problem than a number of far more damaging conditions, about which very little fuss is made— such as alcoholism and tobacco addiction. Moreover, they say, the recent war on drugs emerged at a time when the severity of the drug problem was actually declining Hence, it must have served symbolic functions; it was, in fact, a war against the poor.

The radical constructionist sees law enforcement and the media as working hand in hand with one another. In fact, in the war on drugs, the media and the police are *allies*. Both reinforce the status quo, or existing power and economic arrangements. In fact, in a drug "panic" such as that which erupted in the United States during the period from 1986 to 1990 (or so), lawmakers and law enforcement on the one hand and media attention on the other can be seen as two separate indicators or measures of the same thing: concern about a given problem or condition. In effect, they are both devoted to the same cause: persecuting a scapegoat. Just as police priorities are misplaced in targeting drug violators, media coverage is "cracked" (Reeves and Campbell, 1994), or biased against drug abusers. Law enforcement and the media are two ingredients in the same recipe. The "drug control establishment" and "mainstream journalism" are partners in advancing a hysterical witch-hunt that, during the late 1980s, "helped mask the economic devastation of deindustrialization, aggravated black-white tensions . . . , and, ultimately, helped solidify middle-class support for policies that favored the rich over the poor" (p.3). Although the heat of the drug "panic" of the late 1980s died down by the early 1990s, fundamentally the same processes are continuing today on a more institutionalized and less frenzied basis. And one ingredient in that institutionalization, as we've seen, is more prison sentences, and longer sentences, for drug violators.

Radical constructionists do not see drugs as the enemy. Most argue that drug abuse is the *symptom* of a problem, not the cause of it. The problem is, of course, the gross inequity in society's resources: poverty, unemployment, urban decay, the powerlessness of the poor and racial minorities, racism, a lack of economic opportunities in the inner cities— all combined with the grotesque affluence of the very rich. Drug selling, at least at the street level, is caused not by a character flaw but by a lack of economic opportunity; drug abuse is not an expression of being weak willed but of hopelessness brought on by urban decay (Bourgois, 1995).

The solution to the drug problem is not legalization by itself, which will do nothing to solve the ills and injustices of poverty or the grossly unfair distribution of society's resources. "As long as economic and racial inequities exist, abuse will continue whether drugs are legal or illegal" (Lusane, 1991, p.216). Hence, a "radical redistribution of wealth" and "fundamental economic reform" must be at the heart of any meaningful response to the drug crisis (p.220). After this, more crucial but less grandiose measures must be taken. And high on any reform agenda should be "establishing new approaches to policing and law enforcement" (p.206). Communities must take back their streets; the police must listen to and be responsive to the needs of the people and must discontinue stereotyping, stigmatizing, and harassing poor, inner-city minorities. Alternatives to prison must be instituted, such as community service; prisons are already overcrowded, and African-Americans are hugely overrepresented in the prison population. The "war on drugs" should cease. Law enforcement should stop criminalizing the junkie; drug addiction should be seen as a medical not a criminal matter. Treatment facilities, especially those that involve the community and are drug-free, should be hugely expanded. At the same time, high-level dealers who conspire to poison poor and minority communities should be handed long prison sentences (p.215). In conjunction with these changes, alcohol and tobacco could be restricted in a variety of ways; their sale is profitable to their manufacturers and harmful disproportionately to the poor. Above all, what is needed is *empowerment*—a vastly greater and more effective participation in the political process by the poor, the underrepresented, and members of racial and ethnic minorities. With empowerment will come economic redistribution which, in turn, will bring about a defeat of drug abuse as a major problem in American society.

PROGRESSIVE LEGALIZERS

Unlike the cultural conservatives, progressive legalizers hold a definition of drugs that is based on drugs' psychoactive quality, not on their legality. In fact, legalizers wish to dismantle or at least radically restructure the legal-illegal distinction. Unlike the free-market libertarian, the progressive legalizer does believe in state control of the dispensation of psy-choactive substances. Unlike the radical constructionist, the progressive legalizer argues that the drug laws *are* the problem. Matters of reforming the economy and the political system and redistributing society's resources are important in themselves, but the reform of drug policy, too, is a crucial issue in its own right. Progressive legalizers are more con-cerned with what to do about drugs than with reformulating the politi-cal and economic system generally. They think that there are many things that are seriously wrong with the present system but that the laws pro-hibiting drugs are one of them; they wish to reform the laws so that there will be less pain and suffering in the world.

How does the progressive formulate or *frame* the drug legalization issue? What is the nature of the drug problem, and what is the solution? For the most part, progressive legalizers see the drug problem as a *human rights* issue (Schillinger, 1995, p.21). What they are talking about when they discuss drug reforms "is treating drug addiction as a health problem, like depression or alcoholism, and not as a law enforcement problem" (p.21). Above all, society should "stop demonizing illicit drug users"; "they are cit-izens and human beings" (Nadelmann and Wenner, 1994, p.25). Criminalizing the possession and use of the currently illegal drugs is *unjust, oppressive,* and *inhumane;* it has no moral justification. It represents a kind of witch-hunt, and it penalizes the unfortunate. "Hundreds of thou-sands of young lives have been ruined by imprisonment for what are essentially victimless crimes" (Nadelmann, 1995, p.39). It is the suffering *of the drug user* that is foremost on the progressive legalizer's mind in demanding a reform of drug policy. Says Ethan Nadelmann, the progres-sive legalizers' foremost and best-known spokesperson: "Harm reduction means leaving casual drug users alone and treating addicts like they're still human beings" (1995, p.38). "My strongest argument for legalization," he adds, "is a moral one. Enforcement of drug laws makes a mockery of an essential principle of a free society—that those who do no harm to others should not be harmed by others, particularly by the state." Adds Nadelmann, "to me, [this] is the greatest societal cost of our current drug prohibition system (1990, p.46).

A key to the thinking of the progressive legalizers is their belief that drug use is a sphere of behavior that is influenced by much the same rules of human nature as any other activity. They feel that drug users are no more irrational or self-destructive than are participants in such rou-tine—and far less legally controlled—activities as skiing, boating, eating, drinking, walking, talking, and so on. There is, in other words, no special or *unique* power in psychoactive drugs that makes it necessary for the society to erect laws to control and penalize their use (Nadelmann, 1992, p.108). Why do we penalize people who use drugs but harm no one (perhaps not even themselves), and yet leave the stamp-collecting, chess-playing, and television-watching addict untouched? It is a philosophical tenet of progressive legalizers that it is *unjust* to penalize one activity in which the participant harms no one while, at the same time, other, not significantly safer activities are legally uncontrolled. The assumption that drugs possess *uniquely enslaving* and *uniquely damaging* qualities is not only widely held in American society but also is sharply challenged by the progressive legalizer. "No special or uniquely negative qualities" means that there are no extraordinarily compelling reasons why drugs should be singled out to be criminalized or prohibited. Most drug users are every bit as rational as, let's say, chess players; society has no more cause to penalize the former for their pursuits than the latter.

Another point. Progressive legalizers claim to be serious in considering a cost-benefit analysis, but they insist that others who also claim to do so leave out at least one crucial element in this equation: *pleasure.* Few other perspectives that weigh losses and gains are willing to count the psychoactive effects that users seek—and attain—when they get high as "a positive." But why don't they? Sheer bias, the progressive legalizer would say. Most people take drugs because they enjoy their effects; this must be counted as a benefit to the society. If we are serious about counting positives and negatives, why ignore the most central positive of all—the enjoyment of drug taking? It is what motivates users, and it must be counted as a plus. Clearly, such a consideration would *outrage* cultural conservatives, who see hedonism and the pursuit of ecstasy as signs of decay and degeneracy—part of what's wrong with this country.

The position of progressive legalizers can best be appreciated by a contrast with that of the *progressive prohibitionists,* a position we'll examine momentarily. Advocates of both positions urge reforms in the drug laws; both are, or claim to be, concerned with harm reduction; both attempt to weigh cost and benefit carefully and empirically in any evaluation of drug policy; and both believe that users of the illegal drugs are treated too harshly and that the legal drugs are too readily available. But the differences between these two positions are as important as their similarities. There are three major and profound dissimilarities between the progressive legalizers and the progressive prohibitionists (Nadelmann, 1992, pp.89–94). *First,* in their evaluation of cost and benefit, progressive legalizers weigh the *moral* values of individual liberty, privacy, and tolerance of the addict very heavily (p.91), while the progressive prohibitionists to some degree set these values aside and emphasize concrete, material values—specifically public health—much more heavily. *Second,* in considering the impact of legalization—more specifically, whether it will increase use or not—progressive legalizers are *optimists* (they believe that use will not increase significantly), while progressive prohibitionists are *pessimists* (they believe that use will increase, possibly dramatically). Even if use does increase, legalization is likely to result in increased use of *less*-harmful drugs and decreased use of *more*-harmful substances, the progressive legalizers say (Nadelmann, 1992, pp.100, 123). And *third*, legalizers believe that most of the harms from use of the currently illegal drugs stems from criminalization, while the progressive prohibitionists believe that such harms are more a product of use per se than of the criminalization of those drugs. Harm from contaminated drugs, the grip of organized crime, the crime and violence that infects the drug scene, AIDS, medical maladies from addiction—all are secondary, not primary effects of drugs. And all will decline or disappear under legalization. Progressive prohibitionists are skeptical.

Progressive legalizers have not spent a great deal of time or space spelling out what their particular form of legalization would look like. (Mitchell, 1990, represents one exception.) Still, they do *not* mean by legalization what free-market libertarians mean by decriminalization, nor, indeed, what their critics mean by legalization. "When we talk about legalization, we don't mean selling crack in candy stores," says Nadelmann (Schillinger, 1995, p.21). Unlike free-market libertarians, most legalizers realize that selling drugs in a kind of "supermarket," where any and all psychoactive substances would be as readily available as heads of lettuce and cans of soup, is not feasible for the foreseeable future. Many point to harm reduction strategies that seem to have worked in the Netherlands, Switzerland, and Liverpool. All support steps in that direction: Legalize or decriminalize marijuana, increase methadone maintenance programs, reschedule many Schedule I drugs (such as LSD, ecstasy, and heroin) that may have therapeutic utility, stop arresting addicts, get them into treatment programs, and so on. However, all see these as only stopgap or transitional steps. If not the supermarket model, then what would full legalization look like? One progressive legalizer suggests that the *mail-order model* might work: Sell drugs in limited quantities through the mail (Nadelmann, 1992, pp.111–113). While not the ideal solution, it is the best compromise "between individual rights and communitarian interests" (p.124). It must be noted that, while all progressive legalizers emphasize the unanticipated consequences of prohibition, they do not spend much time or space considering the possible unanticipated consequences that legalization might have.

PROGRESSIVE PROHIBITIONISTS

Progressive prohibitionists (Currie, 1993; Kaplan, 1983, 1988; Kleiman, 1992b; Zimring and Hawkins, 1992) urge many of the same reforms that progressive legalizers argue for—needle exchange, condom distribution, an expansion of methadone maintenance, no incarceration of the addict, rescheduling of many Schedule I drugs, legalization or decriminalization of marijuana, stiffer taxes and more controls on alcohol and tobacco, and so on. (In fact, there are far more similarities between progressive prohibitionists and progressive legalizers than there are between the former and "hard-line" criminalizers, on the one hand, and between the latter and "radical" or "extreme" free-market libertarians, on the other). The progressive prohibitionists draw the line, however, at the legal, over-the-counter or even mail-order sale of drugs such as heroin, cocaine, and amphetamine.

Progressive prohibitionists are not as distressed by the moral incongruity of criminalizing the possession and sale of powerful psychoactive agents and legally tolerating substances or activities that also cause harm. Once again, to demarcate their position from that of the legalizers, they say, to *some* degree, there *is* a special and unique quality in certain drugs that compels *some* users of them to become abusers. This is not a majority of the society, they say, but a sufficiently sizable minority to warrant concern for the public health of the collective as a whole. In fact, to step back and look at their political, ideological, and moral position more generally, progressive legalizers are far more *communitarian* than *individualistic*. While the touchstone of the progressive legalizer is *the rights of the individual,* for the progressive prohibitionist, the guiding principle is *the health of the community.* The individual, they would say, does not have the right to harm the society; certain rights have to be curbed for the good of the society as a whole. If injured, the individual has to be cared for by the community; foolish acts engaged in by the individual are purchased at the price of a very substantial cost to the rest of us (Goldstein and Kalant, 1990). The individual *does not have the legal right* to ignore the seat-belt laws, the helmet laws, or rules and regulations against permitting him or her to be placed in extreme danger—or any other laws, rules, or regulations that attempt to protect individuals from harming themselves. Any humane society must balance freedom against harm, and in this equation, quite often, certain freedoms must be curtailed. In short, compared with progressive legalizers, progressive prohibitionists "are far more willing to limit individual liberty to the extent that they perceive a potential gain in public health" (Nadelmann, 1992, p.91). For instance, coercing addicts and drug abusers into drug rehabilitation programs by arresting them and giving them a choice between imprisonment and treatment is not a moral problem for the progressive prohibitionist, whereas for the progressive legalizer, it is.

It is almost in the very nature of the progressive prohibitionist's argument that there is an assumption of greater use under any possible legalization plan. (Marijuana may very well represent an exception.) This position sees the American population—or a segment of it, at any rate—as being *vulnerable* to the temptation of harmful psychoactive drugs. They are *pessimists* when it comes to contemplating the extent of use under legalization. They do not necessarily see the dire and catastrophic "worst-case" scenario predicted by the cultural conservatives—tens of millions of new cocaine and heroin addicts and abusers. But many progressive legalizers see a doubling, a tripling, or a quadrupling of hard-drug abuse in the United States as an entirely possible outcome of many of the currently proposed legalization schemes. And they find that unacceptable. *Most* Americans will resist the temptations and blandishments of these seductive, dependency-producing substances. But focusing on the potential behavior of "most" Americans is a distraction and an irrelevancy. What counts is whether the small minority who use drugs destructively is likely to grow. Most distressing to progressive prohibitionists: The volume of drug abuse *of current addicts and abusers* is likely to increase and, along with it, the harm that flows from drug abuse.

And last, the progressive prohibitionist sees more *direct* harm from use of the hard drugs—such as cocaine, amphetamine, and heroin—than the progressive legalizer sees. There are, it is true, they say, some secondary harms and complications caused mainly by the legal status of these drugs; certainly HIV/AIDS ranks high among them. But most of these secondary or indirect harms can be attacked through modifications of the current system that fall far short of outright legalization. Certainly needle exchange and condom distribution programs would go a long way in combating the problem of HIV contamination. The fact is, cocaine and heroin are a great deal more harmful than the legalizers claim, say the prohibitionists. Harm has been kept low by the very fact of the drug laws, because far fewer people use currently than would be the case under legalization. Alcohol and tobacco kill many Americans in part because their use is *intrinsically* harmful (at least, given the way we use them) and in part because they are widely used. Cocaine and heroin—considering the many possible drugs that can be harmful—are also intrinsically harmful drugs. (Although they are harmful in very different ways.) *And* they are taken, recklessly, by segments of the population who are far more likely to take extreme risks with their health than the rest of us. If these drugs were to be used as widely and as commonly as alcohol and tobacco are used today, many, many users would die as a result. It is foolish and unrealistic, the progressive legalizer says, to imagine that these drugs are harmful today *entirely* or *mainly* because they are illegal. While the progressive legalizer stresses the *secondary* harms and dangers of the illegal drugs, the progressive prohibitionist stresses their primary harms and dangers.

Again, while the more-progressive prohibitionists and the more-moderate legalizers share many items in their drug policy agenda, they differ on these three major issues: how much they stress individual liberty versus public health; their prediction of whether drug abuse, and its attendant harms, will increase significantly under legalization; and their notion of whether the currently illegal drugs are more intrinsically or more directly harmful or are harmful indirectly, that is, mainly because they are illegal (Nadelmann, 1992, pp.89–94). Ironically, although the progressive legalizers and the progressive prohibitionists stand on opposite sides of the great legalization divide, they share more particulars of their drug policy proposals than any two major positions in this debate. If major changes in drug policy do take place in the next century, they are likely to be drawn from the substantial overlap in these two positions.

SUMMARY

Clearly, then, the various approaches to drug legalization fit more or less comfortably into, and have relevance and resonance for, quite distinct political views or orientations. Drug legalization may be said to be a specific *instance* of, or a specific *issue* for, a more general political, ideological, and moral position. The issue is thought about in terms of a broader image or worldview expressing how things ought to be. In this sense, then, is is misleading to think about the debate strictly in pragmatic or empirical terms. In many ways, it is an ideological debate about which political perspective will dominate policy on drugs in the years to come.

For the *cultural conservative,* the relationship between general ideology and morality on the one hand and the question of drug control on the other hand is extremely close. To legalize drugs is to surrender to the very forces corrupting the society today. Drugs (that is, *illegal* drugs) must be fought, just as abortion, pornography, and crime must be fought, and one weapon in this fight is law enforcement. Legalization is a "cop-out," a surrender to the forces of evil. By itself, it legitimates and endorses drug abuse, and it is also highly likely to produce higher rates of drug abuse. Drug legalization must be fought at every turn.

For the *free-market libertarian,* the issue of drug legalization represents a stage on which broader ideological issues are enacted. Legalization is unacceptable because it represents too much government meddling; on the other hand, a policy of government laissez-faire, "hands-off," or more or less complete *decriminalization* is the answer. Everyone has the right to acquire, own, and use chemical substances because they represent a form of property; the government does not have the power to take that right away from its citizens. Leave the people alone to choose as they wish, and they'll usually be wise in their choice. Even if they are unwise, well, that's their choice.

For the *radical constructionist*, public, media, and law enforcement concern over drug abuse is a smoke screen. It is a "fig leaf" with which the powers that be attempt to hide the patent inability or unwillingness to solve society's most serious problems. By itself, legalization is not the solution to the drug problem, but more humane and more democratic solutions must be found to drug abuse other than law enforcement, which only exacerbates the problem. If society's resources were more equitably distributed, and the poor and the powerless were more adequately empowered, American society would not face the drug problem that now ravages our communities.

For the *progressive legalizer*, the drug user's human rights are paramount. It is *unjust* to penalize participants in a specific activity that does not harm others. Drug use, progressive legalizers argue, is not markedly different from a wide range of other activities in this respect. Any consideration of cost and benefit to determine whether the currently illicit drugs should be legalized must consider the human rights factor. Legalization will maximize the drug user's rights, and, at the same time, minimize the addict's suffering; in addition, it will not place the rest of the society in peril. In fact, in many ways—such as a reduction in drug-related crime and violence, the withering away of organized crime, and the sharp reduction of drug-related medical maladies—nonusers will experience little but benefits from legalization.

For the *progressive legalizer*, the main issue is public health, not the constitutional rights of drug users. Human rights are not without limits, and regulations may be used to control harms that participants inflict upon themselves, even if they do not harm others. The fact is—and this is central to the progressive legalizer's position—it is almost certain that the abusive use of the hard drugs will rise under practically any conceivable legalization scheme and, along with it, harm to the society as a whole. To a significant degree, drug use *is* somewhat different from many activities which the society does not attempt to control, like stamp collecting and playing chess. While a variety of reforms ought to accompany continued criminalization of the hard drugs—including far less reliance on arresting and imprisoning the user, addict, and petty dealer, and, for many progressive prohibitionists, the partial decriminalization of marijuana—the legalization of the hard drugs is a very high risk option; it is likely to do a great deal more harm to the society than good.

6

Legalization and Decriminalization: An Overview

It is against the current punitive policy that all the proposals for change must be measured. According to what criteria should a given proposal be measured? How is the success of a given proposal indicated? In what specific ways would we want a given policy to succeed? Is our goal the reduction in the number of users of all the currently illegal drugs? Or a reduction only in addicts and abusers of the hard drugs? Do we want to see a decline in the illegal drug trade? What about drug-related murders? Drug overdoses? Drug-related diseases, such as infection with the AIDS/HIV virus? Do we seek a reduction in the amount of money the society pays to deal with the drug problem, especially the cost of incarcerated drug offenders? What if a given program helps in one way but harms in another? Is there one overall best drug policy? Would either legalization or decriminalization produce changes we all would regard as desirable? Are the legalizers right? Has our punitive or prohibitionist drug policy failed? Which drug policy is likely to work better; which will be worse? What do we know that will tell us something about the feasibility of one or another drug program?

Beginning in the late 1980s (Kerr, 1988), a taboo, almost unthinkable proposal—the decriminalization or legalization of the currently illegal drugs—began to be advanced with remarkable frequency and urgency. Dozens of books, hundreds of magazine and newspaper articles, uncountable editorials and op-ed pieces, and scores of prominent spokespersons have urged the repeal of the drug laws. Drug legalization has become a major focus of debate in recent years, joining such controversial subjects as abortion, pornography, the environment, the economy, gun control, and homosexual rights, women's rights, minority rights, and affirmative action as yet another battlefield of controversy.

It must be emphasized that legalization is not a single proposal. Instead, it is a *cluster* of proposals that stands toward one end of a *spectrum* of degrees of regulation and availability. As we've seen, very few, if any, legalization advocates argue that there should be absolutely *no* controls on drugs whatsoever—for instance, that minors be allowed to purchase heroin and cocaine from whoever is willing to sell to them. Instead, all agree that *some* sorts of controls will be necessary; the question is, how far along the spectrum of control to decontrol—and whether those controls should be legal or of some other type—the currently illegal drugs should be moved. Consequently, both the similarities and the differences among the various legalization programs have to be considered.

GENERALISM VERSUS SPECIFISM: AN INTRODUCTION

Many observers of and commentators on the drug legalization issue are not very careful about making distinctions among what is in fact a variety of proposals. In fact, the terms "legalization" and "decriminalization" refer to a wide range of different practices. Of the many distinctions between and among the many different legalization proposals we might make, perhaps the most crucial would be between *generalism* and *specifism*. Both reject the legalistic definition of drugs I spelled out in Chapter 1 and embrace a definition based on psychoactivity. Where they part company is on the question of whether legalization applies to *all* psychoactive drugs, or only to some of them. The *generalist* proposes some form of legalization for *all* psychoactive substances, whether currently legal or illegal, whereas the *specifist* is more selective, proposing legalization for some substances and prohibition for others.

GENERALISM

A generalist approach to drug abuse is one that sees *all* psychoactive substances, legal or illegal, as more or less equal in harm and health costs; it approaches drug abuse as a medical matter. This is an "all drugs are created equal" approach, leading to a "one size fits all" solution—legalization for drugs, treatment for drug abusers (Zimring and Hawkins, 1992, p.10). The generalist sees similarities between and among the many psychoactive drugs. Hence—seeing all drugs as basically the same—the generalist is likely to support some form of legalization for *all* psychoactive substances. The distinctions we might make among them are secondary; their similarities, all-important. In a nutshell, the generalist believes that drug use and abuse should be taken out of the realm of the criminal law; as a consequence, when the currently illegal drugs are legalized, the problems we now experience with drug abuse will decline drastically or disappear altogether. Generalists see moral and empirical absurdity in different laws for different drugs; they see an injustice here as well as a policy that can't work. Going beyond the issue of drug use, generalists do not believe that prohibition is possible at all—for drugs or anything else. Generalists see the sin not in use itself but in making drug use a crime. To them, the solution is legalization. Some generalists believe that, with the exception of sale to minors, there should be virtually no restriction on the possession and sale of psychoactive drugs (Szasz, 1992), while others argue that there should be certain restrictions on them—and, in addition, that current restrictions on cigarettes and alcohol should be made *more* stringent—but all should be dealt with in more or less the same fashion (Trebach, 1993).

SPECIFISM

In contrast, the specifist believes that all drugs are *not* created equal; each drug presents a somewhat different problem with respect to control and public harm. Whether the law or the drug causes more harm is an empirical question—one we have to resolve with evidence, not by resorting to rhetoric or moralizing. Specifists agree with generalists in that they also base their definition of drugs on psychoactivity. However, the specifist believes that each drug, while nonetheless psychoactive, should be approached somewhat differently with respect to the law. The specifist is a pragmatist, a utilitarian, and bases drug policy on the principle of *harm reduction.* Forget the moral question of whether certain varieties of drug use constitute an affront to the established order, the specifist says; forget the ideological question of whether users of illegal drugs get a "raw deal" by being regarded as criminals while the users of legal drugs are seen and treated as respectable citizens. These issues pale into insignificance when considering the question of what is best for the society, what policy causes the least harm, what contributes to the public's well-being. The law should be changed where appropriate and enforced when that, too, is worth-while. Yes, the specifist says, some instances of prohibition have worked, and, yes, others have done more harm than good. Our task is to figure out which is which for the substances under consideration. The bottom line, and what should count in the long run and should guide public drug policy, is a detailed *cost-benefit analysis.*

Thus, the heart of the specifist's approach is that the harm a drug causes, and the impact of the drug laws, should be weighed on a case-by-case basis (Zimring and Hawkins, 1992, pp.9–10). Like the generalist, the specifist includes legal substances in a definition of drugs; unlike the generalist, the specifist does not see all drugs as created equal. No sweeping generalizations can be made about the best policy for all drugs; in fact, there is no best policy for all drugs. It is possible that the possession and sale of some drugs should remain a crime and that other drugs should be legalized. The question can be resolved only by looking at the facts, by a practical, pragmatic weighing of the consequences of drug abuse versus the consequences of the law. The moral issue of whether it is "fair" or "just" to prohibit access to one drug and permit access to another is irrelevant, a *non sequitur* (Kaplan, 1988, p.37); it does not enter into the specifist's equation at all. The specifist ranks drugs in terms of *degrees* of harm, and seriously considers the question of which drug represents the "lesser of two evils" (Zimring and Hawkins, 1992, p.12). Neither the use of illegal substances per se nor the use of the criminal law to reduce use and public harm are themselves immoral, according to the specifist. Rather than being concerned about immorality—to the legalist, breaking the law by using drugs; to the generalist, attempting to control drug use by means of the criminal law, and criminalizing some drug users but not others—the specifist focuses on reducing harm to drug users and to the society as a whole. Perhaps the most readily grasped of the specifist's programs is to decriminalize or legalize marijuana and keep the "hard" drugs illegal (Kaplan, 1970, 1983, 1988; Kleiman, 1992b).

FOUR LEGALIZATION PROPOSALS: AN INTRODUCTION

Once we've recognized that some legalization proposals wish to remove criminal penalties from all psychoactive substances while others are selective and aim to legalize some substances and retain penalties on others, we need to make a number of additional distinctions. Legalization is not the same thing as decriminalization, as we'll see momentarily; and requiring the addicted or drug-dependent to obtain their supply via prescription is not the same thing as permitting drugs to be sold to anyone, without benefit of a prescription. More generally, it must be recognized that legalization and prohibition do not represent an either-or proposition. In reality, they form a continuum or a spectrum, from a completely libertarian or "hands-off" proposal—with *no* laws governing the possession or sale of *any* drug—at one end all the way over to the most punitive policy imaginable, let's say Darryl Gates's proposal that even casual marijuana smokers be "taken out and shot" at the other end, with every conceivable position in between. In reality, very, very few commentators advocate a policy of no controls whatsoever on the possession and sale of any and all psychoactive drugs. At the other end of the spectrum, very, very few commentators call for the death penalty for the simple possession of the currently illegal drugs. Hence, what we are discussing in the drug legalization debate is *degrees of difference along a spectrum* somewhere in between these two extremes. In fact, as Ethan Nadelmann (1992, pp.89–94) has argued persuasively, the "moderate" legalizers and the "progressive" or reform-minded prohibitionists share far more in common than the first does with the extreme, radical, or "hard-core" legalizers or the second does with the more-punitive prohibitionists.

Therefore, the issue is not legalization versus prohibition. Rather, the debate centers on some of the following issues: *How much* legalization? *Which drugs* are to be legalized? Under *what conditions* can drugs be dispensed? For instance, are drugs to be dispensed in approved, licensed clinics? *To whom* may drugs be dispensed? To addicts and drug abusers only? Or to anyone above a certain age? *In what quantity* may drugs be dispensed? At what purity? *At what price* are the legalized drugs to be sold? (For these and other questions that legalizers must answer, see Inciardi and McBride, 1991, pp.47–49). Each legalization proposal will answer these questions in a somewhat different way. Hence, there are *many* legalization proposals, and not just one. It is naïve to assume that the broad outlines of drug policy are the only thing that is important, and that the details will take care of themselves. (For just such an approach, see Trebach, 1993.) In my view, this assumption is fallacious. Zimring and Hawkins (1992, pp.109-110) refer to this view as the "trickle-down fallacy"; I call it the "let the chips fall where they may" approach. On both sides of the controversy, observers too often "simply ignore the detailed questions . . . of priority and strategy" (p.109). A specific policy—what should be done about each and every particular—"cannot be deduced" from a general position (p.110). At the same time, there are *some* points that are shared in common by all legalizers and *some* points that are shared in common by all prohibitionists.

To simplify the picture a bit, let's distinguish among the four most commonly proposed drug policy reforms: *legalization, decriminalization,* the *medical* and *prescription models,* and *harm reduction.*

LEGALIZATION

One common legalization proposal refers to placing one or more of the currently illegal and/or prescription drugs under the controls that now apply to alcohol and cigarettes. Under this proposal, psychoactive drugs could be purchased on the open market, off the shelf, by anyone above a certain age. Since the same controls will apply as for the currently legal drugs, presumably, a proprietor would not be able to sell to a minor or an intoxicated individual, or to an inmate of a jail or prison or a mental institution, and could not sell within a certain distance from a house of worship, a school, or an active polling place on election day. Controls may also apply to the establishments that sell the drugs in question; with respect to alcohol, certain types of bars, for instance, must also serve food. Package stores must observe a variety of rules and regulations; some, for instance, are run by the government. Even those that are private enterprises are controlled: They cannot be owned and operated by a convicted felon; they cannot be open on Sunday; they cannot sell substances above a certain potency; and so on. Thus, *legalization* refers to a state licensing system more or less similar to that which prevails for alcohol and tobacco for the currently illegal drugs.

One qualification: Under our current policy of legalization, manufacturing alcohol (beer and wine, for instance), or growing tobacco, for the purpose of *private* consumption—not commercial sale—does *not* come under state control and yet is perfectly legal; the state retains the right to step in and play a role only when selling takes place. In addition, under legalization, *use,* at least in public, is controlled under a variety of circumstances—for instance, driving while intoxicated and public intoxication are illegal. And lastly, for both alcohol and cigarettes, there are restrictions on advertising; cigarette ads and ads for hard liquor are banned from television advertising, current athletes cannot be depicted endorsing alcoholic beverages, and beer cannot be drunk on camera. Presumably, the drugs that are to be legalized will be controlled more or less the same way as alcohol and tobacco now are.

DECRIMINALIZATION

"Decriminalization" refers to the removal of state control over a given substance or activity. (Many observers use the term to refer to what I call "partial decriminalization." *Full* decriminalization is the removal of *all* state controls over a given product or activity.) It is a legal "hands off" policy of drug control. Under decriminalization, the state no longer has a role in setting rules and regulations concerning the sale, purchase, and possession of a given drug. Here, the distribution of marijuana, heroin, or cocaine would no more be the concern of the government than, say, selling tomatoes or undershirts is. Of course, no one may sell poisonous tomatoes or dangerously flammable undershirts, but under a policy of full decriminalization, the rules and regulations that apply to drugs would be *even less restrictive* than those which now apply to the currently legal drugs alcohol and tobacco. Under *full* decriminalization, anyone can manufacture or grow any quantity of any drug and sell it to anyone without any serious restriction at all; the only factor that should determine the sale of drugs—blatant poisons aside—should be the operation of a free and open economic market (Szasz, 1992). Of course, almost anyone proposing this policy is likely to add one obvious restriction, that sale to a minor be against the law. It must be pointed out that full decriminalization for every currently illegal drug, with the possible exception of marijuana, is not a feasible or realistic policy, and is of theoretical interest only. To expect that legislatures will permit the possession, sale, and distribution of substances which have a powerful effect on the mind and great potential for harm be subject to government controls no stricter than those which apply to the possession, sale, and distribution of tomatoes simply beggars imagination. It is not a proposal that has any hope of implementation in the foreseeable future.

There is one exception to this rule, however. Some commentators argue strenuously (and, in some quarters, persuasively) that users be permitted to grow certain natural psychoactive plants—such as the opium poppy, the coca bush, the peyote cactus, psychedelic mushrooms, and, of course, the marijuana or *cannabis* plant—for their own private consumption (Karel, 1991). Thus, one aspect of full decriminalization remains a—marginally—viable subject of debate, while most of the other particulars are so unrealistic as to seem disingenuous.

PARTIAL DECRIMINALIZATION

The term "decriminalization" is often used to refer to what is in fact *partial* decriminalization. Partial decriminalization does not remove any and all legal restrictions on the possession, sale, and/or distribution of a given substance, but it does remove *some* of them. Currently, in one way or another, small-quantity marijuana possession is already partially decriminalized in nine states of the United States, as we saw, and in parts of Europe. The Netherlands pursues a far, far bolder and more radical policy of partial decriminalization for marijuana than that which prevails even in the most liberal states in the United States—in fact, *in practice,* it borders on full legalization.

In the Netherlands, *by law,* small-quantity marijuana possession is technically illegal; however, in practice, the drug is sold openly in "coffee shops" (or "hash bars"), and these transactions are completely ignored by the police. No advertising of marijuana products is permitted; sale to minors under 16—even the presence of minors in an establishment—and the sale of hard drugs will cause the police to shut a shop down. Thus, small-quantity marijuana possession and sale there have been decriminalized *de facto,* that is, in practice—although, again, "legalization" might be a more apt term—but *de jure* or according to the law, they are still technically illegal. The "hard" drugs are unaffected by this policy; sale of heroin and cocaine, especially in high volume, remains very much illegal. In fact, in the Netherlands, the proportion of prisoners who are convicted drug offenders is the same as it is in the United States, roughly one-third (Beers, 1991, p.40). At the same time, possession by the addict or user of small quantities of heroin or cocaine (half a gram or less) is typically ignored by the police. However, the sale of even small quantities of the hard drugs is not permitted to take place openly in legal commercial establishments, as it is with marijuana (Jansen, 1991; Leuw and Marshall, 1994).

PRESCRIPTION AND MAINTENANCE MODELS

The prescription and the maintenance models overlap greatly, although they are conceptually distinct. Both are usually referred to as the *medical approach* to drug abuse, since both see drug abuse as a disease that can be treated by making certain drugs available to addicts or the drug-dependent. Currently in the United States, the prescription model prevails for certain pharmaceuticals deemed to have "legitimate" medical utility; as we saw, certain approved psychoactive substances may be prescribed by physicians for the treatment of their patients' ailments. Under an expanded prescription or maintenance policy, sometimes referred to as a type of *legalization plan,* anyone who believes himself or herself to be dependent on a given drug would be able to go to a physician or a clinic and, after a medical examination, be duly certified or registered. Certification would enable one to obtain prescriptions at regular intervals which, in turn, would make it possible to purchase or obtain the drug in question. Or the drug could be administered directly by a clinic or a physician. Some current prescription models call for an eventual withdrawal of the client or patient from the drug, but they insist that this must be done gradually, since it is both humane and effective. Under the current prescription policy, drugs have to be tested by pharmaceutical companies and reports submitted to the Food and Drug Administration (FDA) demonstrating that they are safe and effective for the ailments for which they would be prescribed. A drug demonstrated to be either unsafe or ineffective cannot be approved by the FDA and hence, cannot be prescribed as a medicine. Presumably, if the currently illegal drugs are to be prescribed to addicts, they must pass muster as safe and effective medicines.

One version of, or variation on, the prescription or medical model is referred to as the *maintenance model* because the addict or drug-dependent person is "maintained" on doses of the drug in question. As we saw, currently, in the United States, some form of maintenance is in effect for roughly 100,000 heroin addicts, most of whom are administered methadone. However, methadone maintenance programs are fairly tightly controlled in most jurisdictions, and most addicts nationwide are not enrolled in them, either because they do not wish to be—for instance, because the restrictions are too severe and the quantities administered are too small—or because the clinics do not have room for all who wish to enroll. To set up a full walk-in program for any and all heroin addicts who want to take part in methadone maintenance therapy would require a *quadrupling* of the current operating budget of this treatment modality. In addition, there is no *heroin* maintenance program in place in the United States, and none for those dependent on any drug other than a narcotic, including cocaine. (Such a program is in effect in Great Britain, in Liverpool, on a provisional basis.) Presumably, a legalization proposal that relies heavily on the medical model would aim to expand the number of addicts currently on methadone; expand the number of possible narcotics used for maintenance programs, including heroin; and possibly even expand maintenance programs to include nonnarcotic drugs, for instance, cocaine. Again, regardless of the particulars, a drug maintenance program sees drug abuse as a medical, not a criminal, matter and aims to legalize the administration of psychoactive substances to addicts or abusers. It is not clear what such a program proposes to do when drug abusers refuse to participate in the program, demand to use other drugs in addition to the legal drugs they are being administered, or demand a significant escalation in the dose they are administered. Or what should be done when someone who is not chemically or psychologically dependent demands quantities of a given drug from the program. This program sees the primary motivation of drug abusers as maintenance, not recreation.

HARM REDUCTION

Harm reduction represents an eclectic or mixed bag of policy proposals. It is, as we saw, a *specifist* legal policy: different programs for different drugs. Harm reduction is the explicit policy that prevails in the Netherlands, Switzerland, and certain jurisdictions in the United Kingdom, such as Liverpool. Its goal is stated in its title: Rather than attempting to wipe out drug distribution, addiction, and use—an impossibility, in any case—its goal is for drug policy to attempt to minimize harm. Legal reform, likewise, is secondary; the emphasis is on *practicality*—what works in concrete practice rather than what seems to look good on paper or in theory. A needle exchange and distribution program stands high on the list of particulars of any harm reduction advocate: Addicts can turn in used needles at distribution centers and receive clean, fresh ones free of charge. This is designed to keep the rate of new AIDS/HIV infections in check. Another particular of the harm reduction advocates relates directly to law enforcement: Make a sharp distinction between "soft" and "hard" drugs, and between users and small-time, low-level sellers on the one hand and high-level, high-volume dealers on the other. In practice, this means de facto decriminalization of small-quantity marijuana possession, attempting to route addicts into treatment programs but not arresting them, but arresting and imprisoning big-time heroin and cocaine dealers.

In short, harm reduction means: Stress treatment and rehabilitation; underplay the punitive, penal, or police approach, and explore nonpenal alternatives to trivial drug offenses. Expand drug maintenance, especially methadone programs; experiment with or study the feasibility of heroin maintenance programs; expand drug education programs; permit heroin and marijuana to be used by prescription for medical treatment. Consider ways of controlling the legal drugs, alcohol and tobacco. Be flexible and pragmatic: Think about new programs that might reduce harm from drug abuse, and if one aspect of the program fails, scuttle it, and try something else. Remember: Drugs are not the enemy; harm to the society and its constituent members is the enemy. Whatever reduces harm by whatever means necessary is all to the good (Beers, 1991).

No one who supports a harm reduction proposal questions the fact that there are theoretical and practical difficulties and dilemmas in implementing such a policy. Some tough and troubling questions demand an answer. For instance, how do we measure or weigh one harm against another? What if our policy results in fewer deaths and more addicts? Less crime and more drug use? If we are truly worried about harm from drug abuse, why concentrate on legalizing or decriminalizing the illegal drugs—why not focus on ways of reducing the use, and therefore the harm, that the *legal* drugs cause? What if our policy improves conditions for one group or category in the population but harms another? And will harm reduction really result in less state control of the drug addict, abuser, and user? Government regulations and programs designed to reduce drug-related harm is likely to result in far *more* state intervention into the lives of persons affected by them. (For a cynical, mechanistic, and ill-conceived critique of harm reduction programs from a radical or left-wing perspective, see Mugford, 1993.) No advocates of a harm reduction program suggest that it is a problem-free panacea or cure-all, but all believe that these and other criticisms are not fatal, and that its problems can be resolved with the application of reliable information and good common sense.

WHY CRIMINALIZATION CAN'T WORK

Proposing that the drug laws and their enforcement be changed implies that the current ones are ineffective and/or harmful. (In fact, the bulk of the legalizers' writings is devoted to criticizing the current punitive policy; only a very small proportion of it deals specifically with the particulars of a viable legalization program.) Consequently, to fully understand the justifications for drug legalization, it is necessary to explain, in the view of the legalizers, *how* and *why* the current prohibitionist program to deal with the drug problem is a failure. Behind the punitive reasoning of criminalization is the assumption that a drug war can and should be fought, that it can be won, and that the principal weapons that must be used in this war are *the law, arrest,* and *imprisonment;* they agree that drug abuse is primarily a *police* matter. In stark contrast, all, or nearly all, legalizers, agree on one point: They *oppose* the current punitive system. They insist that drug abuse is *not* primarily a police matter. They believe that relying on the law and its enforcement is *ineffective, counterproductive,* and *unjust.*

Why do the legalizers and decriminalizers believe that our current, mainly punitive approach to drug control doesn't work? In their view, what are some major flaws in attempting to solve the drug problem by criminalizing the sale and possession of drugs? Why don't drug prohibitions work, according to the legalizers?

Before these questions can be answered, we have to lay down specific criteria as to what constitutes "working" in the first place. No specific drug policy is likely to "work" best in all important ways. It is entirely possible that a given program may work well in one way and badly in another. What do the legalizers *mean* when they say the punitive policy toward drug abuse doesn't—and *can't*—work? In criticizing the current policies and urging drug legalization or decriminalization, they make 10 points.

First, the legalizers say, criminalization makes the illegal drugs expensive and, hence, profitable to sell; because of the profit motive, arresting producers and sellers and taking them out of business simply results in *other* producers and sellers stepping in to supply the shortfall. Therefore, drugs can *never* be stamped out through the criminal law: The demand for drugs is constant and inelastic; the criminalized status of illegal drugs makes them expensive, and therefore highly profitable to sell. Therefore, it is *inevitable* that suppliers will remain in business; ironically, it is criminalization that *guarantees* "business as usual."

Second, they say, the currently illegal drugs are less harmful than the prohibitionists say and, in fact, *less harmful than the currently legal drugs*. Hence, drug criminalization is both aimed at the wrong target and discriminatory as well. If anything, controls ought to be applied to cigarettes and alcohol—which kill many more people—and not to the far safer currently illegal drugs.

Third, the legalizers insist, prohibition is futile because criminalization does *not* deter use. Drug abuse is as high now, under a punitive policy, as it would be under a policy of legalization; legalization would not produce an increase in use. Anyone who wants to use is doing so now. Prohibition is a logistical impossibility; there are simply too many holes in the net of social control. Drugs will always leak through the net. Hence, the very *foundation* of prohibition is invalid, they insist. Moreover, since the demand for drugs is *inelastic*—users will pay any price, no matter how exorbitant—raising the price through legal harassment cannot work.

Fourth, the legalizers argue, prohibition encourages the distribution and therefore the use of *harder, stronger, more dangerous* drugs—and discourages the use of softer, weaker, safer drugs. This is the case because criminalization places a premium on selling drugs that are less bulky and easier to conceal, drugs that show a greater profit margin per operation. This has been referred to as the "Iron Law of Prohibition": The more intense the law enforcement, the more potent the prohibited substance becomes (Thornton, 1992, p.70). In contrast, under legalization, they say, less potent and less harmful drugs (such as cocaine leaves, cocaine gum, opium, and marijuana) will be substituted for the more potent, more harmful illicit drugs now in use (crack, heroin, "ice," and methamphetamine) (Goldstein, 1986).

Fifth, they say, drug dealers sell in a market in which there are no controls whatsoever on the purity and potency of their product. Hence, users are always consuming contaminated—and dangerous—substances. In contrast, legalization would enforce strict controls on purity and potency; as a consequence, death by overdose would be virtually eliminated.

Sixth, the legalizers say, by undercutting the profit motive, organized crime would be forced out of the drug trade. As a result, the stranglehold that criminal gangs and mobs have on the throat of the community would be released; residents would be able to reclaim their neighborhoods, and democracy would triumph.

Seventh, legalizers say, the current level of drug-related violence is solely a product of the illegality of the drug trade. Drug-related murders

are the result of disputes over dealing territory or "turf," robberies of drug ✗
dealers, assaults to collect a supposed drug debt, the punishment of a
worker, a drug theft, and a dealer selling bad or bogus drugs (Goldstein et
al., 1989). Eliminate criminalization, and the profit motive will be eliminated, and so will drug gangs and the violence they inflict. The murder
rate will decline, and neighborhoods and communities will be safer.

Eighth, by placing such a huge priority on the drug war and encour-
aging the arrest of dealers, the government has opened the door to the
violation of the civil liberties of citizens on a massive scale. False or mis-
taken arrests or rousts, the seizure of the property of innocent parties,
corruption and brutality—these are the legacies of prohibition. Under
legalization, such violations would not occur. The police would not be
pressured to make questionable arrests, nor be tempted by bribes from
dealers; consequently, they will be better able to serve the community
(Ostrowski, 1990; Wisotsky, 1990a, 1990b, 1993).

Ninth, consider the enormous cost and the staggering tax burden of
enforcing prohibition; billions of our tax dollars are being wasted in a
futile, harmful endeavor. Under legalization, not only would this waste
not occur, but the sale of drugs could be taxed, and revenues could be
raised to treat drug abusers. In an era of fiscal austerity, surely the bud-
getary argument should weigh heavily. Legalization would represent
using the tax dollar wisely.

And *tenth,* under legalization, useful therapeutic drugs, now banned
by the government, will be reclassified so that they will find their right-
ful place in medicine. Marijuana, a Schedule I drug, is useful in the treatment of glaucoma and in reducing the nausea associated with
chemotherapy; heroin, also completely banned by virtue of its Schedule
I status, is an effective analgesic or painkiller. In addition, a current
Schedule I classification is the kiss of death for scientific experimentation. The book has been prematurely closed on some drugs, such as
MDMA ("ecstasy") and LSD—both Schedule I drugs—which have enormous potential for unlocking the secrets of drug mechanisms and, possibly, valuable therapeutic application as well. Our society cannot afford
to remain ignorant about drugs with such complex and potentially
revealing effects as these (Beck and Rosenbaum, 1994, pp.146ff.;
Grinspoon and Bakalar, 1993).

Taken as a whole and at first blush, these arguments might seem
forceful and persuasive. But are they really valid? We'll examine a few of
them in the next two chapters.

7

Business as Usual?

The sale and distribution of illegal drugs is a business—a huge business. Estimates range from between $40 billion and $150 billion for the yearly sales of illegal drugs at the retail level in the United States. This is an enormous range, of course, but, given the clandestine nature of drug sales, a precise, definitive, and authoritative figure is impossible to come by. Suffice it to say that tens of billions of dollars are earned by the American drug trade each year; perhaps the total is roughly $100 billion. If drug sellers were arrested in large numbers, would the drug trade and, hence, illegal drug use be eliminated as a consequence? Would busting these dealers, sellers, growers, and distributors wipe out drug abuse? Is this the way to fight the "war on drugs"? Prohibitionists and criminalizers argue that this is an extremely effective strategy. In contrast, the legalizers say this line of attack is futile—worse than futile, counterproductive.

STAMPING OUT DRUGS AT THEIR SOURCE?

Is stamping out drugs at their source an effective means of prohibiting, eliminating, or controlling use? Looked at superficially, the idea seems appealing. After all, what could possibly work better than pinching off the flow of a substance at the very peak of a pyramid-shaped distribution system? Cut off the head of the monster, and the monster will die—or so the saying goes. Does it apply in this case? A closer look at how drugs make their way to the consumer demonstrates the flaws in every prohibitionist plan that is based on wiping out drugs at their source. Indeed, historical experience with this program has demonstrated its fallaciousness time and time again.

The drug trade has become an international or *multinational* enterprise. Drugs used on the streets of American cities now have their origin in dozens of countries around the world. Why? Consider the current international picture. The Soviet Union has collapsed, replaced by 15 separate, independent nations. Each one faces economic problems; those in central Asia are sparsely populated, remote, impoverished, and marked by relatively weak central governments. In 1992, Kazakhstan legalized the cultivation of the opium poppy. Over the past decade or two, Third World countries have experienced shrinking gross national products; political instability in the form of conflict between and among ethnic, racial, tribal, and religious groups; and the growth of terrorism. Centralization has receded in China; its economy is moving toward privatization. National currencies in most of the Third World are nonexchangeable and essentially worthless outside the borders of each specific country. The motivation for drug dealing by greedy entrepreneurs, insurgent groups seeking weapons, peasants who recognize the difference between starving to death and achieving a comfortable way of life, businesses seeking hard currency, even governments struggling to keep afloat, is often irresistible. The result: a proliferation in drug producers world wide (Bonner, 1995; Flynn, 1993). The fabled "Silk Road," which, in times past, brought wealth to Central Asia and spices, carpets, and silk to Europe, has been reincarnated in a new role: the transportation of opium. "Propelled by the dissolution of the Soviet Union in 1991, economic and political chaos, civil war, borders that cannot be controlled and the aggressive anarchy of Afghanistan . . . , this rugged, often unassailable region has become the ultimate drug runner's dream come true" (Specter, 1995, p.A1).

Stamping out drugs at their source is a fatally flawed policy for four reasons, each of which is related specifically to the illegality of the drug trade. *First,* an almost infinite number of entrepreneurs are willing to take a risk to earn a profit; arresting one results in another's stepping in and taking over the business. *Second,* logistically, growing, transporting, and selling drugs are impossible to detect and eradicate because the drug trade does not require much space and can be easily shifted around when necessary. *Third,* the drug business contributes to the wages even of low-level workers and the economy of regions, even entire countries; hence, it is deeply entrenched and widely supported. And *fourth,* the enormous profits of the drug business translate, for distributors, into enormous resources which enable them to evade detection, corrupt officials, and purchase personnel and equipment to combat law enforcement.

PUSH DOWN/POP UP

All four of these factors can be traced to a broader master principle; in general, eliminating the drug trade at its source cannot work because of a phenomenon that has been referred to as the "push-down/pop-up" factor (Nadelmann, 1988, p.9). Whenever drug production is wiped out in one location, growers and distributors in other areas step in to supply the shortfall. And the reason why this happens is that the sale of drugs is enormously profitable. Imagine the automobile industry's being wiped out overnight; within hours, steps will be taken to replace it, again, because it is an enormous source of profits. But what makes the drug trade different is that it is *illegal,* say the legalizers, and that makes it *even more* profitable than a legal industry. The risk of arrest in a given transaction is fairly small; and, at the top of the distribution pyramid, the chance of earning huge sums is extremely high. Eliminating one grower or distributor means greater sales for the ones who remain, and creates a business opportunity for those who are thinking about taking the plunge. In other words, criminal law yields to "a higher law," economic law—"the law of the marketplace, the law of supply and demand" (Wisotsky, 1990b, p.8).

In 1975, the U.S. government financed a program to supply the Mexican government with the resources to spray illicit marijuana fields with Paraquat, a poisonous insecticide, which killed the plants. For a time, this program (albeit temporarily) practically eliminated Mexico as a source of marijuana imported to the United States. Rather than allow this multibillion-dollar need to languish unmet, entrepreneurs from a wide range of countries—including Colombia, Jamaica, and Belize—began growing and exporting marijuana on a massive scale. In addition, understandably, home-grown marijuana became more popular—and far more potent. Reacting to this trend, in 1989, President Bush launched "Green Merchant," a program of arresting domestic, especially indoor, marijuana growers. Growers, in turn, became more sophisticated, efficient, and secretive. The result? In the 1970s, home-grown marijuana made up less than 10 percent of the market; by 1989, this had grown to 25 percent; and by the mid-1990s, this had grown to roughly half (Pollan, 1995). Whenever the source of illicit marijuana was wiped out ("push-down"), it managed to "pop-up" somewhere else. And the reason is always the same: the profit motive.

In the early 1970s, most of the heroin consumed on the streets of the United States began as opium poppies grown in Turkey; they were processed in France, Italy, or Lebanon and exported to New York. At that time, President Nixon, with the cooperation of the Turkish government, initiated a major program to wipe out illicit poppy cultivation in Turkey and sever the "French Connection." The plan worked; heroin which had its origin as Turkish poppies ceased to make its way into the veins of American junkies. But by 1975, Mexico had become a major opium grower and the main source of illicit heroin. Subsequently, in the wake of the push to eliminate Mexico as a source of illegal drugs in the mid-1970s, within only five years, Southwest Asia (Pakistan, Iran, and Afghanistan) and Southeast Asia (Burma, Thailand, and Laos) became the country's principal suppliers. Today, 70 percent of the heroin sold on the street in the United States originated from opium poppies grown in Burma (whose proper name is Myanmar). Today, after vast, multibillion-dollar efforts to wipe out heroin at its source, the drug is much more abundant than it was a decade ago, and much more potent; in the early-to-mid-1980s, illicit heroin was 3 or 4 percent pure, whereas, by the 1990s, the average purity of heroin nationwide grew to between 35 and 40 percent (Treaster, 1993). Clearly, severing the Turkish-Italian-French pipeline did not cut off the supply of heroin to the United States; although there was a reduction in the short run, within a matter of a few years, demand stimulated entrepreneurs in a variety of locations around the world to supply the drug. At one time, the Medellín cartel supplied most of the illicit cocaine sold in America. In the 1980s, a massive crackdown all but eliminated that city from the drug distribution picture. Within a matter of a few months, Colombia's sister city, Cali, became the center for cocaine exportation to the United States.

THE LOGISTICS OF ERADICATING DRUGS AT THEIR SOURCE

The fact is, illegal drugs can be grown and manufactured in very many places, in very small spaces, and it is enormously profitable to do so. American addicts consume roughly 10 to 20 tons of heroin a year, which can be made from 100 to 200 tons of raw opium. This is less than 5 percent of the world's opium production, most of which is legal; if only one-twentieth of the world's legal opium production is diverted into the illegal manufacture of heroin, this would satisfy all the drug needs of all narcotic addicts in the world. The entire world's illicit heroin supply can be grown on a mere 25 to 50 square miles of poppy fields. This can be accommodated by growing plants in tens or hundreds of thousands of widely scattered fields that are virtually immune to electronic or satellite surveillance. In Burma, the principal source of America's illicit heroin supply, vast territories are not under the control of the central government at all; they are controlled by warlords in command of large, well-armed and well-financed armies whose business is to protect the poppy fields and make sure the supply of opium and morphine makes its way to refineries in Laos and Thailand (Brookes, 1990). In 1996, Kung Sa, the most powerful of the Burmese opium barons, was arrested (Shenon, 1996). Will his removal put a dent in the heroin supply shipped to the

United States? (U.S. State Department officials believe the deal Kung Sa worked out with authorities entails his staying in business.) Or will another group, gang, or cartel step in and take over his business? It's too early to tell; drug experts are not optimistic.

The coca plant is the source of cocaine. Its leaves are a legal crop in Bolivia and Peru; they are chewed by a substantial number of Indians in those countries to offset fatigue and hunger. Less than 1,000 square miles of land worldwide is devoted to the cultivation of coca. According to the senior senator from New York, Daniel Patrick Moynihan, citing a report by the Department of Agriculture, coca plants can be grown in practically any location in the world which receives between 40 and 240 inches of rain a year and has no frost or swamps; in South American alone, these characteristics fit 2.5 million square miles. Brazil has what is one of the vastest unpatroled jungle territories in the world; if coca production is stamped out in Peru, it can be relocated to Brazil (Gonzales, 1985; Nadelmann, 1989, pp.939–940). With the government crackdown on marijuana growing in the United States, cultivation has become increasingly sophisticated. Today, enough plants to generate profits of nearly $200,000 a year can be grown in an indoor area the size of a pool table. Within a very few years, some claim, "virtual" marijuana gardens can be cultivated which will be self-regulating; their ownership will be almost untraceable, the grower appearing only to harvest the product, replant some seeds, and, once again, disappear into anonymity (Pollan, 1995).

THE DRUG TRADE AS AN EMPLOYER

There is far more to eradicating drugs than the logistical problem of locating and destroying them at their source. Thinking about how the illegal drug trade works means that we have to consider its *economic contribution* to an entire region or nation. Considering the economic factor should *not* be construed as an argument that claims that eradicating the drug trade is impossible—only that it will be a much more difficult task. In addition, the economic factor means that, if successful, eradication will almost inevitably have serious and, in all likelihood, deleterious consequences. (The same may apply to the impact of legalization as well.) Considered strictly from its economic contribution, selling drugs is no different from any legal business. Indeed, up and down the hierarchy, from the grower to the importer to the lowliest worker, wages are higher in the illegal than in the legal sector. But more than this: It isn't only those at the top who profit; it is anyone who derives employment from it. All workers who earn a wage spend it in the legal sector—on food, clothing, shelter, as well as other necessities and luxuries. Hence, we have

to consider the influence of the drug in "spreading the money around"—
what is sometimes referred to as the economic "ripple" effect. Again, considered strictly from an economic point of view, eliminating an illegal
industry is no different from eliminating any legal industry. Wiping out
the drug trade worldwide would devastate the economy of a large number of countries throughout the world.

In Colombia, the cocaine trade is as profitable as the coffee business.
Try to picture Colombia's coffee business wiped out overnight; the result
would be economic catastrophe for the country as a whole. In principle,
this is no different for the cocaine trade. The marijuana crop in the
United States is more profitable than the corn crop (Pollan, 1995).
Picture the entire corn industry obliterated from the face of the earth.
Again, it would impact not only the growers and sellers but everyone
who is dependent on their business, and everyone who does business
with them, and so on down the line—that is, the entire country. One reason why the drug trade is so deeply entrenched at the supplier level is
that entire regions and even nations are dependent on it, even citizens
who have no idea that they are. Drug trafficking is estimated to bring
between $3.5 and $7 billion into Colombia's economy. The current
crackdown on its cocaine trade has brought about a shortage of income
within the Cali cartel, sales of real estate by its members, a devaluation of
the peso against the dollar, a recession in the construction industry, and
a decline in the Colombian stock market (Anonymous, 1995). The
remarkable feature about the economy is that it does not distinguish
between income earned by "moral" and "immoral" enterprises; while
both income streams could have *additional* impacts, the money that
flows through an economy is completely without a conscience.

Half of Bolivia's foreign trade derives from the coca business
(Gonzales, 1985, p.242). Bolivia is a poor country. What is going to
replace this revenue in the event of the loss of the cocaine trade? The
Drug Enforcement Administration estimates that Jamaica earns more
from exporting marijuana than from all other exports combined; if this
source of income is obliterated, how can it be replaced? What industry
can possibly contribute as much to these and other countries' gross
national product? What economic sector are the jobs that are eliminated
going to come from? The reason why drugs cannot be eradicated at their
source by convincing peasants to grow potatoes and wheat is that there
is an endless supply of entrepreneurs willing to take risks in order to earn
huge sums of money and to employ any number of laborers to work at
jobs which pay them 10 times what they would earn producing a legal
crop (Gonzales, 1985, p.238). But note: The fact that the drug trade is a
viable and lucrative employer is relevant to both the prohibitionist *and*
the legalization arguments since, under legalization, drug profits would

presumably plummet. If legalization threatens to become law, would drug entrepreneurs resist it as forcefully as they have resisted law enforcement? Or, if legalization is instituted, would they become the legal suppliers of formerly illegal drugs? At the present time, we can only speculate.

DRUG PRODUCTION AS A VIOLENT ENTERPRISE

One Colombian drug dealer is reputed to earn $20 million a month; his private army of several thousand heavily armed men represents a force that is larger than the entire personnel of the federal Drug Enforcement Administration (Gonzales, 1985). In Burma (or Myanmar), in vast territories, there are no federal authorities whatsoever; the territories are ruled by warlords who command huge armies. Their business: the production and transportation of opium poppies (Brookes, 1990). In order to capture a drug baron and put his operation out of commission, the Burmese government must expend enormous resources and, often, engage in open, bloody, and extremely costly warfare. These territories are, in effect, outlaw nations unto themselves. (Kung Sa was captured only because a portion of his private army mutinied.) Some powerful drug sellers are personally worth billions of dollars and control entire towns and even regions with an iron fist. In Colombia, even honest judges let arrested drug traffickers go free because they know that they and their entire families will be murdered if they do not; they are given a choice: "a big payoff or a bullet" (Riding, 1988)—in Spanish, *plata* (silver) or *plombo* (lead). In locales where drug selling is deeply entrenched, corruption is not even the issue; there, law enforcement has simply ceased to function. Drug dealers are often more powerful than the government; they have more money and command larger armed forces, with superior weapons. In some areas, law enforcement against illegal drug production is simply impossible without massive federal intervention; in other areas, it is possible, but extremely difficult and dangerous.

In 1995, against overwhelming odds, the Colombian government launched a concerted campaign against illegal drug sellers located mainly in and around Cali (Brooke, 1995b). One of the fruits of their efforts: the arrest of Henry Loaiza Ceballos, a cocaine kingpin nicknamed "the Scorpion." Loaiza owns 30 luxurious ranches, 5,000 head of cattle, and several apartments and beach houses. In an attempt to win over the loyalty of the populace in the towns and regions in which he operates, he has paid for the repair of Catholic churches, purchased a fleet of buses and given free rides to those unable to pay the fare, sponsored beauty pageants and distributed free rum to the audience and motorcycles to the contestants, and handed out candy to children at Halloween. Loaiza also commands a large army of ruthless killers. In 1990, peasants in one town where he owns a ranch talked about organizing a union. In a reign of terror lasting a year, 107 suspected unionists were rounded up, tortured, and cut to pieces with chain saws; their body parts were found in a nearby river. A Catholic priest complained of the killings; several days later, his "decapitated and dismembered body" was pulled out of the river. A local fruit picker went to Cali and complained about the killings; he was arrested and never heard from again. While the ruthlessness of such enterprises does not argue for the impossibility of rooting them out, it does highlight its difficulty. Indeed, the arrest of Loaiza demonstrates that law enforcement under such circumstances is possible. Still, some observers speculated that the Scorpion will be released within a few years in a generous plea bargain with the government. Commenting on Loaiza's "blazer, blue jeans, designer tie, and engaging smile," *La Prensa,* one of Bogotá's leading newspapers, marveled, he "doesn't look like a . . . killer. . . . Anyone would say that he is a math teacher" (Brooke, 1995a).

SMUGGLING: INTERCEPTING DRUGS AT THE BORDER

Policies succeed or fail not because the general principle on which they are based is wise or foolish, but because of specific, nuts-and-bolts features pertaining to their implementation. Think of intercepting drugs at the border as a military campaign; think of the nuts-and-bolts or *logistical* problems entailed in stopping the drug flow at this point. Roughly 10 to 20 tons of heroin and 120 to 150 tons of cocaine enter the United States each year across its borders, including from international waters. This sounds like a huge quantity until one realizes how much legal freight enters the country from abroad. A total of roughly 100 *million* tons of cargo comes into the United States annually. In addition, there are more individual border crossings into the country than there are residents— over 300 million. What cargo gets checked by customs officials? Which persons are searched? In 1991, for example, nearly two million containers came through the Port of Newark, of which customs officials were able to inspect only 15 to 18 a day (Flynn, 1993). Tracing the many inlets, islands, and harbors along the waters lapping the shores of this country produces nearly 90,000 miles of coastline where small, drug-laden boats could dock silently, surreptitiously, without attracting attention.

Checking every item of cargo and every person crossing the border is a literal impossibility; it represents a tactical horror story for law enforcement officials as well as a massive inconvenience for people entering the country for legitimate reasons. A lesson can be taken from "Operation Intercept" (1969), when every person and vehicle crossing the U.S.-Mexican border was subject to inspection. Traffic backed up for as much as six miles, waits ran to two or three hours, and complaints flooded American officials; the policy hurt tourism, hurt business, and seriously inconvenienced Mexican workers and American travelers returning home. Moreover, the plan resulted in no major drug seizures; the total quantity of marijuana confiscated was no more than was true before it went into effect, 150 pounds a day. After 20 days, Operation Intercept was abandoned. The policy did have two effects, however. It stimulated an increase in marijuana importation from Vietnam, as well as an increase in home-grown marijuana (Gooberman, 1974; Inciardi, 1992, pp.42–43).

After the problem of the sheer *volume* of persons and cargo entering the United States, there is the problem of the remarkable *inventiveness* of smugglers in hiding drug cargo. Quantities of illegal drugs crossing the border have been hidden in baby diapers, fresh fruit, frozen fruit pulp, hollowed-out religious statues and other relics, clothing mannequins, electronic equipment, the hulls of ships, panels and gas tanks of cars, bags of coffee, surfboards, books, furniture, concrete fence posts, ice-packed cases of vegetables, aerosol cans, sneakers, and pillows strapped around someone's waist. Heroin and cocaine have been stuffed into condoms and swallowed by couriers; animals have been surgically cut open and, again, had heroin- or cocaine-filled condoms inserted into their bodies, were sewn shut, and were then transported across the border; drugs have been placed in airtight containers in a liquid—such as olive oil, gasoline, liquor, mouthwash, shampoo, and the water tropical fish swim in—and smuggled into the country. Cocaine has been molded into a bust of Jesus and spray-painted a light-gray color; 15 pounds of cocaine were chemically bonded into two fiberglass dog kennels; half a ton of cocaine was packed into hollow plaster shells shaped and painted to look like yams (Speart, 1995). The possible ways that drugs can be shipped across the border are almost infinite, limited only by the smuggler's imagination. These are only a few of the gimmicks we know about, since they resulted in detection and confiscation. It almost boggles the mind to try to imagine what some of the *successful* attempts have entailed.

When the Coast Guard targeted large ships carrying huge drug loads, smugglers shifted to smaller loads and smaller, faster boats. When one coastline attracted the Coast Guard's attention, another coastline was chosen for offloading drug shipments. When long-haul, large-load planes were detected and busted, smugglers turned to faster, lower-flying planes. When large loads generally attracted surveillance, detection, and arrest, smugglers shifted to sending in a large number of couriers, each with a fairly small load, on the assumption that the majority will get through. When operations which moved drugs directly from the source country to the United States became vulnerable to detection, arrangements were made with intermediaries in offshore Caribbean islands to bring drugs into the United States indirectly, in more graduated stages. And throughout the past two decades or so, the watchword has been *diversification*—not only of techniques but also of the national and ethnic backgrounds of importers and smugglers. No longer the exclusive domain of a small number of nationalities or ethnic groups, drug smuggling is conducted by Colombians, Cubans, Mexicans and Mexican-Americans, Italians and Italian-Americans, Chinese, Nigerians, Israelis, Iranians, White Anglo-Saxon Protestants—in fact, quite possibly, every imaginable racial, national, and ethnic category on Earth.

As important as the logistical problem of surveillance and inspection is the fact that the persons crossing the border smuggling quantities of an illegal drug are almost always couriers—"mules" or "Smurfs" who are paid to deliver the goods and know next to nothing about the operation of the organization they work for. Each has been paid a few thousand dollars for taking a risk; if any one of them is arrested, it represents only a small loss to the total operation. Arresting them and confiscating their shipment amounts to little more than a tariff or "tax" levied against smugglers to continue doing business. Customs officials estimate that between 5 and 10 percent of the total volume of illegal drugs entering the United States is confiscated. And of this fraction, again, only a small fraction results from border inspections per se; most confiscations result from tips or intelligence in advance of the crossing itself. As things stand now, for drug smugglers, having a certain proportion of their goods confiscated represents little more than the cost of doing business.

Busting at the border does have a number of effects; none, unfortunately, has anything to do with drastically reducing drug abuse. The authorities can report an increasing number of arrests and seizures and claim that they are doing their job to bring drug abuse to a halt, that the seizures are "taking drugs off the street" and the arrests are "putting dangerous drug dealers behind bars." The statistics on seizures and arrests can be used to back up these claims, since they are specific, concrete, and quantitative. After all, seizing two tons of cocaine is twice as good as seizing one; arresting a dozen smugglers is twice as good as arresting six. The effort is largely symbolic, however; at the level of seizures and arrests that currently prevails, it has nothing to do with reducing the supply of illegal drugs. A ton of cocaine seized at the border does not translate into a ton less cocaine on the street; in the short run, it may mean a bit more dilution and a bit higher price. In the medium run, it means another smuggler using a different technique to import more cocaine into the country. In the long run, it means nothing.

In 1986 and again in 1988, two federal bills were passed which required that the U.S. military be a party to intercepting illegal drugs coming into the country. The most important of the provisions of these bills allocated resources, mainly equipment and personnel, to interdict illegal drugs at the border. Officials at the Department of Defense, long aware of the low interdiction rate and the improbability of success in this venture, commissioned a study by the Rand Corporation to evaluate the feasibility of "sealing" the country's borders off from incoming illegal drugs (Reuter, Crawford, and Cave, 1988). The report concluded that it is "extremely difficult" to reduce cocaine consumption in the United States by even as little as 5 percent, even if the government were to put into operation the most stringent and thorough interdiction program feasible. Drug smuggling, the report said, is too sophisticated, decentralized, diversified, flexible, versatile, adaptable, resourceful, and intelligent an operation to be slowed down by a few seizures and busts. There is too much to gain by getting illegal drugs into the country, and too much to lose by giving up the business as a result of a few busts and seizures. It simply can't be done, concluded the Rand report. The military agrees, but to keep up symbolic appearances (and for the purpose of relative deterrence), the operation continues. News reports, complete with photographs of politicians and high-level police brass standing next to huge piles of confiscated cash and drugs, convince the public that "something is being done" about the drug problem. The coverage is always good for a few votes at election time.

Consider one truly sobering statistic: Only 12 percent of the retail cost of cocaine stems from producing, refining, importing, and smuggling the drug. Even if *half* the cocaine that comes into the country from abroad were to be seized—which is unrealistic in the extreme—cocaine prices would increase by only 5 percent. "Since prices are already so low, such increases would not affect consumption" (Falco, 1992a, p.8). Not only is it logistically impractical to rely on border seizures as a means of controlling drug abuse in the United States; from an economic standpoint, its basis is completely illusory. But recall our distinction between *absolute* and *relative* deterrence: If there were *no* inspections at the border, it is certain that the volume of drugs entering this country would be many times greater than what it is today. (Yes, relative deterrence *does* work.) But relying on border seizures to shut down or seriously reduce the size of the drug trade is almost unbelievably naïve. (No, absolute deterrence does *not* work.)

ARRESTING AT THE DEALER LEVEL

As we've learned, the value of the American drug trade is an estimated $100 billion a year at the retail level. Clearly, here, as elsewhere in the world, a great many people depend on the sale of controlled substances for their living. In principle, the economic impact of this business is not a particle different from any other industry, such as producing and selling hamburgers, doughnuts, motorcycles, hang gliders, sporting goods—or tobacco and alcohol. A decade and a half ago, a journalist estimated that, in New York City alone, a quarter of a million people earned their primary livelihood from the sale of illegal drugs (Pileggi, 1982). These people not only earn that money but also spend it, and contribute to the livelihood of others. Can anyone seriously entertain the belief that, through the routine enforcement of the drug laws, this immensely lucrative business will be closed down? Remember: It is not only at the top of the pyramid where these benefits accrue, but at every level, from top to bottom, and horizontally as well, that is, as I said, persons outside the industry with whom drug-trade workers spend their money.

If it weren't for the fact that there are many Americans who still believe in the myth of a "Boss of All Bosses," it might not seem necessary to refute it. A surprising number of my students still believe that the illegal drug trade is highly centralized, that there is a single, big-time, high-level dealer in the United States who directs the sale of illicit drugs nationwide. He is swarthy, in all probability, Latin or Mediterranean; he wears dark sunglasses, sits at a very large desk, and speaks into a telephone with a deep, gravelly voice. And they believe that, if he were arrested, drug sales in the country would come to a screeching halt. But—the myth continues—he is protected by corrupt police officials and politicians at the highest levels of power, possibly even up to the presidency of the United States. If only we could clean up the corruption and arrest "Mr. Big," we could wipe out drug abuse in the country overnight! This belief would be amusing if it weren't so pervasive. The fact is, drug dealing in this country is highly decentralized, and has become increasingly so in the past generation; different dealers operate in hundreds, possibly thousands, of independent enterprises. Illegal drugs are smuggled into the United States from several dozen different countries. Certainly there are one, or several, Mr. Bigs in some countries or regions, and in the United States, there are, again, one or several *local* Mr. Bigs—cartels and monopolies that operate at the community or neighborhood level; still, to imagine that any single powerful figure, or even a small number of players, could run the whole show in the United States demonstrates an almost unbelievable childlike naïveté.

Does busting at the dealer level within the borders of the United States work? It is important to make a distinction between high-level and low-level drug sellers. In all likelihood, arresting the high-level dealer cannot have an impact that is appreciably different from attempts to eradicate drugs at their source. Again, the dealer's risk is small, while the rewards are great. But what about the street-level dealer, that is, the person who sells drugs directly to the customer? Would arresting the petty, small-time drug seller (who is usually a user, even an addict, as well) be effective in reducing drug abuse nationally? At first glance, it might seem an extremely ineffective way of going about fighting the drug war. Why harass and arrest the poor, miserable junkie and street-level dealer, while permitting major drug suppliers to roam the streets, free as a bird? It might seem that a policy of concentrating on smaller sellers rather than a neighborhood Mr. Big represents a policy with a misplaced or inverted emphasis, perhaps little more than a cynical police ploy to pile up a large number of meaningless arrests to little or no practical purpose. Doesn't it make more sense, this logic would hold, to arrest a small number of major dealers who supply tens of thousands of addicts, and shut down their operations, than to arrest large numbers of petty dealers with no more than a few dozen customers?

It is true that crippling an entire drug-dealing organization through the arrest of all or most of the high-level figures in it is likely to interrupt the flow of drugs into a community, at least temporarily. However, it is rare for the police to be able to apprehend the key players in an entire drug operation. More often, one or a small number of key players are arrested, and they can almost always be replaced. Of course, each time an arrest of a drug figure is made, the police attempt to get dealers to testify against their colleagues; this effort is more likely to fail than to succeed. If truth be told, the police prefer to arrest large-scale dealers—corruption aside—largely because it carries with it publicity, professional pride, and a symbolic message to all concerned that they are doing an effective job in their war against illegal drugs. The police refer to these busts as "quality" arrests, while they call the arrest of petty street-level dealers "garbage" collars. Unfortunately, arrests of big dealers are difficult; they require a huge investment of time and resources. Moreover, these figures are often successful in avoiding conviction and imprisonment by hiring expensive, sophisticated legal counsel. In contrast, street-level busts are easier to make, and petty dealers have fewer resources with which to fight conviction and incarceration. In addition, and obviously, there are a great many *more* street-level dealers at the bottom of the distribution pyramid than there are Mr. Bigs at the top. Moreover, street-level dealers may make one or two dozen observable, public transactions a day, maximizing their vulnerability to arrest, whereas a high-level, high-volume dealer may make one or two well-concealed transactions a month. Hence, there are logistical reasons why there is a vastly greater likelihood that the police will arrest the petty, small-time drug seller-user than the high-level, high-volume dealer.

But the far greater likelihood that the police will be far more likely to make petty or street-level dealer arrests than at the top of the drug distribution ladder may have a practical rationale as well as a logistical or operational dynamic. Again, disrupting an entire operation aside, ironically, high-level busts generally have very little if any impact on the distribution and availability of drugs in an area. The reason is simple: The temptation for allied or competitive dealers to step in and continue business as usual is enormous. In contrast, there is a possibility, some observers feel, that many low-level busts will have something of a more long-term impact. Why? Consider this. Today, almost all experts are agreed that eradicating the *supply* side of the illegal drug equation is hopeless. Given the vastness and versatility of the drug production and distribution enterprise, and the huge economic incentive, there is no possibility of wiping out drug abuse by attacking its supply. But drugs would not be used if there were no demand for them. What about attacking the *demand* side of the illegal drug equation? Many drug experts believe that demand is influenced by supply, and by arresting the ultimate seller, the dealer who transacts with the user and addict, demand and therefore use are *most likely* to be affected. Again, why is this?

Studies of police "crackdowns" or "street sweeps" in neighborhoods and communities in which drug dealing is rampant demonstrate that their impact is inconsistent; even in areas where a reduction in selling and drug-related crime can be demonstrated, they are almost always short-lived. Mark Kleiman studied the effect of saturation arrests in two heavy-drug-dealing communities in Massachusetts. In one, the arrests were followed by a two-year reduction in the robbery and burglary rate and an increase in new enrollments to drug treatment programs, indicating that drug supplies had dried up. However, after two years, these changes were wiped out, and in some categories, the situation was worse than before. In the second community, following the crackdown, there were no reductions in the availability of drugs, and rates of violent crime actually increased (Kleiman and Smith, 1990, pp.80–81, 89). In 1984, the New York Police Department launched "Operation Pressure Point," a massive crackdown on drug-selling arrests in the city's Lower East Side. Soon after the program was launched, certain crime indicators were down, but experts eventually concluded that both crime and drug dealing had been displaced to other neighborhoods. In 1986, Operation Clean Sweep was initiated in Washington, D.C.; again, a detailed study of its impact showed, drug markets were displaced to other areas, and they reopened in the original neighborhoods when the police stopped saturation arrests (Kleiman and Smith, 1990, pp.80–81).

On the other hand, such police efforts may make other contributions. Says criminologist Jerome Skolnick, commenting on police crackdowns of street dealers in Oakland, while such efforts have not driven dealers off the street, they have reduced the "wide-open marketplace atmosphere" in the worst areas; says a police respondent interviewed by Skolnick, "you don't have the swarms of people all night long. They're still dealing, but not twenty-four hours a day. At least we've thinned it out so people can get in and out of their own driveways" (quoted in Currie, 1993, pp.206–207). Thus, such neighborhood sweeps may reclaim the streets for the community's law-abiding citizens. In addition, they may convince residents that something is being done about the drug problem, that the police are not corrupt agents of drug dealers (Wilson, 1990b, p.533).

As we'd expect, something of the same "push down/pop up" effect we looked at on the international stage applies to the distribution of drugs within the country's borders. The removal of one drug dealer through arrest will result in some temporary disruption in the distribution of drugs, which, in turn, results in another dealer's stepping in as a replacement. When the police crack down in one neighborhood or community, business will move elsewhere; when the intensive enforcement campaign is eased, typically, business resumes in the first locale. Moreover, busting dealers makes it more profitable for those who are willing to take the risk of arrest. How could things be otherwise? One suitcase full of cocaine or heroin can earn a dealer hundreds of thousands of dollars in a single transaction. Can anyone possibly imagine that, as a result of possible arrest, *no one* can be found who is willing to take the risk? The profits will always attract enough daring, enterprising traffickers to ensure an uninterrupted flow of illegal drugs (Pileggi, 1982). There is enough talent to go around to keep the ranks of drug dealing well supplied with personnel who will guarantee that drugs continue to flow from their source to their target. The risk is simply too low, and the profits too great, to expect that there will be a dramatic interruption in the flow of heroin and cocaine as a result of drug busts (Kaplan, 1983, pp.85–86).

There are some striking differences between busting at the top and busting at the bottom of the distribution chain, however. Unless busting at the top disrupts an entire organization, it is likely to have little effect, since other entrepreneurs will inevitably step in and take over the arrested dealer's business. On the other hand, *some* impact can be felt at the community level as a result of police "street sweeping." For one thing, petty dealers are a great deal more visible and more vulnerable to arrest than high-level dealers are. And even a temporary disruption of business is a good thing; it makes dealing less visible and residents more mobile and less intimidated; and it may convince skeptical but law-abiding citizens that the police are honest and trying to deal with the drug problem. Even these small gains are not necessarily obtained by scattering arrests all over a city, however; they can be made only by saturation arrests in one area or a small number of areas. It's something like cleaning up the litter a little bit in parks all over a city versus cleaning up a few parks thoroughly; saturation street sweeps will have some impact on the targeted neighborhoods, while a few busts in neighborhoods all over the city will accomplish next to nothing (Kleiman and Smith, 1990, p.89). In sum, although the "push down/pop up" factor does work *to some extent* for low-level busts, there is some evidence that focused saturation arrests of petty dealers will have a modest impact on the affected neighborhoods.

8

Will Drug Use/Abuse Rise under Legalization?

Attacking the *supply* or manufacture and distribution side of the drug-use equation is extremely unlikely to work, as we just saw. Clearly, the lure of the profit motive is too great for at least some of our citizens, even with some measure of risk involved. What about the *demand* or user side? The motives for selling and use, although intertwined, are at least analytically distinct. *Can* law enforcement deter use? More generally, does the law and its enforcement deter *any* activity? If there were no laws and no enforcement, would currently illegal activities become more common? If a product or service is criminalized, does the demand for it remain constant? Will just as many customers be willing to pay for it *regardless* of whether it is legal or illegal? Just how inelastic is the demand for certain products and services? The legalizers are insistent that "prohibition doesn't work"—indeed, *can't* work (Carter, 1989; Hyse, 1994; Morgan, 1991; Priver, 1993). Is this true for *all* products and services, under *all* circumstances? More specifically, is it true for the currently illegal drugs?

As a general rule, strongly condemned and punished activities are less commonly engaged in than are tolerated and approved activities. The "forbidden fruit" argument—that condemnation makes an activity more attractive and, hence, more frequently enacted—may apply, in certain limited instances, to *experimentation* with an activity but certainly not continued participation. I suspect that criminalization actually *does* lower the demand—as well as the supply—of *certain* products and services. To put the matter another way, legalization *would* result in an increase in the incidence of many activities. As a general rule, the more *elastic,* more *substitutable,* and more *sensitive to price* a demand is, the more effective criminalization is in discouraging its satisfaction; the less elastic, less substitutable, and less sensitive to price a demand is, the less effective criminalization is (Wisotsky, 1990b, p.8). Outlawing leaded gasoline, for instance, has not produced a huge illegal market for it—customers who are willing to pay hundreds of times its previous, legal, price and manufacturers who are willing to supply it, thereby risking arrest. For practically all motorists, an adequate substitute exists in unleaded gas; hardly any customers are willing to pay huge price increases for marginally superior performance. The sale of automobiles in the United States is restricted to those that meet certain standards, for instance, with respect to emission controls. Has that resulted in a huge underground sale of cars that do not meet these standards? No; in this case, the "prohibition" of nonstandard cars works, more or less. The number of times customers visit prostitutes and, hence, the number of prostitutes, are almost certainly smaller, all other things being equal, where it is *illegal* than where it is *legal.* Can anyone seriously doubt that a substantial proportion of men would visit prostitutes more frequently if the public sale of sex were completely legalized? Prostitution is a major business in Nevada, where it is legal; elsewhere in the country, studies show, sex with prostitutes is only a minor sexual outlet for men (Michael et al., 1994, p.63). For many men, where it is illegal, sex with a prostitute affords a sordid, even risky sexual option, as the British actor Hugh Grant discovered in Hollywood in 1995. Risks come not only in the form of arrest (extremely low, although, with sporadic police campaigns, they are there) but also in the form of criminal victimization from the prostitute and her colleagues and from denizens of the environs in which prostitution is likely to take place, and, for some, in the form of social stigma in the event of discovery following arrest. Hence, the "prohibition" of prostitution must be counted as at least a partial success.

PROHIBITION

Some legalizers argue that *no* ban or prohibition on an activity or substance that is desired by a sizable number of citizens can ever be successful. The legalizers may be referred to as *anti-prohibitionists.* Most adopt a broad, sweeping view of the failure of prohibitions in general; their guiding model for this stance is national alcohol prohibition (1920–1933). The Eighteenth Amendment, also referred to as the Volstead Act, is the only constitutional amendment to have been repealed in U.S. history. Everyone knows that Prohibition was a clear-cut failure—very possibly the biggest domestic legal mistake in the federal government's entire history. We've all learned about the history of Prohibition—Al Capone, organized crime, gangland violence, bootleg liquor, bathtub gin, speakeasies and illegal nightclubs. Since Prohibition was such a disastrous failure, it follows as night follows day that our current policy of drug prohibition will also fail. "Prohibition can't work, won't work, and has never worked" (Carter, 1989), we've learned. True or false?

Remember that policies may work well in one way but badly in another. Prohibition is an excellent example of this principle. Interestingly, national alcohol prohibition *did* work in at least one sense—it reduced the level of alcohol consumption in the American population. Historians, medical authorities, and policy analysts have put together indicators from a variety of sources—arrests, automobile fatalities, hospital admissions, medical examiners' reports, as well as legal sales before and after Prohibition—and concluded that the consumption of alcohol declined significantly between 1920, when the Eighteenth Amendment took effect, and 1933, when it was repealed. (Actually, most *state* laws prohibited alcohol sales by 1916, so the decline in use took place even *before* 1920.) In 1911, the death rate from cirrhosis of the liver, a reliable measure of alcohol consumption, stood at 29.5 per 100,000 men; in 1929, it was 10.7. Admissions to state mental hospitals for alcohol psychosis was 10.1 per 100,000 in 1919, and 4.7 in 1928 (Moore, 1989). Legal alcohol sales were twice as high in the 1911–1915 period (2.56 gallons of absolute alcohol per adult) as in 1934, the first full year of repeal (0.97 gallons). This indicates that a substantial number of Americans discontinued the use of alcohol during Prohibition and did not pick up the habit again until a few years later. (Of course, keep in mind the fact that repeal did not legalize the sale of alcohol; it authorized "local" or state options. Some states opted to legalize, while others retained some form of prohibition, at least temporarily. This is a point in favor of the prohibitionist argument, of course, since, as more and more states legalized over time, alcohol consumption increased in those states.) It was not until after the early-to-mid-1940s that legal sales matched the pre-Prohibition levels—1.20 gallons in 1935, 1.54 in the 1936–1941 period, and 2.06 in 1942–1946 (Lender and Martin, 1987, pp.206–207). The conclusion is inescapable: *In the narrow sense of reducing alcohol consumption,* Prohibition *did* work. Far from being a failure, *in this one respect,* it was a *resounding* success.

But again, in most other important respects, Prohibition was a *disastrous* failure; in this sense, the anti-prohibitionists are correct. It may have switched millions of drinkers from beer, a less potent beverage, to distilled spirits, a far more potent—and more harmful—beverage; it encouraged the consumption of harmful, poisonous substitutes, such as methyl alcohol; it certainly gave organized crime an immense boost, pouring billions of dollars into the hands of criminal gangs, consolidating their power, and effectively capitalizing their other illegal enterprises; it encouraged corruption and brutality on the part of politicians and the police on a massive scale. In these crucial respects, Prohibition did *not* work; in fact, it was clearly a catastrophic failure. (It was also a failure from the point of view of *absolute* deterrence: Many Americans *did* get their hands on illegal alcoholic beverages.) The lesson from Prohibition should *not* be that drug prohibitions cannot work; it should be that, in instituting a drug policy, impacts come in packages. Some of the contents in a given package may be desirable, while others may be most distinctly undesirable. Another package will contain a different mix, with entirely different positives and negatives. Which package one selects depends on values, not science—that is, depends on a preference for certain results over others. There is no policy that will yield results that everyone—or anyone—will regard as entirely or uniformly positive. As the saying goes, "You pays your money, and you takes your chances."

LEGALIZATION AND USE: TWO ISSUES

Regardless of whether or not prohibition generally does or does not reduce the incidence of an activity (for certain activities, it does; for most, it doesn't)—and regardless of whether or not Prohibition specifically did or did not reduce the consumption of alcohol (as we saw, it did)—the results of one of the various versions of legalization have to be considered separately. The fact that "trickle-down" thinking is a fallacy reminds us that a policy that looks good on paper may not work in the real world, one that works in general or in most instances may fail in a specific case. The assumption of the legalizers is that abolishing the criminal penalties for the possession and sale of the currently illegal drugs will not result in a substantial rise in their use and abuse. (Some of legalization's most optimistic advocates even argue that use will actually decline; this view is not widely shared.) Is this true?

The question of the impact of legalization on the incidence and frequency of use pivots on two separate questions, one *empirical* and the second *moral* and *ideological*. The empirical question is familiar to us all and can be stated simply, although answered with difficulty and only tentatively: What evidence do we have that addresses the issue of the impact of legalization on use? The moral question is a bit harder to spell out, but need not detain us here, since it is essentially unanswerable: If legalization *does* result in an increase in use, how many more users and abusers represent an acceptable increase, given the beneits that this change will bring about? Dennis (1990, pp.128–129) estimates that legalization will result in a 25-percent increase in the number of abusers and addicts. Even if the figure were to double, he finds this acceptable, considering that legalization will unburden us from criminalization's enormous monetary and human costs. I suspect that even if we were all to agree on Dennis's numerical prediction, not all of us would accept his conclusion. Again, the moral question has to be disentangled from the empirical question. Empirically, what is likely to happen under some form of legalization? Will the use of the presently illegal drugs rise—or remain at about the same level?

WORST-CASE SCENARIO

One critic of the drug laws claims that their supporters argue that legalization will mean that "countries will plunge into anarchy, families will disintegrate, and most of us will become drugged zombies" (Mitchell, 1990, p.2). Some supporters of the drug laws actually do feel that way, or very nearly so. Former drug "czar" William Bennett estimates that under legalization—a plan he vigorously opposes—some 40 million to 50 million Americans would become hard core heroin and cocaine abusers. William Pollin, former director of the National Institute of Drug Abuse (NIDA) estimates even greater numbers for cocaine alone. Since cocaine is the most pleasurable (or "reinforcing") drug in current use, it makes sense that if there were no law enforcement, "the number of cocaine users would be right up there with smokers and drinkers. . . . We'd have 60 to 100 million cocaine users instead of the 6 to 10 million current users we now have. . . . Viewed in this light," Pollin adds, our punitive law enforcement policy "is 90 percent effective" (Brinkley, 1984, p.A12). Would we become a nation of "drugged zombies" under legalization?

I do not believe that the use or abuse of cocaine or heroin will increase 10 times if any of the currently debated legalization plans were put in place. In other words, I believe that Bennett's estimate of 40 million to 50 million addicts for heroin and cocaine and Pollin's estimate of 60 million to 100 million regular cocaine users are seriously wide of the mark. Regardless of how alluring, seductive, or reinforcing these drugs are, the tens of millions of Americans Bennett and Pollin project who will become involved in the use of these seriously mind-transforming drugs for the pleasure they afford—and risk destroying everything they now value, including job and career, marriage and family, money, possessions, and their freedom—simply do not exist. At the same time, I do believe that, if one or another legalization proposal were to be instituted, the number of Americans who will take, and become seriously involved with, the currently illegal drugs, including heroin and cocaine, would increase more than modestly, possibly even dramatically, possibly along the lines of two to three times. In other words, there will be a significant increase, but the "worst-case scenario" will not come to pass. My estimate contradicts both the legalizers, who argue that there will be no, or an extremely modest, increase; and the criminalizers, who argue that the increase will be monstrous, almost uncontrollable. Here, I am a firm believer in relative deterrence: Yes, use is lower than would be the case *without* law enforcement, but no, law enforcement does not and *cannot* eliminate or drastically reduce use. Perhaps some justification of my estimate is in order.

Three different sets of evidence can be used to address the question of the impact of legalization on frequencies of use. The first is related to what we know about human nature generally. The second is related to the intrinsic nature of each drug, how it is used, and what its effects are. And the third is what is known about actual or concrete frequencies of use under more restrictive, and less restrictive, conditions.

HUMAN NATURE

All predictions of what is likely to happen under certain conditions are based on specific assumptions about human nature—a general theory of behavior, if you will. Legalizers and prohibitionists hold contrasting sets of assumptions about human nature; perhaps it will be worthwhile to look at them under a microscope.

The legalizers see human nature as basically rational, sane, temperate, and wise. "Inform a normally intelligent group of people about the tangible hazards of using a particular substance and the vast majority of them will simply stop" (Gazzaniga, 1990, p.39). That is, the *reason* why drug abuse will not rise sharply under legalization is that most people are cautious and not willing to take risks; since currently illegal drugs entail a certain likelihood of harm, it is extremely unlikely that they will be taken up by many people who are not currently already using. In contrast, one of the reasons that prohibitionists cite in support of their argument is their assumption—as we saw with Bennett and Pollin's predictions—that many people are not nearly so rational and moderate in their behavior as the legalizers believe. Many, many Americans will experiment with and use heroin and cocaine, the prohibitionists believe; of this total, a substantial proportion will become compulsively involved with them to the point of abuse and addiction. The reason why this will happen, the prohibitionists believe, is that many of us are willing to take dangerous risks; they feel that a substantial number of us believe that bad things happen to *other* people but not to *us,* that we, somehow, are somehow lucky enough to do potentially dangerous things, yet not get hurt. A lot more people are reckless risk-takers than the legalizers think, the prohibitionists argue. In fact, they say, this is precisely the reason why we have criminal laws outlawing certain activities: By introducing the risk of arrest, society can dissuade the *slightly* foolhardy from engaging in high-risk activities, leaving only a fairly *small* number of *very* foolhardy souls who will be willing to do so.

Many decades ago, Ruth Benedict published a classic in the anthropological literature, *Patterns of Culture* (1934). In that book, she made a distinction between two approaches to life—the *Apollonian* and the *Dionysian*. In the ancient Greek and Roman religions, Apollo was the god of poetry, music, light, healing, and manly beauty, while Dionysus was the god of fertility, wine, and drama. Hence, the Apollonian approach to life is a "classical," measured, graceful, traditional, rational way of living, while the Dionysian approach is pleasure-seeking, lustful, hedonistic, selfish, risk-taking, even violent and dangerous. Some cultures stand more at the Apollonian end of this spectrum, while others stand at the Dionysian end. Likewise, some people are more Apollonian, others are more Dionysian. The legalizer's general theory of human nature (or, at least, the American version of it) is Apollonian; the prohibitionist's is Dionysian.

In my view, the argument between the criminalizers (who see human nature as closer to the Dionysian pole) and the legalizers (who see it as more Apollonian) is misplaced. To put it another way, both sides are partly right—and partly wrong. In fact, while most Americans are not Dionysian risk-takers, this is irrelevant. The crucial issue is not the orientation of *most* Americans, but the orientation of a *minority*. There are *enough* Dionysians in this society who, under the right social and legal conditions, would be inclined to experiment with drugs and seriously disrupt the lives of the rest of us. In spite of the practical, hard-working, sober veneer of most Americans, many of us are a great deal more Dionysian than we are willing to admit. There are many among us who want to drive fast cars, get intoxicated on psychoactive drugs, engage in a variety of sexual adventures, neglect our workaday and family obligations, eat fattening foods without restraint, dance until dawn, and commit a wide range of criminal acts, but who are afraid of the consequences—social, monetary, and, for some of these actions, legal consequences. The removal of legal penalties outlawing one of them—getting intoxicated on drugs—would make drugs more attractive to a substantial number of Americans. My contention is that the threat of arrest and imprisonment is one of the mechanisms that keeps the wilder side of the *moderate* Dionysians (if such a creature is not a contradiction in terms) in check, while the small minority of *extreme* Dionysians remain undeterred by any manner of risk, legal or otherwise.

But here's an extremely important point: The legalizers are correct in assuming that *most* of us are *not* true Dionysians. Most Americans would *not* experiment with heroin or cocaine, and, of those who would, most would *not* become unwisely and abusively involved with them. There is almost *no* chance that, under legalization, heroin or cocaine would ever become as popular as cigarettes or alcohol. The vast majority of Americans would shun the recreational use of the currently illegal drugs, and the vast majority of those who would use them would be temperate and moderate in their use. Comments one critic of the current policy, "while certain drugs can produce physical dependence, most individuals *will not willingly take* those drugs, even after experiencing their effects" (Gonzales, 1985, p.105). Still, this is irrelevant. What is important is that *more* people would use under almost any conceivable version of legalization than is true today, and more would use compulsively and abusively.

I do believe that most people do not want to harm themselves. I believe that the evidence shows that, however inaccurately, people generally do calculate cost and benefit before engaging in certain actions. (Indeed, this is one of the reasons behind enacting and enforcing criminal laws.) But *risk* is not the same thing as *harm;* risk entails taking chances—it is not a guarantee of being harmed. A certain proportion of motorcyclists refuse to wear helmets. For most of them who take that risk, not wearing helmets will make no difference to their life or limb, because most will not get into a serious accident. The same applies to motorists do not want to wear a seat belt; for most of them, not wearing a seat belt is in fact *not* harmful. However, harm enters into the picture not in each and every case but in the overall picture. Injury and fatality statistics are very clear about this: You are *more likely* to be seriously injured and die if you do not wear a helmet or a seat belt. *Some* (not all, not even most) motorcyclists are harmed because they didn't wear a helmet; *some* motorists are harmed because they didn't wear a seat belt. The law convinces a very substantial proportion of motorcyclists and motorists to wear these protective devices; even more persuasive than a law by itself is a law with real penalties and vigorous enforcement.

Again, it is simply irrelevant to argue that most "normally intelligent people" will give up an activity if they are aware of the "tangible hazards" of an activity or substance (Gazzaniga, 1990, p.39). The fact is, the risk an activity entails is not always clear-cut, obvious, or immediately apparent. Indeed, the danger in question may *never* manifest itself because, once again, risk is a statistical, not an absolute, affair. Most people are not harmed *at all* by a great many very risky activities. The two crucial issues are, first, the absolute number who are harmed, not the proportion, and, second, the number who are persuaded not to take a given physical risk because of an entirely separate risk—the likelihood of arrest. In my view, if that second risk were removed, a substantial number of people *would* engage in harmful, abusive drug taking. (Why do the legalizers empha-size the dissuasive power of physical risk but ignore the power of the threat of arrest and imprisonment?) Not a majority, not even remotely close to Bennett and Pollin's tens of millions of Americans, but a sub-stantial number. Seeing the American population as far more Dionysian than the legalizers do leads me to conclude that legalization *will* result in a significant rise in drug use and abuse.

USING DRUGS, DRUG EFFECTS

A second piece of evidence relevant to the question of the impact of legalization on drug use bears on the effects of the drugs under consid-eration and the ways they are used. Although all drugs are by definition psychoactive, not all drugs are used in the same way; while all drugs are used for their pleasureable effects, the way that that pleasure is experi-enced and integrated into the lives of users is far from identical for all drugs; while all the psychoactive drugs possess a potential to generate a dependence in users, that potential varies enormously from drug to drug.

The mechanics, logistics, and effects of each drug influence the degree to which it can be woven into everyday activities. The effects of cigarettes, as they are currently used, are mildly stimulating. Most users can continue to puff cigarettes more or less throughout the day without disruption—while working, studying, interacting, talking, driving a car, walking about, and so on (Kaplan, 1988, p.41). Only (as it turns out, a growing) social disapproval cuts smokers off from nonsmokers; in other words, the intrinsic nature of the use of the drug and its effects do not preclude their integration into routine living. Although alcohol is not quite so readily integrated into everyday life, in moderation, it is com-patible with a wide range of pleasureable activities, it tastes good to most of us, it goes well with food, it is typically a lubricator of sociability; it does not usually isolate drinkers from nondrinkers except at the point of heavy consumption. Unlike many drugs, the effects of alcohol are linear; one does not have to be drunk or intoxicated to enjoy its effects. One can enjoy extremely mild effects of alcohol, whereas for some drugs (heroin, for instance), achieving only subeuphoric effects is more likely to be experienced as frustrating than enjoyable. As they tend to be used, most of the currently illegal drugs are taken specifically to get *high;* this is typ-ically an all-or-nothing proposition.

As a hypothesis it may be stated that the more readily a given form of drug use can be adapted to everyday life, other things being equal, the more popular it is likely to be. Contrarily, the more disruptive its use is, the less potential it has for widespread popularity. In contrast to cigarettes and, to a lesser extent, alcohol, drugs like heroin, crack cocaine, and especially psychedelics such as LSD are *highly* disruptive drugs; their effects jolt the user out of routine activities and away from sociability with others, particularly nonusers. Using these drugs requires a much greater commitment to use and a much greater willingness to suspend whatever else one may wish to do, at least for a time. We may place marijuana and powdered cocaine midway along a continuum between cigarettes at one end and heroin, crack, and LSD at the other. Smoking marijuana and "snorting" or taking powdered cocaine intranasally are moderately disruptive, are usually confined to periods when the focus is more or less on getting high and enjoying oneself. Again, few users seek a mildly pleasureable sensation; most wish to become high or intoxicated. Hence, the use of these drugs will create an *interactional barrier* between the users and the nonusers—and often among users themselves. Thus, with respect to the connection between the way these drugs are used and their effects, tobacco is *least* disruptive to everyday life and requires the *least* commitment to use, while heroin and, most especially, crack cocaine and LSD stand at the opposite end of the continuum; they are highly disruptive and require a great deal of commitment to use regularly and frequently. Hence, legalizers predict, under legalization, heroin, crack cocaine, and LSD and the other psychedelics, could *never* attain the popularity of the currently legal drugs. Given the basic fact of the disruptive nature of heroin, crack cocaine, and LSD, it is *almost inconceivable* that they would be taken up on an abusive scale by more than a small fraction of users, even if they were to be legalized. Their use will remain marginalized and indulged in by a very small minority (Nadelmann, 1989, p.945).

On the other hand, there is the issue of how *reinforcing* the drugs in question are, a factor which Bennett and Pollin stress in their predictions of use patterns after legalization. With respect to drugs, "reinforcement" refers, roughly, to how enjoyable a substance is, its capacity to deliver an orgasm-like jolt or "rush" of unmodified, undiluted, unsocialized pleasure. "Reinforcement" refers to the reward an organism achieves upon taking the drug and the commitment it has to continue taking it. To put the matter in more formal terms, the more reinforcing a drug, the harder an organism will work to continue taking it. The reinforcing potential of drugs can be determined even among nonhuman organisms; rats, mice, and monkeys find cocaine (and, to a lesser degree, heroin and amphetamine) *immensely* pleasurable; they will press a bar hundreds of times in order to receive a single dose of the drug. In a laboratory situation, they will take it as much as they can and will even risk their lives to do so. They will take cocaine in preference to food and water, and will even kill themselves, self-administering cocaine. Moreover, if they have taken cocaine over a period of time and the drug is suddenly discontinued, they will continue doing whatever they did previously that rewarded them with doses of cocaine, but now go unrewarded, for a longer period of time than for any other drug, including heroin (Bozarth and Wise, 1985; Clouet, Asghar, and Brown, 1988; Eckholm, 1986; Johanson, 1984). Psychologists regard whatever produces such slow-to-extinguish previously rewarded behavior as extremely reinforcing.

In this respect, then, cocaine stands at the top of all widely used psychoactive drugs; it possesses the greatest *immediate sensual appeal;* this means that previously inexperienced subjects who are administered a range of drugs without knowing what they are being given are most likely to say they liked cocaine and most likely to say they want to take it again (Grinspoon and Bakalar, 1976, pp.191–194; Lasagna, von Felsinger, and Beecher, 1955). Most pharmacologists and psychologists now argue that psychological reinforcement, not physical dependence, is the key to dependence. Drugs that are highly pleasurable in a direct, immediate, sensual way are most likely to produce addict-like behavior in users, *whether or not* these drugs produce a literal, physical addiction, that is, withdrawal symptoms (Ray and Ksir, 1996, pp.40–42). In this respect, then, among all widely used psychoactive drugs, cocaine possesses the greatest potential for producing dependence.

At the same time, we must be skeptical of any automatic extrapolations from laboratory experiments, whether on humans or animals, to real life. Wilbanks (1992) warns us against the "monkey model" of addiction—the fallacy of thinking that what monkeys in cages do with drugs automatically tells us everything we want to know about what humans will do on the street. After all, animals do not like the effects of alcohol or tobacco; it is difficult to induce them to take these drugs, use them, or become dependent on them. Yet we know that they are extremely widely used—and abused—among humans in their natural habitat.

Still, laboratory experiments cannot be dismissed out of hand. They remind us of the *potential* for dependence that specific drugs possess. And cocaine possesses that potential in greatest abundance: It is most reinforcing, immediately pleasurable, appealing, sensual, and seductive. Remember, this is only one factor out of a range of factors that influence use. By itself, it does not dictate the popularity of drugs. But knowing this one fact about cocaine should make Bennett and Pollin's prediction understandable. I think they are wrong in the *magnitude* of that prediction, but it is not difficult to see how they came up with it. Again, regardless of the exact *size* of the predicted increase, other things being equal, the pharmacological properties of cocaine (and, to a much lesser extent, heroin) should lead anyone to predict an increase in use. There is, in other words, sufficient ground for genuine concern when it comes to sharply reducing the cost and increasing the availability of cocaine, given its intrinsically pleasure-inducing and reinforcing property. A great deal of contrary evidence would have to be marshaled to convince evidence-minded observers that cocaine abuse would *not* rise sharply under legalization—and, as yet, no such evidence has been forthcoming. In the absence of such evidence, most of us will have to remain convinced that, in the words of John Kaplan (1988, p.33), legalization "ignores basic pharmacology." It almost defies logic to assume that, when criminal penalties are removed, the use of an entire array of pleasureable, highly reinforcing drugs will not rise significantly.

FREQUENCIES OF USE

What *direct* evidence do we have that bears on the impact of legalization on drug use? Contrarily, what evidence bears on the impact of the criminalization of drugs and enforcement of the drug laws on use? Does drug use/abuse rise when drugs are legalized and fall when they are criminalized? Or, as the legalizers assume, does law enforcement have little or no impact on the incidence and volume of use? What circumstances make drugs more, or less, available? Is there a *variety* of controls which influence use, and not merely legal ones? What does the use picture under *nonlegal* controls tell us about the impact of *legal* controls?

We already know that national alcohol prohibition in the United States (1920–1933) *did* discourage use: Fewer Americans drank, and fewer contracted cirrhosis of the liver during Prohibition than before and afterward. (Prohibition brought about a number of *other* changes, as we saw, but they are separate from the issue of volume of alcohol consumption.) We also know that the partial decriminalization of small quantities of marijuana in nine states of the United States has *not* resulted in a significant increase in the use of this drug (Cuskey, Berger, and Richardson, 1978; Johnston, 1980; Single, 1981). It is entirely possible that marijuana is a case apart from cocaine and heroin. At any rate, cocaine and heroin are the drugs most Americans fear and worry about the most. A number of observers have endorsed the legalization of marijuana and yet oppose the legalization of hard drugs such as heroin and/or cocaine (Kaplan, 1970, 1983; Kleiman, 1992b). And the Dutch policy (often mistakenly referred to as "legalization") is based on making a sharp distinction between "soft" drugs such as marijuana and hashish and "hard" drugs such as cocaine and heroin (Beers, 1991; Jansen, 1991; Leuw and Marshall, 1994). Hence, the case for or against heroin and/or cocaine legalization will have to be made separately from the case for or against the legalization of marijuana.

Several pieces of evidence suggest (but do not definitively demonstrate) that when the *availability* of certain drugs increases, their *use* increases as well. It has been something of a cliché among legalizers that criminalization doesn't work. Look around you, they say. Go to certain neighborhoods, and see drugs openly sold on the street. Drugs are getting into the hands of addicts and abusers right now. How could the situation be any worse under legalization? Those who want to use are already using; selling drugs to addicts, abusers, and users legally would not change anything, they say.

The fallacy in this line of reasoning is that, currently, under our punitive policy, addicts and abusers are *not* using as much as they would like. Under almost any currently proposed legalization plan, the currently illegal drugs would be more available; if that were so, current abusers and addicts would use a great deal *more* cocaine and heroin than they do now. The fact that we can look around on the streets of the country's largest cities and see drug selling taking place means next to nothing. The fact is, there is the "hassle factor" to consider. Addicts are *pulled into* use by the fact that they enjoy getting high, but they are *pushed away* from use by the fact that they have to commit crime to do so. Street crime is difficult, risky, and dangerous; use is held down by that fact. If drugs were less of a "hassle" to obtain, the majority of addicts and abusers would use it more. The vast majority of heroin and cocaine abusers want to get high, are forced to commit a great deal of crime to do so, and are not getting high as often as they want because their drugs of choice are too expensive, and the crimes they commit are too much of a "hassle," for them to use as much as they want. Mark Moore (1973, 1976) refers to this as the "search time" for illegal drugs; says Moore, as "search time" goes up, demand decreases. Careful ethnographic and interview studies of street addicts and abusers have shown that *getting high*—not mere maintenance—is their prime motivation. Most are *not* technically addicted, their day-to-day use varies enormously, and most would use *much more* frequently if they could (Johnson et al., 1985; McAuliffe and Gordon, 1974). In this sense, then, the drug laws and their enforcement have cut down on the *volume* of drug use among a substantial proportion—very possibly a majority—of our heaviest users and abusers. Again, the distinction between relative and absolute deterrence comes into play here; these addicts and abusers use a *substantial quantity* of illegal drugs—but a great deal less than they would if these drugs were legal or freely available to them. Ironically, the drug laws are *most* effective against the drug use of the *heaviest* users, those, who, moreover, are arrested *the most*.

Goldstein and Kalant (1990) base their opposition to legalization on the observation that use is directly related to availability, and availability can be influenced by a variety of controls, including criminalization and cost. Under all legalization plans, the currently illegal drugs would be sold or dispensed at a fraction of their present price. Indeed, that is the advantage of this plan, say its supporters, because the high cost of drugs leads to crime which, in turn, leads to a panoply of social harms, costs, and problems. But Goldstein and Kalant argue exactly the opposite: that the high cost of the illegal drugs is *specifically* what keeps their use down. If drugs were to be sold or dispensed at low prices, use would almost inevitably rise—in all likelihood, dramatically. This relationship is demonstrated, they say, with a variety of drugs in a variety of settings. For instance, as measured by constant dollars, cost and the per-capita consumption of alcohol—and the rate of cirrhosis of the liver—were almost perfectly correlated in a negative fashion in the Canadian province of Ontario between 1928 and 1974: During periods when the price of alcohol was low, the use of alcohol was relatively high; when the price of alcohol was high, use was relatively low. Price and use were mirror reflections of one another. In addition, observe Goldstein and Kalant, the purchase of cigarettes, and therefore smoking, varies *directly* and *negatively* with the level of taxation on cigarettes: The higher the taxes on cigarettes, the lower their sales. "These data suggest that anything making drugs less expensive, such as legal sale at lower prices, would result in substantial increases in use and in the harmful consequences of heavy use" (p.1515).

There are two additional pieces of evidence bearing on the relationship between the availability of psychoactive drugs and their use: first, the immense rise in the use of and addiction to narcotics among servicemen stationed in Vietnam, and the sharp decline in use and addiction upon their return to the United States; and second, the higher rates of certain types of psychoactive drug use among physicians and other health workers—who have greater access to drugs—than is true of the population as a whole.

Robins (1973) reports that almost half of a sample of U.S. military servicemen serving in Vietnam in the 1970s had tried one or more narcotic drugs (opium, heroin, and/or morphine), and 20 percent were addicted to opiates. *Prior* to their arrival in Vietnam, however, only a small fraction had ever been addicted, and *after* their return to the United States, use and addiction fell back to their pre-Vietnam levels. (This study cross-checked self-reports on drug use with urine tests; hence, we can have a high degree of confidence in the answers on use and addiction.) This study's findings are significant for at least two reasons.

First, the fact that the vast majority of addicted returning veterans discontinued their dependence on and use of narcotics on their own, without going through a formal therapeutic program, has major implications for the study of drug treatment. And second, and more central for our purposes, the fact that use and addiction increased *massively* in Vietnam, where drugs were freely available (although technically illegal), and returned to their previous, extremely low levels when these veterans returned to the United States, gives us a glimpse of what may happen under legalization. The fact that 95 percent of those who became addicted in Vietnam *had not been addicted in the United States,* and a similar 95 percent who became addicted in Vietnam *ceased* their addiction when they returned to the United States, tells us that there must have been something about the conditions that prevailed in Vietnam that *encouraged* use and addiction, as well as something about those conditions that prevailed in the United States that *discouraged* them. Some observers have attributed the high levels of drug abuse that prevailed in Vietnam to the combat stress that these servicemen experienced (Gazzaniga, 1990), but it is unlikely that this is the whole explanation. It seems almost *incontestable* that the greater availability of drugs in Vietnam induced an enormous number of servicemen to use, and become addicted to, narcotics who otherwise would not have become involved. Their low level of narcotic addiction in the United States, both before and after their Vietnam experience, was almost certainly influenced by the fact that opiates are illegal here.

There are three aspects of physician drug use that are significantly higher than is true for the population at large.

First, as a number of studies have shown, the fact that recreational drug use among medical students and younger physicians is strikingly higher than among their age peers in the general population, again, suggests that availability is related to the likelihood of use. In one study, 73 percent of medical students had at least one recreational experience with at least one illegal psychoactive drug (McAuliffe et al., 1986). In comparison, for 18- to 25-year-olds in the general population at roughly the same time, the figure was 55 percent, and for 26- to 34-year-olds, it was 62 percent. For cocaine, the comparable figures were 39 percent for medical students and, in the general population, 18 percent for 18- to 25-year-olds and 26 percent for 26- to 34-year-olds (NIDA, 1991, pp.25, 31).

Second, rates of *self-medication* among physicians are strikingly higher than is true among the general population. In the study of physician drug use cited above, four out of 10 physicians (42 percent) said that they had treated themselves with one or more psychoactive drugs one or more times, and 7 percent said that they had done so on 60 or more occasions; one-third of medical students had done so once or more, and 5 percent had done so on 60 or more occasions (McAuliffe et al. 1986, p.807). This represents an extraordinarily high rate of self-medication with psychoactive drugs.

And third, the proportion of physicians reporting drug *dependence* is extraordinarily high—3 percent of physicians and 5 percent of medical students said that they were currently dependent on a psychoactive drug (McAuliffe et al., 1986, p.808), far higher than for the population as a whole. Other surveys have produced similar results (Epstein and Eubanks, 1984; McAuliffe et al., 1984; Sethi and Manchanda, 1980). While occupational stress, once again, has often been cited as the culprit which causes high levels of physician drug use, abuse, and dependence (Stout-Wiegand and Trent, 1981), as with the Vietnam situation, it is difficult to deny that *availability* plays a substantial role. And it is greater availability that every proposed legalization plan offers; to the extent that some "legalization" proposal does *not* offer availability, then clearly, at that point, as with the current system, illegal market processes take over.

CONTINUANCE RATES

As we saw earlier, *legal* drugs tend to have *high* continuance rates, while *illegal* drugs tend to have far *lower* continuance rates. That is, out of the total universe of everyone who has ever taken a given drug, the proportion who continue to use it (let's say they used it once or more in the past month) tends to be fairly *high* for the legal drugs and fairly *low* for the illegal drugs. As we saw, nearly six out of 10 of all at-least-one-time drinkers consumed alcohol during the previous month and can be said to still be drinking; for tobacco, the comparable figure is under four in 10. In contrast, for marijuana, the continuance rate is only 15 percent, and for most of the other illegal drugs, less than one at-least-one-time user in 10 used in the past month. The same relationship holds up in Amsterdam, where marijuana (but not the hard drugs) is de facto decriminalized and users and small-time dealers of the hard drugs are rarely arrested. There, alcohol's continuance rate is 80 percent, tobacco's is 63 percent, marijuana's is 24 percent, that of most prescription drugs falls somewhere in between tobacco's and marijuana's rates, and that of the illicit, criminalized drugs is under 10 percent (Sandwijk, Cohen, and Musterd, 1991, pp.20–21). The fact is, although many factors influence a drug's continuance rate, other things being equal, if a drug is *legal*, users tend to stick with it longer; if it is *illegal*, they tend to use it less frequently and more sporadically, and they are more likely to give up using it altogether. Clearly, then, it is simply not true that, under criminalization, illegal drugs are as freely available as are the legal drugs. Criminalization makes drugs more difficult to obtain and use on an ongoing basis; for many would-be regular users, the "hassle factor" makes use simply not worth it.

9

Drugs and Crime

Drugs and crime are intimately related in the public mind. When a gangland execution is reported in the media, most of us immediately begin thinking about a possible drug connection. Drugs are behind the extraordinarily high murder rate in the nation's largest cities, we feel. Innocent bystanders are gunned down on the street—and behind every such slaying, drugs are seen as being responsible. Decent, honest, law-abiding citizens are held hostage to drug dealers, afraid to leave their apartments at night. Robbery, burglary, auto theft, simple larceny—these and other property crimes are committed on a massive scale to pay for millions of drug habits. Assault, rape, reckless endangerment, child abuse, automobile fatalities: Much of it is committed when the offender is under the influence.

The connection between drugs and crime is real, of course, although somewhat exaggerated in the public's mind, and in the media as well. All researchers recognize that determining the causal link between drug use and criminal acts is not an easy matter. If the police discover a body in a known crack house, was the killing drug-related? Not necessarily. The deceased may have died of natural causes, or as a result of actions completely unrelated to drugs. To some degree, the designation "drug related" is a construct, not an objective reality (Brownstein, 1993). Even the fact that drugs and crime are frequently found together or *correlated* does not demonstrate their *causal* connection. Still, all observers agree that the drugs-crime connection is strong. Drug users do have a significantly higher than average crime rate. In fact, the recreational users of *all* drugs—alcohol and tobacco included—have a substantially higher crime rate than do drug abstainers. (Let's return to this theme momentarily.) What's behind this connection? What causes it? And what can we do about it? Quite obviously, the criminalizers and the legalizers have precisely the opposite solution. The criminalizers think that severe penalties will take the criminals off the street, discourage potential offenders from breaking the law, and lower the crime rate. The legalizers think that removing criminal penalties from the currently illegal drugs would sever the drugs-crime connection by removing the motives for property crime (because drugs would be cheap) and violent crime as well (because there would be no illegal empire to protect). How would it work? And would it be successful?

One building block of the legalization position is that it is law enforcement itself that is largely responsible for the high rate of crime in our society. If the currently illegal drugs were to be legalized, they say, the crime rate would decline sharply and drastically. Legalization would "take the crime out of drugs," its advocates argue. This will take place in at least four distinctly different ways.

First, since, under legalization, drug possession would no longer be a crime, not arresting addicts and users—and, in all likelihood, petty, street-level user-dealers as well—would free up the criminal justice system to the tune of hundreds of thousands of arrests per year, and keep hundreds of thousands out of the nation's prisons, and put them into treatment programs.

Second, since drugs would be sold legally and at low cost, addicts and drug abusers would no longer be forced to commit crimes in order to obtain their substances of choice. Their current crime rate is a function of the illegality of cocaine and heroin; transform that legal status, and the crime rate of hard-drug users will plummet, again, freeing up our criminal justice system so that it can focus largely on the violent criminal.

Third, legalization would result in the deflation of the profits earned by dealers which, in turn, would result in the virtual elimination of gang "turf" wars and other violent disputes that erupt around the drug trade. As much as half the urban street violence can be traced to the drug trade; eliminate drug profits, violence will decline, and many lives will be saved.

And fourth, legalization would virtually wipe out organized crime, at least that sector of it that earns its livelihood by selling the currently illegal drugs. A major source of the underworld's profits will be eliminated overnight; organized crime will shrink correspondingly.

Do these arguments in favor of legalization make sense? Will legalization reduce or "take a bite out" of crime? Are these points empirically sound? What evidence do we have to address these points? Conceptually, at least, we have to make a distinction between crimes committed by users in the course of their everyday lives and those committed by dealers in the course of their illicit business. In addition, we have to keep the distinction between crimes of violence and property crimes fresh in our mind. These two distinctions will become relevant as our discussion unfolds.

DRUG CRIMES

If drug possession and sale are legalized, by definition all the current drug crimes would no longer be against the law. In this sense, legalization would produce a direct and immediate drop in the crime rate as a result of taking the drug laws off the books. Or would it? This depends entirely on the specific legalization program under consideration. The details of the plan under consideration are far from a trivial matter. Details represent a series of conditions which determine or influence what the targeted population is likely to do, and that is different for different conditions.

Many legalization plans propose controls for the currently illegal drugs similar to those now in place for alcohol. Alcohol is a legal substance; anyone above a certain age may purchase it. Let's be clear about this: In the United States, there are far more arrests related directly to the use, possession, and sale of alcohol, a *legal* substance, than is true for all the illegal drugs. In 1994, according to the Federal Bureau of Narcotics, arrests for drug abuse violations numbered 1.3 million. But there were just under 1.4 million arrests for driving under the influence, over half a million for violations of the liquor laws, and nearly three-quarters of a million for drunkenness. (This does not count the arrests for violations that are code words for alcohol-related offenses, such as disorderly conduct and vagrancy.) Of course, this statement must be met with a strong qualifier: Though there are many alcohol-related *arrests,* and consequently, a sizable segment of jail or temporary holding facilities is devoted to them, there are very few arrests that result in *prison incarceration.* In contrast, over 60 percent of federal and 26 percent of state prisoners (and a third of newly incarcerated state offenders) are incarcerated for drug offenses (Butterfield, 1995). Alcohol offenses tie up a huge proportion of police and jail resources, but practically none in prisons. In any case, if the laws and their enforcement against the now-illicit drugs were similar to those now operating for alcohol, it is clear that this would *not* eliminate drug crimes or arrests on drug charges. It is not inconceivable that, under legalization, the current drug arrest figures may actually *rise* as a result of two developments: One, as I argued, under legalization, more people will use drugs; and two, the police will use charges like public intoxication and driving while under the influence as a new means of controlling drug abuse. In any case, an alcohol-type legal control system will *not* eliminate drug arrests—and it may actually increase them.

The marijuana decriminalization or "harm reduction" program that now prevails in the Netherlands is often cited by legalizers as a model drug plan the United States might adopt. Yet, it has not resulted in the disappearance of drug crimes. Recall that in the Netherlands, the posses- X sion and sale of small quantities of marijuana, while technically against the law, are tolerated in practice; the possession and sale of large quantities of marijuana remain a crime—both in the law and in its enforcement. Moreover, the possession and sale of the hard drugs by users, addicts, and petty street dealers, again, while illegal, results in very few arrests. Yet, as we've seen, in the Netherlands, roughly a third of the prison population is made up of drug offenders; most were arrested for the sale of substantial quantities of the hard drugs. This is comparable to the United States, where, again, just over a quarter of the state prison population is made up of drug violators (Butterfield, 1995). Clearly, then, *certain* legalization or decriminalization programs will not eliminate drug crimes.

Picture a far more modest legalization scheme: some form of drug maintenance or a prescription plan. In the United States at present, as we've seen, roughly 100,000 narcotic addicts are enrolled in methadone maintenance programs. Under these programs, narcotic addicts are not granted complete, free, or unrestricted access to any psychoactive substance they wish to take. Instead, they are administered maintenance doses of methadone, a slow-acting narcotic. These doses are administered orally rather than injected, so that they do not produce a high or intoxication. However, only a minority of the nation's narcotic addicts are enrolled in these programs (100,000 out of between half a million to a million), partly because funding for them is limited and partly because most narcotic addicts do not want to be maintained—they want to get high. *Most* enrollees violate the terms of the program by taking illegal drugs; most drop out of the program against the advice of the staff, presumably to return to a life of addiction; most continue to commit criminal behavior, even when they are enrolled in the program. However, roughly a third to 40 percent, as I pointed out earlier, are helped in some major way, as a result of a significant decline in their use of heroin and other drugs, as well as a reduction in their crime rate. If drug legalization is to look anything like the current methadone maintenance program for narcotic addicts, then what we should expect is a significant drop in the overall rate of illegal drug use for enrollees as a whole (to perhaps one-half or one-third of their previous level). However, roughly a third of all enrollees will continue to take illegal drugs frequently, and will drop out of the program; a third will take them less frequently, and will bounce in and out of the program; and a third will remain semi-abstemious as a result of the program (Hubbard et al., 1989). Again, while this is an improvement, it does not result in an *elimination* of drug crimes among addicts. If legalization is to look like our present methadone maintenance program, we should expect similar results. In fact, perhaps we should expect *poorer* results, since, now, methadone programs only enroll the addicts who are *most* committed to giving up illegal drug use. If these programs were to be expanded, they will inevitably enroll a far higher percentage of less-committed addicts and, hence, a higher volume of drug violations.

Considering methadone maintenance programs forces us to face an obvious dilemma in "fine tuning" the dispensing of drugs in any legalization system.

On the one hand, if the restrictions are as strict as they are for our current methadone maintenance program, many users, abusers, and addicts will not be willing to enroll because it does not give them the drug they want, or the drug in sufficient doses, or administered the way they want. Most users want to get high, they do not wish simply to be maintained and, hence, refuse to enroll in a maintenance program. As a consequence, a restrictive program, such as the methadone programs we now have, will result in *many* drug violations among users, including enrollees.

On the other hand, under a viable legalization program, what are our criteria for eligibility to be? Should anyone above a certain age be allowed to obtain any quantity of any drug, no matter how large, at any level of potency? What would the price of newly legal drugs be pegged at? The price of the currently illegal drugs is hugely inflated above what what they cost to manufacture under free-market conditions—by a factor of 20 to 50 times. Should drugs be priced at what the market will bear? If this means selling crack at 50 cents a dose, within the budget of any sixth-grader—so be it? If not, will an illicit market step in and supply what the market wants, but cannot obtain legally?

The fact is, under almost any conceivable form of legalization, that is, one with some restrictions, an illicit market will "continue to thrive alongside the legal one" (Kraar, 1990, p.71). The lower legal prices are (and the more accessible drugs are), the smaller this illicit market will be; the higher legal prices are (and the less accessible drugs are), the larger it will grow. If there is an "iron law of prohibition" it is this: *An illicit market in a hugely desired product will shrink only to the extent that the demand for that product is satisfied; to the extent that it is not, the illicit market will grow correspondingly.* The claim that legalization will dry up an illicit drug market seems extraordinarily naïve, given that it fails to stipulate the single most crucial factor: the price and availability of the newly legalized substances. Is it really possible that any informed observer imagines that free and ready availability of drugs will not significantly increase their use and abuse and, hence, multiply the damage they cause?

Hence, the dilemma can be stated quite simply: The more restrictive the program, the larger the volume of illicit use, and therefore the more frequent the drug crimes; the less restrictive the program, the smaller the volume of illicit use—but, almost certainly, the greater the legal use (Moore, 1990a, p.16). Programs with *many* restrictions will have little licit but much illicit use, whereas programs with *few* restrictions will have much licit but little illicit use. Programs which claim to wipe out drug distribution crimes will do so only at the expense of distributing psychoactive substances to anyone who wants them, and will encourage use; to the extent that there are restrictions, an illicit market will arise to meet that demand. The same economic market principle operates for less-than-full legalization programs as for our current punitive policy. The only legalization plan that would result in eliminating drug-related crimes or arrests for sale and possession is a complete free-market or laissez-faire program (Szasz, 1992), which calls for virtually no restrictions on drugs whatsoever. This plan has no likelihood whatsoever of implementation in the foreseeable future. As I said earlier, it is difficult to imagine any legislator or serious policy analyst urging a program that calls for controls on powerful and dangerous psychoactive drugs that are no more stringent than those that apply to the possession and sale of tomatoes.

THE DRUG USE–PROPERTY CRIME CONNECTION: THREE MODELS

Currently, drugs and crime are connected in very specific ways; their connection bears directly on the issue of whether or not property crime would decline under legalization. At least three "models" spell out the different *ways* they could be connected: the "enslavement" or "medical" model, the "criminal" model, and the "intensification" model.

The *enslavement* (or "medical") model is the one that has been adopted by the legalizers. It goes as follows. Addicts and abusers become "enslaved," unable to control their use of they drug; they spend so much money on it that they are unable to support their habit by working at a regular, legitimate job. Consequently, they *must* engage in crime; they have no choice in the matter. The enslavement model argues that addiction came first and crime followed as a consequence; addicts turn to crime *because* of their addiction. In the absence of addiction, those persons who are now enslaved to a drug would not commit moneymaking crimes, at least not to the same degree. Under legalization, in contrast, heroin and cocaine would cost just a dollar or so per dose, and a huge slice of crime would be wiped out virtually overnight (Inciardi, 1992, pp.150, 153, 159, 248, 263). The enslavement model makes two assumptions: first, that addicts and abusers are motivated to use their drugs of choice primarily because they want to avoid painful, body-wracking withdrawal symptoms and, second, that they will be satisfied with maintenance and will not seek intoxication or a high.

The *criminal* model argues that it is not *addicts who turn to crime* but *criminals who turn to drugs.* Long before they become dependent on hero- X in and cocaine, those who eventually do so were *already* engaging in a variety of criminal activities. Persons who eventually become drug addicts and abusers were delinquents and criminals *first;* only later do they turn to drug use. The *type of person* who engages in criminal behavior—moneymaking crimes included—is the same type of person who experiments with and becomes dependent on drugs. Addiction has nothing to do with their criminal behavior; they are not enslaved to a drug so much as *participants on a criminal lifestyle.* Their drug use is a *reflection* or an *indicator* of that lifestyle; it is a later phase of a deviant *tendency* or *career.* Take away the drugs and they would still commit a great deal of crime; make drugs inexpensive, and they would still commit a great deal of crime; make drugs legal, again, and they would still commit a great deal of crime. Such persons belong in prison, this argument holds; legalization isn't going to reform their criminal tendencies (Inciardi, 1992, pp.151, 160–163).

The *intensification* model represents something of a blend or compromise between the enslavement and the criminal models (Inciardi, 1992, pp.158, 163, 248). It argues that, yes, criminal careers are *already* well established long before someone abuses, becomes dependent on, or even uses illegal drugs. Take away the drugs and, indeed, these same persons would *still* commit crimes vastly in excess of the rate of the general population. Legalization will *not* eliminate their criminal activities; indeed, most drug-dependent persons are deeply entrenched in a criminal lifestyle—dependency or no dependency, drugs or no drugs. Drug abuse and criminal activity are simply *part and parcel* of the way some people live. Drugs and crime are not causally connected so much as manifestations of the same deviant tendencies. *On the other hand,* the heavy use of cocaine and heroin certainly *intensifies* the likelihood that addicts and abusers will commit crimes, especially moneymaking crimes. Researchers have followed samples of heroin addicts over a period of years. The number of days on which these addicts committed crimes was extremely *high* during periods of nonaddiction (that is, during abstention or when enrolled in a methadone maintenance program)—but *strikingly lower* than the number of days during which they remained addicted (Anglin and Speckart, 1988; Nurco et al., 1988). The conclusions are inescapable: Drug abuse does not *create* or *cause* criminal behavior, but it does *intensify* or *drive* it. Legalization would not *wipe out* moneymaking crime among addicts and abusers, but it may very well *reduce* it (Inciardi, 1992, pp.158, 163, 248).

Would some form of drug legalization reduce the incidence of moneymaking crimes among drug addicts and abusers to practically zero? Almost certainly not. Most are involved in crime as a way of life; very few have a legitimate job; very few have enough education to make them marketable. Most commit crimes just to stay alive. In the world of chronic street-drug abuse, criminal activity is routine, deeply entrenched. It is simply how a certain segment of the abuser population earns money to obtain what it wants. Legalization is not going to change this very much. On the other hand, would legalization *reduce* the likelihood that heroin addicts and cocaine abusers would commit moneymaking crimes? In all likelihood, yes. Now, as we've seen, the total amount of crime committed by addicts who are enrolled in treatment programs declines to between one-half and one-third of its former level (Hubbard et al., 1989). Remember, however, that methadone maintenance clients represent a fairly small, self-selected sample of addicts who are motivated to succeed; if all addicts were able to walk into such a program whenever they felt the impulse to rehabilitate themselves, would their crime rate be as affected as is the case now, with a more restrictive program? If legalization were to increase the number of addicts and abusers significantly and strikingly, the total crime rate may very well increase along with it. And under legalization, would users, who would then spend less money on drugs, begin spending the same amount on other goods and services and, as a consequence, commit the same amount of crime? This is a distinct possibility.

DRUGS AND VIOLENCE: THREE MODELS

As we saw, crimes of violence must be at least conceptually separated from property crime. Their dynamics are not necessarily the same; in fact, their motives are quite different. (At the same time, most of the same persons who commit crimes of violence also commit property crime.) The legalization model, at any rate, rests on a sharp distinction between them. As with the connection between drug use and moneymaking crimes, we encounter three models of the drugs-violence nexus, or why violence is more common among drug abusers than the rest of our citizenry: the *psychopharmacological* model, the *economic-compulsive* model, and the *systemic* model (Goldstein, 1985; Goldstein et al., 1989). They do not correspond exactly to the three models for moneymaking crimes I just spelled out, although the economic-compulsive model is similar to the enslavement model above, and the systemic model corresponds more or less to the criminal model. It is important to note that these three models are *not* mutually exclusive; that is, one is not right, while the other two are wrong. In fact, one could be right in explaining the dynamics of a particular criminal event, while, for another specific crime, another model best explains its unfolding. All may be right in explaining the drug use–violence link for different specific crimes; on the other hand, it is possible that one of them best explains a great deal *more* drug-caused acts of violence than the other two.

The *psychopharmacological* model says that drugs cause violence because of their *direct* effects. As a result of taking a specific drug, this model argues, users become irritable, excitable, impatient, and irrational and, hence, are much more likely to engage in criminal behavior. Judging by their direct or pharmacological effects, it might seem reasonable that narcotics would depress or reduce violent behavior because of their soothing, calming, soporific effect; marijuana as well is more likely to lower the user's violent tendencies and hence, reduce the incidence of violent behavior as well. In contrast, again, simply going on their direct pharmacological effects, cocaine and amphetamine would seem to increase the criminal behavior of users as a result of these drugs' tendency to stimulate overall activity, alertness, edginess, suspicion, paranoia, and behavioral fixations. It should also be said that heroin and the narcotics could generate an excitable, impatient, irritable state *during withdrawal* (Inciardi, 1992, p.161).

The *economic-compulsive* model argues that what causes the higher rate of violence among addicts and abusers is not so much the direct or pharmacological effects of drugs but the fact that users are dependent on drugs and, thus, engage in a great deal of violent crime that is a *by-product* of that dependency. In supporting a costly drug habit, addicts and abusers have to commit such crimes as theft, prostitution, and robbery; in committing them, they come into abrasive and sometimes violent confrontation with victims, bystanders, and the police. Moneymaking crimes *become* violent crimes inadvertently, by accident, without design, simply because victims and others fight back or because drug abusers often lack good judgment about using the most effective means of carrying out the deed. They are not "really" violent criminals, this reasoning goes, they're just involved in moneymaking activities that unwittingly *force* them to become violent upon occasion. Their violence is an extension of their "enslavement" to drugs.

The *systemic* model argues that drug abusers are more likely to be violent than the rest of us because drug abuse is densely woven into a lifestyle that is, by its very nature, violent. This is especially the case when we consider drug selling in addition to the use and abuse of illegal drugs. One cannot be a drug dealer, especially in the inner city, without facing the possibility of violence; it is a world that is *saturated* with violence. In a study of over 400 homicides in New York City, Goldstein et al. (1989)

found that over half were "drug related." Four out of 10 of *all* these homicides, and eight out of 10 the drug-related homicides, specifically involved cocaine. The connection in nine out of 10 of the cases of cocaine-related homicides was *systemic* in nature. It was *the social context of the drug trade* that generated the vast majority of these killings; these homicides were results of territorial disputes, robbery of a drug dealer, assaults to collect a debt, punishment of a drug worker, disputes over a drug theft, and disputes involving a dealer's selling bad drugs.

In other words, the world of selling cocaine, especially in certain contexts, is an ugly, brutal, violent, *inherently disputatious* world. Arguments are frequent. Predators roam the street looking for opportunities to rip dealers off or muscle in on their territory. Dealers dilute the merchandise for a fatter profit. Users attempt to acquire merchandise without paying for it. Huge sums of cash are exchanged; valuable merchandise—illegal drugs—is moving from one location to another, from hand to hand, apartment to apartment, vehicle to vehicle. The temptation to cheat, steal, and shortchange is always great. Violence is a means of social control in such a world; it is an ever-present reality.

But we can take this a step further: It is not only the world of drug dealing in which violence is common (although this is especially the case); so is the street world of drug abuse generally. A later study by the same research team (Goldstein et al., 1991) obtained detailed, day-by-day accounts of the criminal activities and drug use of nearly 300 street cocaine users for eight weeks, or 56 days. The sample was divided into nonusers (former cocaine users—that is, they were nonusers for the period of this study), "small" users (who spent less than $34 per day on cocaine during the study), and "big" users (who spent more than $34 per day on cocaine). The researchers sampled men and women equally. This study provides a somewhat different slant on the reality of the connection between drug, especially cocaine, abuse and violence than the study cited earlier.

About half the sample were involved with at least one seriously violent episode during the eight weeks of the study (55 percent for the men, 59 percent for the women). However, the violence in which men were involved was mainly as a *perpetrator,* while the violence most of the women were involved in was as a *victim.* Moreover, as volume of cocaine use increased, the men were increasingly likely to be involved in violence as a perpetrator, while for the women, as cocaine use increased, the likelihood of being a victim of violence increased (pp.356, 357). For men, violence as perpetrator was related to involvement in robbery; for women, violence as victim was related to domestic disputes with lovers, boyfriends, and husbands, as well as to disputes with friends and acquaintances. In this study, alcohol played a prominent role in violent episodes, and an extraordinarily high proportion of the violent events reported by the sample stemmed from the psychopharmacological dimension, and far less from the systemic or economic-compulsive dimensions (p.361). And in most of these events, alcohol—not cocaine—was the drug most intimately connected to violence. Interestingly, of all the categories in the sample, the "big" male cocaine users were the *most* likely to be involved in violence, but their violence was *least* likely to be related to cocaine use or distribution (p.364).

The conclusions we can draw from this study seem clear. Heavy, chronic street abusers of illegal drugs are involved in a great deal of violence. Heavy (or "big") male cocaine users are often victimizers; they frequently engage in a variety of crimes, both economic and violent. The specific motive of paying for and supporting a drug habit is almost beside the point. Rather, most engage in crime more or less as a way of life. Even crimes with an economic motive, such as robbery, often turn violent. Many of their acts of violence are alcohol-related. Women, too, are frequently implicated in acts of violence, but more often as a victim than as a perpetrator. It is almost inevitable that women who are involved in the illegal street drug scene will be victimized; in fact, the more they use cocaine, the greater that likelihood is. Drug use either places them in vulnerable situations or is a measure or indicator of their involvement in the violence-saturated street drug scene. It is extremely unlikely that legalization will transform the violent nature of the world of heavy, chronic drug abuse very much. That violence is a part of the way that frequent, heavy drug users live their lives; it is *systemic* to their subculture. In assuming that the ordinary, routine, day-to-day, garden-variety violence will decline substantially if the currently illegal drugs were to be legalized, the legalizers do not make a terribly compelling argument.

THE DRUGS-CRIME
CONNECTION GENERALLY

The connection between drug use and criminal behavior is strong, intimate, and, in all probability, ineradicable. But is it causal in nature? If so, what is the *nature* of the causal relationship between them? As we've seen, the causal connection is extremely complex. Certainly illegality and, hence, the cost of illegal drugs influence the crime *rate*, that is the exact *magnitude* of crime. But illegality and cost do not determine *criminality*. Recall that, among cocaine abusers, the drug that was most intimately connected with violence was alcohol, not cocaine, and that the more that they used cocaine, the less that cocaine played a role in their violence (Goldstein et al., 1991).

The role of the unexpected is made stunningly clear when we examine the correlation between *legal* drug use and criminal behavior. The relationship between alcohol and tobacco use and the commission of crime is strong and significant. Practically every study that has ever been conducted on this relationship has found that drinkers and smokers are *more likely* to engage in criminal behavior of all kinds—both property crime and crimes of violence—than is true of substance abstainers. Moreover, the more that one drinks, at any rate, the greater this likelihood is (Akers, 1984; O'Donnell et al., 1976, pp.82, 83). Again, what's the causal connection? And if this is true of crime's connection with *legal*—and fairly inexpensive—drugs, what does this say about the impact that legalization will have on the criminality of users of the currently *illegal* drugs? Then, too, if systemic violence is characteristic of heavy users of illegal drugs (cocaine and heroin, at any rate), what accounts for the higher crime rate of drinkers and smokers? After all, most consumers of alcohol and tobacco are presumably not members of a criminal subculture; where does their higher rate of criminality come from?

Let's be clear about this: *Most* drinkers and smokers are law-abiding; most do not engage in crime—serious crime at any rate—and most are not "criminals." When criminologists assert a connection between drug use and crime, they are talking about a correlation, a *statistical,* not an absolute, relationship. *In comparison with* alcohol and tobacco abstainers, drinkers and smokers have a higher rate of criminal offenses. Of course, there are many drinkers and smokers in the population, so this does add up to a lot of crimes, but *very few* of them commit the crimes that are likely to lead to arrest and incarceration. Still, when we're talking about differences, they are significant. And they do shed light on what is likely to happen if the currently illegal drugs were to become legalized. So, what accounts for the relationship? What's the explanation?

The explanation, according to some criminologists, is quite simple. Crime does not cause drug use, and drug use does not cause crime; attempting to determine a causal relationship between them is "a waste of time and money" (Gottfredson and Hirschi, 1990, p.234). It is not even necessary to refer to a criminal subculture, they say. (Although it may be a factor in the equation.) What's important is that "*crime and drug use are the same thing*—that is, manifestations of low self-control" (pp.233-234; the italics are mine). Essentially, this argument goes, the *type of person* who uses psychoactive substances (alcohol and tobacco included) is also the type of person who commits criminal offenses. Both drugs and crime "provide immediate, easy, and certain short-term pleasure" (p.41). Both entail engaging in an activity that satisfies a hedonistic desire for something that involves a measure of danger, risk, or harm, either to oneself or to another. And who is willing to take such risk, to expose oneself to such danger, to harm oneself or another? An actor who lacks self-control. After all, the pleasure is immediate, but the pain takes place over the long run. Hence, it is an inability to control one's desire for risky pleasures that is the key here, and that may be found both in substance abuse and in criminal activity.

Again, this is not to say that all or most substance users engage in (nondrug) crime. Or that all or most criminals are substance users or abusers. (Although the second statement probably is true.) What it is to say is that drug users and criminals are essentially the same people, at least those who use drugs and commit crime at a certain level of frequency and seriousness; these two denizens are cut from the same cloth. The kind of person who engages in one activity is likely to engage in the other; they are, in fact, motivated by the same impulse.

This fundamental fact has important implications for what is likely to happen if the currently illegal drugs were to be legalized. The fact is, the routine, garden-variety criminal behavior of the vast majority of heavy substance abusers is likely to be fundamentally *unchanged* under a program of drug legalization. Currently, the day-to-day lives of drug abusers is saturated with crime and violence; under legalization, by what magical formula is this going to be transformed overnight? If drugs were distributed inexpensively, would our current abusers commit the same level of crime to obtain more nondrug commodities? Hard-core drug abusers are typically uneducated (most are not even high school graduates), unskilled, and essentially unemployable. How will legalization change this? How will abusers obtain the basics, such as food and shelter, to live after drugs are legalized? It is not clear that legalization can transform a way of life very much. Sure, among current abusers, moneymaking crimes may decline, but this is likely to be purchased at the cost of drawing a greater number of users into the drug scene, and increasing their involvement in the drug subculture. Being able to obtain drugs legally will not change the fact that most drug abusers, now and in the future, are low impulse control, high-crime perpetrators. It is difficult to imagine what will turn them into law-abiding citizens, although some feasible programs could, conceivably, lower their crime rate a bit.

VIOLENCE, DEALING, AND ORGANIZED CRIME

Would legalization eliminate or substantially reduce the volume of violence that stems from drug dealing? It depends on the exact program in question. Extremely liberal programs relying on the ready availability of drugs on demand may very well eliminate the need for an illicit drug market, and thus have the projected impact. But as with users generally, without a source of income and essentially unemployable in legitimate jobs, how will the dealers of today earn their livelihood? Will crime, including violence, become their only source of income? What will replace what they now have? And will legalization wipe out or weaken organized crime? (Keep in mind that "organized crime" is a good deal *less* organized—that is, far more decentralized—than most people think.) The repeal of Prohibition didn't wipe out organized crime in the 1930s; in fact, Prohibition capitalized the later enterprises, some of them legal, that organized crime turned its attention and talents to. What would these ambitious, daring entrepreneurs have in store for us if a major source of their income were to be eliminated overnight? Would they become more ruthless in taking over legal enterprises? Would they turn their attention to more or less legal financial speculation? Would their new enterprises entail more, or less, danger to the public than the sale of drugs does now? Or, would the old organized criminals now be selling legal drugs? Would they then be in much the same position that purveyors of alcohol and tobacco are now? After having "gotten rich from illegal drugs," would dealers then "launder their images and play key roles in the now-legal distribution system" (Jacobs, 1990, p.29)? Would their new, legal source of income magnify their power and influence? It's anyone's guess. But one thing is certain: A legal change is not going to force them out of business. They'll do *something*, but whether this will involve more—or less—mischief for the rest of us has to remain in the realm of speculation.

Of course, the other side of the equation is that, to the extent that legalization programs are more restrictive, an illicit market will be correspondingly larger. As we've seen, illicit drug dealing can be shrunk down *only* to the extent that the current demand for these drugs can be met. To the extent that restrictions block access to them, an illicit market will flourish correspondingly. And, of course, as I've argued, increases in use are an extremely likely consequence of less-restricted access. An illicit market can be diminished, and whatever benefits there are in a reduction in the crime rate along with it, only at the expense of an increase in availability and therefore use. As with use specifically, this represents one of the central dilemmas in the issue of legalization.

SUMMARY

If a knowledgeable observer were to summarize the probable impact of legalization on criminal behavior, it would go something like this.

Legalization is likely to reduce economic crimes among current heroin and cocaine abusers to a certain extent, although probably not dramatically. But drug abusers commit a great deal of crime in their day-to-day lives, and most of that volume is not going to be affected very much. Moreover, we do not know what the impact of increased use is likely to have on the crime rate of current nonusers. And what are current dealers, high and low, going to do once their livelihood is taken away? To imagine that they will turn into law-abiding citizens overnight is fanciful. An experienced gambler is not likely to wager much money on the bet that legalization will have a dramatic impact on the crime rate.

10

Alcohol and Tobacco: The Real Dangerous Drugs?

James Q. Wilson (1990a) asks us to perform a mental experiment. Imagine, he says, that in the 1920s, alcohol had been criminalized, and cocaine and heroin remained legal. Would the criminalization of alcohol have produced a criminal underworld of users and addicts? In contrast, would the two currently illegal drugs have become socially acceptable and widely used? If so, would the legalizers now be claiming that it is *cocaine* and *heroin* that are the more dangerous drugs, and that *alcohol*, being safer, should be legalized? In short, are the legalizers being duped into thinking that legal drugs are the more dangerous, not because of their intrinsic qualities, but simply because they are more widely used? Shouldn't we be worried about what will happen when cocaine and heroin are legalized and, hence, much more widely used? There's a lesson to be learned from this mental experiment, Wilson warns.

Legalizers claim that the legal drugs, alcohol and tobacco, are more dangerous than has been acknowledged and, in fact, more dangerous than the illegal drugs—heroin, cocaine, marijuana, LSD, methedrine ("ice"), PCP (Sernyl, or "angel dust"), and the prescription drugs (when used for the purpose of intoxication rather than medication). Consequently, they say, the law and its enforcement are targeting the wrong drugs. As a result, prohibition is both discriminatory and ineffective. Why waste tens of billions of dollars, ruining hundreds of thousands of lives in the process, by criminalizing the users of comparatively *safe* drugs while the use and sale of *more* dangerous drugs are tolerated, even encouraged?

Let's go back to a point I made early in the book and separate two entirely different issues here: the *moral/ideological* and the *empirical* issues. The *moral* or ideological issue says, arresting illegal drug users but permitting consumers of alcohol and tobacco to go their merry way is *unfair* and *discriminatory*. The *empirical* issue says, alcohol and tobacco are medically more harmful than cocaine, heroin, and the other illegal drugs. The first issue, that of fairness, is essentially unresolvable; it has its roots in philosophy and even theology. Once again, it is a non sequitur, a "So what?" argument. To say that it is unfair to arrest drug users and sellers but tolerate drinkers and smokers and that, *therefore,* the former substances should be legalized, does not logically follow. There may be a variety of reasons why a given activity or substance is banned while another is permitted; their relative dangerousness is only one of them. For instance, penalizing one activity may result in far more negative consequences than the other; the total damage may tip the balance in favor of cracking down on one and tolerating the other. Consequently, let's concentrate on the second issue, the *consequentialist* or *empirical* question, and ignore the first, the moral issue. More specifically, let's examine the evidence on the relative harm of the substances in question.

What is the scorecard on harm? There is no doubt whatsoever that the legal drugs are a great deal more dangerous than most of us believe, while it's possible that the illegal drugs are less so. It's hard to imagine any public health expert questioning this point. But what about the harm of the illegal relative to the legal drugs? The legalizers argue: Let's compare the number of deaths from legal drugs with the number of deaths from illegal drugs. Pile up the bodies, and which source wins? It's legal drugs, hands down. But they also make a second empirical point as well; they argue that *if* the currently illegal drugs were to be legalized, their medical harm would decline, just as with crime and violence. Legalized, heroin and cocaine would cause less disease and fewer deaths than they do now.

As to the first point, let's look at the medical record, they say. We've already seen that the two legal drugs cause or significantly contribute to the loss of well over half a million American lives per year—430,000 for tobacco and between 100,000 and 150,000 for alcohol. The methods by which these estimates were reached are complex and technical, and widely accepted; they need not detain us here. The important point is that our legal drugs kill hundreds of thousands of users—and nonusers as well, counting victims of homicide, accidents, and passive smoke. In contrast, the legalizers say, the total number of deaths from illegal drugs adds up to a mere 3,500 in a recent year, according to one advocate (Nadelmann, 1989, p.943). Are legal drugs almost 150 times more dangerous than illegal drugs? Are alcohol and tobacco far more dangerous than heroin and cocaine? Is this possible? *Are* the legal drugs more dangerous than the illegal drugs?

The legalizers make a second and even stronger point: It is *criminalization* that makes the currently illegal drugs *as harmful as they are.* Legalize them, and they would be *even less* harmful. Here's what legalization would do, they say: regulate the production and sale of the now-illegal drugs, standardize the dose, make certain that they contain no impurities, distribute clean needles and condoms, make sure that treatment and maintenance programs are available to addicts and abusers on a walk-in basis. All these changes would result in a dramatic reduction in drug-related deaths (Nadelmann, 1989, p.942).

Legal or illegal drugs: Which category is more dangerous? While legal drugs *do* cause more deaths, there are at least four problems with the legalizers' comparison between legal and illegal drugs as sources of death. First, the comparisons that are most often made are between apples and oranges. For the *legal* drugs, deaths from *all* sources, as well as for the *entire country,* are tallied; for the *illegal* drugs, deaths from only *certain* sources and only in certain *areas* of the country are tabulated. Second, the figures on drug-related deaths are meaningless until they are connected to the *extent* and *frequency* of use. Third, as I've emphasized, we don't know whether or how these figures will change under legalization. The legalizers are placing their money on no increases in the use of heroin and cocaine under legalization; the rest of us aren't so sure about this. What if use skyrockets? And fourth, the legalization tally makes no mention of an absolutely crucial measure in the field of public health: *number of years of life lost.* But the legalizers do insist on a crucial point, one that is in their favor: A distinction must be made between *primary* (or direct) and *secondary* (or indirect) drug harms.

APPLES AND ORANGES

Let's start with the "apples and oranges" issue; for the illegal drugs, we need to estimate roughly the overall total deaths they cause. We've already seen that DAWN estimates that 430,000 drug-related emergency room episodes took place in the coterminous United States. During the same period, 8,500 drug abuse–related deaths were tallied by DAWN, but only 43 metropolitan areas were included in the program (HHS, 1994b, 1994d, 1995b). If we use the same formula DAWN used to extrapolate from the emergency rooms they studied to the country as a whole, we come up with a total of 16,500 acute drug-related deaths. Some of these deaths entailed the use of alcohol in combination with illegal drugs, and some entailed the recreational use of, or suicides by taking, prescription drugs, that is, the illegal use of legal prescription drugs. A few are the result of taking overdoses of over-the-counter drugs like aspirin and Tylenol. Even so, 16,500 deaths is a very long way from the tally racked up by the legal drugs—430,000 for cigarettes and roughly 100,000 to 150,000 for alcohol.

Of course, these medical examiners' reports on drug-related and drug-caused deaths only entail *acute* reactions, as well as deaths from fairly *direct* medical causes. We know nothing from the DAWN data about deaths from *chronic* illegal drug-related causes. We know that most of the deaths that legal drugs cause are from *chronic,* not acute, causes—for instance, lung cancer as a result of cigarette smoking and cirrhosis of the liver from excessive drinking. Yes, the major slice of the deaths that the illegal drugs cause is acute in origin. This is partly because most drug addicts, unlike drinkers and smokers, do not live long enough to become victims of many chronic drug-related illnesses. But at least two additional sources of death are worth mentioning; one is nonacute in nature and the other is not, strictly speaking, medical in origin: the first, contracting the AIDS/HIV virus, and the second, drug-related violence.

Half the roughly half a million to a million needle-using heroin addicts in the country are infected with the HIV virus. It is not unlikely that almost all of them (that is, a quarter to half a million) will die within a decade or two. And a very high proportion, perhaps as many as 10 percent, of the heaviest chronic cocaine and crack-dependent abusers are similarly infected, some through the use of needles and some as a result of engaging in unprotected sex (McCoy and Inciardi, 1995); hence, they share the same medical fate as the infected heroin addicts. Clearly, then, drug abuse is a prodigious—and growing—source of AIDS-related death. It is possible that, as a result of their use of heroin and cocaine, 25,000 to as many as 50,000 Americans *a year* will die of AIDS in the early years of the twenty-first century. The legalizers argue that these deaths are largely or entirely due to the current ban on needle exchange programs; their numbers would drastically decline under the plan legalizers propose. And AIDS is a *secondary* consequence of drug use, but that's a separate issue. And violence? Here, we're relying on a bit more speculation than for AIDS-related deaths. Roughly 25,000 Americans are murdered each year. How many are drug-related? A common estimate is that half of all large-city criminal homicides, or perhaps a quarter of the total, some 6,000 to 8,000, are causally related to the use of illegal drugs. This is a lot of people, but the total is unlikely to exceed the deaths racked up for alcohol. We discussed the issue of whether this total would rise, fall, or remain the same under legalization in the last chapter.

Suffice it to say that, if the total sources of yearly death from illegal drugs are tallied for the country as a whole, we'd come up with a total many times higher than Nadelmann's 3,500 figure. Illegal drug use is a great deal more dangerous than the legalizers claim.

EXTENT AND FREQUENCY OF USE

Second point. To me, the key question here relates to the extent and frequency of use: Under legalization, would the use of heroin and cocaine rise and, with it, the damage their use causes? Many observers say yes. I agree. As John Kaplan says, denying that it would simply ignores one of the most basic generalizations in the field of pharmacology (1988, p.33). Statistics on harm must be considered with reference to total use, or prevalence. I've already summarized the statistics on prevalence rates for the legal and illegal drugs. Not only are there more *users* of legal than illegal drugs, but their continuance rates, likewise, are considerably higher. Suffice it to say that *legal* drugs are used *vastly* more often than the *illegal* drugs are, on an episode-for-episode basis. Roughly 60 to 70 billion "doses" of alcohol (that is, drinks containing one ounce) and something like 500 billion "doses" of nicotine (that is, individual cigarettes) are consumed in the United States each year. The point is, when discussing the dangers of these two legal drugs, we must keep in mind their total number of users and the total number of *episodes* of their use. In contrast, there are between half a million and a million heroin addicts or more-or-less daily abusers, and between two and three million Americans taking cocaine weekly or more (Goldstein, 1994, p.241; Kleiman, 1992b, p.288), which add up to vastly smaller use figures for the illegal drugs than for alcohol and cigarettes. Estimating the total number of times addicts as well as the more casual users of these two drugs take heroin and cocaine is likely to be tricky; still, it is unlikely to be more than a tenth the number of doses of alcohol and one one-hundredth that of cigarettes.

On an episode-for-episode basis, which is more dangerous: using legal or illegal drugs? We may not come up with a clearly more dangerous category. Different drugs kill in different ways, and our evidence is quite messy and inexact. In the absence of more precise measures, it should be sufficient to say that, while, *descriptively,* the legal drugs kill many more Americans than the illegal drugs do, *relative to the extent of their use,* we may have something of a tie. To answer the question definitively, we'd need more data. Both categories certainly kill a lot of people; both categories include very dangerous drugs. Consider the fact that heroin appears almost as often in DAWN's lethal "overdose" statistics as cocaine—and the fact that, in the United States, cocaine is used something like 10 times as often as heroin. It seems almost certain that there is something *intrinsic* about heroin itself, not the mere fact that it is illegal, that is related to its capacity to kill.

YEARS OF LIFE LOST

Another point concerning the legalizers' flawed argument: ignoring years of life lost. Legal and illegal drugs do not kill their victims at the same age in the life span. The legal drugs kill *older* victims, and, hence, there are fewer years of life lost per victim; the average victim of the illegal drugs tends to be younger, and, hence, for each death, far more years of life are lost. Tobacco and alcohol are most likely to kill persons in their fifties, sixties, and seventies—tobacco kills those a bit older, alcohol those a bit younger; but taken as a whole and on average, they kill the middle-aged to the elderly. In contrast, heroin and cocaine are most likely to kill victims in their twenties and thirties. The fact that AIDS, almost entirely contracted from drug-addicted mothers, is the number-one killer of children age one to four in New York City is dramatic evidence that age cannot be ignored in any evaluation of harm. Thus, on a death-by-death basis, far more years of life are lost as a consequence of the use of the illegal drugs than of the legal drugs. This point cannot be ignored in any public health tabulation of the relative harm of these two categories of drugs. Even factoring this into the equation, we're still a long way from parity for the two drug categories as a source of death, but it does tip the scales a bit.

PRIMARY VERSUS SECONDARY HARM

One problem with any exercise which equates sources of death as a result of the use of different drugs is that it is difficult to separate the contribution that drug use per se makes to drug-related medical problems, death, accidents, violence, and other measures of harm and dangerousness from the legal status of these drugs. That is, are the correlations between drug use and harm a *primary* effect of the drug itself or a *secondary* product of the circumstances of use, including the drug's legal status? Says Mark Kleiman: "The failure to distinguish between the bad effects of drug abuse and the bad effects of drug abuse control sometimes reduces public discourse about drugs to gibberish" (1992b, p.17). At the same time, in some cases, this distinction is not always easy to make. "Some aspects of the drug problem defy division into results of pharmacology and results of legislation" (p.17). We know that, by itself, heroin does not make the user sick, and that moderate and controlled doses do not cause the user to die. On the other hand, heroin addicts are taking a drug that can kill them; it is *heroin* that causes addicts to overdose if they take too much. It is not legal policy by itself that causes the medical problem addicts experience, nor is it the pharmacology of narcotics alone. We must free ourselves from the clutches of either-or thinking; we must stop imagining that drugs, by themselves, are magical substances that have harmful effects—*and* that law enforcement alone is responsible for the medical harm we see in addicts and abusers. It is a combination of the two.

Nonetheless, if the currently illegal drugs were legalized, would they inflict less—or more—harm on the American public? Would as many users die of drug overdoses? Of drug-related disease? The legalizers claim that, in comparison with the legal drugs, not only are the currently illegal drugs relatively safe but they also would be a great deal *safer* if they were to be legalized (Nadelmann, 1989, pp.941–942). In opposition, the prohibitionists argue that the statistics measuring the relative harm of legal versus illegal drugs is an artifact of their legal status. Legalize the currently illegal drugs, and they will become a great deal *more* dangerous, not less. It is only because of their illegality that heroin and cocaine are expensive, difficult to obtain, and therefore relatively infrequently used; legalize them, and more people will use them—and more will become sick and die as a result (Wilson, 1990a).

As I've already argued, here I agree with the criminalizers far more than with the legalizers. The evidence is extremely strong that more people would use the currently illegal drugs if the drugs were legalized and made more readily accessible. More important, the current addicts and abusers of heroin and cocaine would use a great deal *more frequently*—and more abusively—if they found that they could obtain these drugs with less cost and less hassle than is true now. It is difficult to imagine that anyone would discount the role of opportunity in use; regardless of the restrictions that legalization might place in the path of cocaine and heroin users, the restrictions would inevitably be less binding than is true under criminalization. To the extent that restrictions would apply, addicts and abusers would simply seek out the illicit market for their needs. No amount of good intentions will alter that fact.

Still, the legalizers do make several good points. First, state-distributed drugs will be purer and more dosage-controlled than are the illicit drugs currently sold on the street. Contamination is not *the,* or even *a,* major problem for drugs sold on the street; a certain proportion of the batches of illicit drugs are contaminated, of course, but dealers who sell such goods are not likely to stay in business very long. (Marijuana sprayed with Paraquat, once a serious problem, hardly ever shows up any more.) Potency and purity vary greatly from one batch to another and can pose a serious problem for any user, but users tend to be foolhardy about the number of doses they take at one time as well as taking several different drugs at the same time. Variations in potency and purity simply adds another problem on top of several others that will still prevail, whether legalization is instituted or not. Keep in mind the fact that the rate of death among heroin addicts in the United Kingdom and the United States (mostly drug overdoses in both places) is the same, about 2 percent a year (Goldstein, 1994, p.241). Although Great Britain is a long way from legalization—some of its jurisdictions, such as Liverpool, are a great deal closer to it than others—it is also a system that is far more liberal and flexible, and less punitive, than is true of the United States. The fact that Great Britain has a somewhat different system but practically identical rates of drug-related death among addicts does not speak strongly for the legalizers' argument on harm.

Their point on expanding drug treatment programs (along with a reduction in law enforcement directed at drug violators) is well taken. The problem is, hardly any drug expert questions it. It has become almost a truism that our priorities are misplaced; instead of a budget that allocates 25 percent to treatment (and education) and 75 percent to law enforcement, including interdiction and incarceration, we should have one where this ratio is reversed. Methadone maintenance programs should be expanded; so should therapeutic communities. Needle exchange and condom distribution programs promise to keep the rate of HIV and AIDS among addicts and drug abusers from rising (Lee, 1994). Clinics in mobile vans can search out addicts who are unwilling to come into an established program and can distribute methadone, needles, condoms, medical care, and information. There are many ways that the harmful consequences of drug abuse can be kept in check short of outright legalization, and many experts support a number of them. If nothing *aside from the factors that legalizers discuss* were to change, of course, legalization would produce less disease and fewer deaths among addicts and abusers. The problem is, drug use is a dynamic and volatile proposition; many observers believe that many of the changes that legalization would bring about would result in more medical harm, not less.

THE SCORECARD

After all the possible sources of death are considered—and we have considered only a few—what does our scorecard look like? Which is the more dangerous category of drugs: legal or illegal? Are alcohol and tobacco more capable of causing harm—or heroin and cocaine? Focusing narrowly on *acute* medical effects, there is absolutely no doubt that heroin and cocaine—especially heroin—are far more likely to cause a medical emergency and lead to death by overdose *on an episode-by-episode basis*. Their contribution to DAWN's lethal medical examiners' reports is truly prodigious. (Alcohol causes many overdoses, most not counted by DAWN, but it is a far, far more widely used drug.) In contrast, focusing narrowly on direct, *chronic* medical effects, heroin and the narcotics do not cause the medical pathologies that alcohol and tobacco cigarettes do. (Incredibly, overdosing aside, narcotics cause no life-threatening medical pathologies of any kind.) It would be difficult for any drug to match alcohol's ravaging impact on the liver or tobacco's carcinogenic impact on the lungs. (The exact nature of the long-term impact of cocaine—and amphetamine—on the brain remains to be seen; we already know that in large doses over a long period of time, alcohol does damage the brain.) In addition, the illegal drugs are *indirectly* implicated in death in at least two major ways: the transmission of the HIV virus, through contaminated needles and unprotected sex, and murder resulting from dealing-related conflicts.

All in all, the sources of drug-related death from both legal and illegal substances are considerable. It is difficult to select one category over the other as incontestably safer or more dangerous. Certainly criminalization contributes to some sources of illegal drug-related death (violence and AIDS), but it may inhibit others (acute and chronic medical pathologies). In the process of weighing the relative dangers of these two drug categories, it is difficult to come away with anything other than a mixed scorecard. Legalization is extremely unlikely to result in all the medical benefits legalizers argue for it. Addicts and drug abusers lead extremely unsafe lives; a surprisingly high proportion of them drink heavily—a substantial minority of methadone maintenance patients drink at alcoholic levels—take a variety of drugs simultaneously, use wildly different quantities and potencies of heroin and cocaine from one day to the next, use unsterile needles, are oblivious to nutrition, engage in dangerous illegal activities (such as robbery), are often arrested, and so on. While some of these factors will probably change under legalization, the total picture is not likely to change very much, for the one burning factor the legalizers are unable to dismiss is a rise in drug use following legalization. This renders their argument shaky if not specious.

CONTROLS ON ALCOHOL AND TOBACCO

As I said at the beginning of this chapter, the question of whether it is fair or just to criminalize the possession and sale of heroin and cocaine while keeping alcohol and tobacco legal is essentially unanswerable; it is a moral and ideological, not a sociological, issue. However, there is no contradiction between advocating legal reform for the currently illegal drugs—even legalization—*and* tighter restrictions on the legal drugs. In fact, following the "harm reduction" line of reasoning, it is likely that more lives will be saved by making tobacco and alcohol less accessible than by instituting any conceivable drug legalization or decriminalization program. In fact, Ethan Nadelmann, a major legalization spokesperson, has argued for control strategies aimed at tobacco and cigarettes (1989, p.945), and Mark Kleiman, a drug reformer who advocates limited legalization of marijuana, supports a variety of controls on the legal drugs (1992b, 203ff., 317ff.). The logic? Again, consider the numbers: Alcohol and tobacco kill many more people than the illegal drugs do because they are much more widely used; in the case of tobacco, roughly 50 million addicts use it dozens of times each day. The legal drugs are harmful because too many people use them far too frequently. Said another way, the legal drugs are far too readily available; too many people are finding it far too easy to get their hands on them. There is practically no "hassle factor" involved in obtaining and using them. (It is only after many episodes of use—in the case of tobacco, after literally decades of use—that the debt for use must be paid.) Hence, the question becomes, how do we lower the use of alcohol and tobacco? If we are serious about rewriting legal policy to reduce harm, this is an extremely important question.

Please note that the following discussion of harm reduction strategies aimed at the legal drugs is not a display of my ideological or moral biases. I am not endorsing them as strategies so much as proposing that *if* they are adopted, fewer people will get sick and die as a result of use-related ailments. This is an empirically defensible exercise. Also note that, for tobacco at least, *almost all* smokers began the habit by age 19. Hence, any strategy that delays the onset of smoking will prolong life. This means that the most meaningful and most viable harm reduction strategies should be aimed at teenagers. The earlier in their lives that potential smokers are targeted, the greater the possible impact such a strategy is likely to have.

Can we control tobacco and alcohol abuse through the vehicle of taxation? In fact, why not kill two birds with one stone? We could increase taxes to reduce use and, at the same time, offset the costs that smokers and drinkers impose on the rest of us by charging them more for using those substances. We already know that the cost of a psychoactive substance is correlated with its use—the higher the cost, the lower the use. What increases the cost of legal drugs? Why, an increase in taxation, of course; increase the taxes on tobacco and alcohol products, and use will decline (Goldstein, 1994, p.278; Goldstein and Kalant, 1990). The data supporting our ability to kill (or at least wound) the bird of high-volume use is fairly clear-cut and unambiguous. Of course, with higher taxation comes its inevitable by-product: a certain volume of clandestine, illegal, or underground sales of the product that is taxed. But once again, choosing a total package—lower use and a larger black market versus higher use and a smaller black market—is a political and ideological not an empirical question.

The other bird isn't so easy to kill or wound, in part because the figures are more difficult to come by. Weighing the economic cost that smoking and drinking impose on the society versus the tax revenue that these products generate is an exceedingly complicated exercise. Tracing out all the economic costs, direct and indirect, of indulgence in these two legal drugs is not an easy matter; as soon as we alter one factor, the entire picture changes. Moreover, what do we include in the picture? In the case of alcohol, do we include the increased cost of an already-substantial criminal justice system? How do we measure the decline in productivity that takes place when the drinker can't show up for work? Or a decline in efficiency on the job the morning after an alcoholic binge? Another consideration: Often, observers fail to distinguish between costs that public facilities or nonsmokers incur ("external" costs) and those costs that are paid for directly by the smoker ("internal" costs). And do we calculate the costs incurred by a smoker's or a drinker's family as "external" or "internal" costs? Likewise, consider the following: Smokers get sick more often than nonsmokers and, hence, cost the rest of us far higher medical bills. However, they also tend to die at a significantly younger age; thus, they are less likely to need medical care and collect Social Security and retirement benefits when they become aged—because they more rarely *live* to be aged. Hence, ironically (at least in this one respect), the smoking habit actually *saves* the society a great deal of money! And, while heavy drinking is also related to an earlier demise, this is offset by the fact that alcoholics are more likely to *retire* significantly earlier than nondrinkers and moderate drinkers and, hence, are likely to draw public benefits for a longer period of time. Again, it should be clear that calculating the strictly economic costs of the use of the legal drugs is an exceedingly tricky proposition.

Alcoholic beverages are taxed about 25 cents per ounce of absolute alcohol; this has actually declined, relative to inflation, over the past half century. For cigarettes, the current total for local, state, and federal taxes—averaged out nationwide—is about 53 cents per pack. To put a very long and complex equation into extremely simple terms, economic experts who have studied the question say that alcohol taxes do *not* pay for the costs they impose, while taxes on cigarettes *do* pay their own way. Taxes on alcohol would have to be approximately *doubled* to reach a breakeven point (let's say to 50 cents per ounce of absolute alcohol); in contrast, all things considered, each pack of cigarettes sold only costs the society 33 cents in economic cost, for a net saving of 20 cents (Gravelle and Zimmerman, 1994; Kotata, 1989; Manning et al., 1989; Viscusi, 1995;

Warner et al., 1995). One major difference between smokers and heavy drinkers is the fact that drinkers are more likely to harm other parties in addition to themselves (accident and crime victims, for instance), while smokers are more likely to harm only themselves.

Whether we are killing one bird or two, taxation can be used as a policy both to discourage use and to pay for the costs legal drug users impose on the rest of us. To reduce the harm inflicted on society *and* reduce use, one expert has tentatively proposed a tax of $1 per alcoholic drink and $5 per pack of cigarettes (Kleiman, 1992b, pp.248, 352). Of course, the tax rate would have to be standardized—or at least the differences minimized—for all states to keep the level of smuggling to a minimum. For tobacco at least, increasing taxation "offers the single greatest opportunity for reducing the toll drug taking takes on American life. There is no comparable opportunity for improving health through policy regarding any of the currently illicit drugs" (1992b, p.354). Another consideration: The likelihood that a proposal entailing hugely increased taxes on cigarettes and alcohol will be enacted within the next two decades is very nearly zero, however much sense it makes from a public health standpoint; too many powerful vested interests would oppose the measure and, chances are, would also convince the public that it is in their interest to oppose it as well. Still, restrictions on both alcohol and cigarette consumption are taking hold nationwide on a piecemeal basis; perhaps, eventually, the wisdom of control through taxation, likewise, will begin to occur to harm reduction reformers. Kepp in mind that younger users and potential users, who have the least amount of money, will be most likely to be affected by tax increases. And keep in mind, too, that the further down the income ladder we look, taxes on alcohol and cigarettes will take up a greater proportion of the user's total income.

Harm reduction control strategies need not remain the exclusive domain of federal, state, and local government; private citizens, too, could explore ways to reduce the harm that the legal drugs cause. Aside from increasing taxes, some possible strategies might include:

> *Ban all cigarette vending machines.* This not only would reduce availability and possibly use overall but also would almost certainly reduce use among underage smokers. Although only one pack of cigarettes in 20 purchased by a teenager is obtained from a vending machine, roughly 10 times as many 14-year-olds as 18-year-olds obtain cigarettes from a vending machine. Harm reduction strategy dictates that vending machines dispensing cigarettes be banned altogether—or, at the very least, that they be banned in areas that are accessible to minors.

Enforce the law against cigarette sales to minors. Some 90 percent of teenagers say they purchase their own cigarettes (Kleiman, 1992b, p.343). Unlike establishments that sell liquor, vendors selling cigarettes do not have a license to lose; hence, violations are common. Knowing that selling to minors is illegal, nearly three-quarters of vendors questioned said that they would be willing to sell cigarettes to an 11-year-old girl (DiFranza et al., 1987). A 1993 study commissioned by the New York City Department of Consumer Affairs found that 48 of 60 stores sold *loose* cigarettes (for 15 to 20 cents apiece) to 12-to-14-year-old undercover agents; *all* the rest sold *packs* of cigarettes to these same teenagers (Messenger, 1995). Perhaps licensing for the sale of cigarettes could be explored: If vendors violate the law by selling to a minor, they lose the right to sell cigarettes. One study of 6,000 teenagers found that nearly half (45 percent) were *never* asked for proof of age (Feder, 1996).

Increase negative advertising. The alcohol and tobacco industry could be taxed to support a vigorous and effective campaign designed to reduce heavy drinking and smoking. In addition, cigarette ads blatantly aimed at children (such as the current "Joe Camel" campaign) could be banned altogether. The misleading and false disinformation distributed by the tobacco industry—the alcoholic beverage industry has not launched comparable campaigns—could be offset by counteradvertising and valid information that have a concrete impact on use. The distribution of free samples of cigarettes could be outlawed. The effectiveness of banning *all* cigarette and alcohol advertising could be explored. Would a ban it be effective? If evidence says yes, outlaw it.

Ban the export of American cigarette products abroad. As the number of cigarettes sold domestically declines, tobacco companies are targeting sales to other countries. All too often this means sales to developing Third World countries, which can least bear the burden of crushing medical expenses and the premature death of substantial segments of their populations. Should the American tobacco industry have the legal right to export death abroad? Jesse Helms, a senator from the tobacco-growing state of North Carolina, has put strong pressure on some countries that import U.S. tobacco to lift any and all tobacco restrictions. (Recall that Helms urged that federal support for AIDS be reduced because its victims brought the disease on themselves.) Such complicity with death might be exposed, publicized, and counteracted (Goldstein, 1994, p.279; Kleiman, 1992b, p.348).

Enact legislation outlawing the use *of tobacco by minors.* The fact is, purchasing a pack of cigarettes takes a few seconds, while smoking a cigarette takes a number of minutes—and, hence, the latter is much more vulnerable to detection. Such laws should *not* fall in the realm of the criminal law—entailing, as they could, arrest, jail, prison, and an arrest record—but should be regarded as minor offenses, somewhere in between a speeding ticket and a citation for driving while intoxicated. Fines, community service, or meaningful reeducation programs would be appropriate penalties (Kleiman, 1992b, pp.344–345).

Enact legislation further restricting public smoking. This has begun to take place in some locales—for instance, in restaurants in San Francisco, in restaurants above a certain size in New York City, on most airline flights, and in many work sites nationwide. Citizens could urge legislation further restricting where smokers are allowed to blow smoke in the faces of nonsmokers. The nonsmoking majority should make it clear to legislators that they endorse their right to breathe uncontaminated air.

Enforce the drunk driving laws. At present, penalties for drunk driving are ludicrously light and only fitfully applied. In Scandinavia, a loss of one's license is the penalty for first offenses, and jail sentences are imposed for second offenses; the impact of such penalties is not clear, with some observers arguing that the policy is effective and others claiming that it has no effect. An experiment in Oklahoma (Grasmick, Bursik, and Arneklev, 1993) showed that, when legal sanctions and the threat of public embarrassment and shame for drunk driving are combined, drunk driving declines. A variety of possible sanctions should be explored; what counts is what works. For the most part, however, alcohol-related auto fatalities have declined in the United States over the past two decades, from half to a third. Even among teenagers, the decline has been significant and striking. We must be doing something right.

Restrict the sale of alcoholic beverages. Should beer and wine be sold in supermarkets? In fact, perhaps the sale of all alcoholic beverages could restricted to a small number of state-run Alcoholic Beverage Control or "package" stores. Abolish all "happy hours" and all other special occasions in bars during which large discounts are offered to customers. Abolish all sale and use of alcoholic beverages at sporting events, on college and university campuses, on public transportation, and at all government functions (Goldstein, 1994, p.280). While none of these, by themselves, is likely to have a measurable impact on drinking, they send a message and set a climate that may signal a move to greater moderation in drinking.

Four additional points. First, the goal of such proposals is not to catch offenders but to reduce drinking and smoking and therefore harm; enforcement should be flexible and pragmatic, not vindictive. Second, policy should always maximize citizen-based initiative and minimize government intervention; the latter becomes necessary only when it becomes clear either that private citizens do not have certain powers or that they are unwilling to exercise them. Third, to repeat a point worth repeating, my speculation that these proposals will reduce harm to the society are empirical in nature, not moral or ideological. They may sound Puritanical and anti-hedonistic. Personally, I am very much in favor of pleasure; I indulge in it myself. But pleasure should not be purchased at the cost of far greater pain. Worldwide, in the twentieth century, tens of millions of human beings have died as a result of indulgence in the *legal* drugs. Does not such a tragic loss of life deserve—demand—effective intervention? How many will die in the twenty-first century? If we do nothing, the figure could be far greater than the number of bodies that have piled up already. And fourth, again, to repeat an important point, very few of these proposals have any hope of implementation in the near future, at least in the form in which I've stated them. Right now, they are in the realm of utopianism. But consider, as Trebach does (1993, pp.81–82), the fact that before 1990, hardly anyone would have given the peaceful collapse of the Soviet Union much of a chance. He feels that this indicates that the very long shot of some form of legalization might be possible in the United States by the year 2000. I disagree, but my guess is, some of the preceding controls over alcohol and tobacco are a great deal more likely. In 1995, the American Medical Association recommended some of these reforms (Maier and Yu, 1995). And beginning in 1996, several former employees of the tobacco industry, a scientist and an executive, presented documentation that high-level managers were aware of tobacco's addicting properties and lied about this fact under oath. Perhaps these revelations will yield valuable resources for future lawsuits against the industry and will cripple its capacity to sell a dangerous drug to the public. Some of the proposals outlined above may be adopted here and there in the near future, and perhaps many of them will be implemented during the twenty-first century. If not, it is our loss.

11

Summary and Conclusions

Beginning in the late 1980s, an almost "unspeakable" proposal (Kerr, 1988) has been advanced with great urgency and frequency: Should the currently illegal drugs be legalized? The proposal has touched off a virtual firestorm of controversy; judges, a few politicians, journalists, physicians, drug researchers, the general public, and even a few police officers have entered the fray, voicing support for the proposal. What ignited the controversy? Why now? And does it make sense?

Critics of the present policy toward drugs—"Lock 'em up, and throw away the key"—are legion. The system doesn't work, or works extremely badly, and desperately needs fixing. We are told that "everyone knows" that arresting addicts is "a failure." Tens of billions of dollars of law enforcement money are being expended on criminalizing and imprisoning hundreds of thousands of drug violators—perpetrators of a crime whose only victim is themselves. Three prison cells out of every 10 in America are now reserved for the user, the addict, the drug seller. As we saw, in 1970, there were 200,000 prisoners nationwide; in 1995, that figure surpassed a million for the first time in the history of the United States. In the earlier year, the first-time drug violator could look forward to probation; today, increasingly, it is imprisonment. We are getting tougher on drugs. Has this worked? Over the past half-dozen years, illicit drugs on the street have been getting purer, more potent, more abundant, and cheaper. Something's not working. Between 1980 and 1990, the use of illegal drugs declined sharply, but after 1990, it began rising again, albeit slightly. However, drug overdoses are increasing, new admissions to drug treatment programs are increasing, and seizures of illegal drug shipments are increasing. As law enforcement steps up the pressure, the problem seems to grow apace. How do we put an end to drug-related crime and violence, the grip of criminal drug gangs in the inner city, drug overdoses, drug use in the sixth grade? Perhaps we are doing something wrong. Perhaps the problem is law enforcement, not drug use itself. Perhaps we need a fresh look at the problem, a new solution. What about legalization?

Certainly the many criticisms of our current regime make a great deal of sense. Some of them are accompanied by impressive empirical evidence. Because drugs are illegal, they are expensive and hence, they are hugely profitable to sell. The financial incentive to go into the drug business is immense. And herein lies the rub. Drugs cannot be "stamped out" at their source, nor can they be intercepted at the border in sufficiently large proportions to make interdiction worthwhile. In fact, considering the obstacles to such efforts, it seems astounding that anyone retains a shred of faith in them. Drugs can be produced on small tracts of land in countless locations around the world. When they are stamped out in one locale, they "pop up" somewhere else. In some locales, such as Burma (or Myanmar), there is virtually no effective central government to oppose or confront drug producers; it is the drug lord who controls the territory in which drugs are produced. In others, the local or federal government has been seriously compromised or corrupted by drug producers. And smugglers are almost infinitely imaginative and resourceful in figuring out a way to get drugs through. Shipments of illegal drugs are seized, and such seizures are routinely publicized. But most officials estimate that the seizures make up anywhere from two to 10 percent of the total. Most of it gets through. But the picture is even more daunting than this: Even if half the bulk of illegal drugs were seized before distribution—an outrageous logistical impossibility—this would make a difference of only a tiny fraction of the total price of this bulk. There is no doubt about it: Stamping out drugs at their source and seizing them at the border cannot put an end to the illegal drug trade—can't even make a dent in its volume. In spite of law enforcement efforts, it's "business as usual."

Legalization turns out to be a great deal more complicated than most of both its advocates and its critics imagine, however. Hidden behind the word is a host of very different proposals, each one of which is likely to have its own special and unique set of consequences. Do we legalize marijuana only or the hard drugs as well? Do we legalize the now-illegal drugs while, at the same time, restricting access to the currently legal alcohol and tobacco? Should we put the illegal drugs on a control schedule similar to that which currently applies to the prescription drugs? If so, what is the medical justification for dispensing cocaine to a polydrug-dependent 17-year-old? And will we have to submit data, as we have to do now for the prescription drugs, demonstrating that the to-be-legalized drugs are "safe and effective"? Safe in what sense? Effective for what? Do we permit the over-the-counter sale of the now-illegal drugs in a kind of federal drug "supermarket"? Does it make sense to demand prescriptions for Valium, yet permit off-the-shelf sale of heroin? If drugs are relatively easy to obtain today, wouldn't their availability increase after legalization? Who would be able to purchase them? Who wouldn't? Who is legally liable if a teenager dies of a drug overdose after purchasing a supply of heroin from a state-controlled "drugstore"? If former smokers who get sick as a result of smoking can sue tobacco companies, can addicts sue the government for dispensing heroin and cocaine? At what dose should these newly legal drugs be sold? In what quantity? Will we permit advertising of drugs in the media? Will their manufacturers encourage consumption as aggressively as is now the case with beer, cigarettes, and automobiles? (See Inciardi and McBride, 1991, for similar queries.)

Critics of legalization schemes are far more numerous than their proponents. Many envision a "worst-case scenario" of tens of millions of new addicts dotting the urban landscape, standing on street corners, staring, zombielike, into space, or passed out in the gutter. Advocates assure us that this will not come to pass, that most Americans will be moderate in their use. Some even claim that, under the new regime, users will naturally gravitate to less harmful, less potent drugs, such as cocaine chewing gum, opium, marijuana, and peyote. But even if there is an increase in use, the advocates of legalization claim, look at all the evil consequences of the present criminalization policy; they will melt away like snow in a warm April rain. We can end drug-related crime and violence, the grip of drug gangs in the inner cities, death and sickness from contaminated drugs and drugs of variable or unknown potency, corruption and brutality of the police, the violation of the civil rights and civil liberties of citizens. Consider the advantages of legalization. Consider what we will gain. Consider what we will no longer be burdened with. The proposal sounds tempting.

But would legalization result in a greater volume of drug use? What evidence do we have that can answer the question? No one can be sure about what will come to pass under legalization. Still, some scenarios are more likely to happen than others. We do know some facts that address (but do not definitively answer) the question. We know, for example, that, in the limited sense of reducing the consumption of alcohol, Prohibition "worked"; that is, there was less alcohol consumption during Prohibition than before and after. (There were also a number of additional nasty consequences, but that is another matter.) We know that current addicts and abusers do not use as much heroin or cocaine as they'd like, that they'd like to use a great deal more than they do now. Some days they don't use at all; they can't raise the cash to make a purchase. Or they are too tired or too sick to go out and find someone to victimize for a "score." If they were able to purchase a supply of cheap, medicinally pure heroin or cocaine at a government drugstore, well, that would be different! There would be no "hassle" involved in getting their hands on what they want, and, in all likelihood, they'd use a lot more. We also know that when drugs are or were readily available (among physicians and other health workers, or as was the case among soldiers in Vietnam), use and abuse rise significantly.

We know that, for alcohol and tobacco at least, price is related to sale: The higher the price, the lower the sale. We also know that the continuance rates for the legal drugs are high: Users are very likely to continue taking them, relatively few give them up. But for the illegal drugs, continuance rates are quite low; a small minority continues to use them. Is this the "hassle factor" once again? Most knowledgeable observers know that most of us will not become addicts or abusers if the currently illegal drugs were legalized. But that is quite a different matter from recognizing that a large increase in a small minority of heavy, chronic, abusive users can inflict a great deal of damage on themselves and on the rest of us. A reading of the evidence indicates to many knowledgeable observers that, yes, the abuse of heroin and cocaine would increase under legalization. Most of us would not use these hard drugs, and even most of those who would, would do so moderately and nonabusively. It's that small minority that we have to worry about, and it's what they are likely to do that makes legalization an extremely risky proposition.

And crime and violence? Will legalization make a dent in what has become one of the nation's paramount concerns? The logic of the argument appeals to common sense. After all, drug abusers and addicts commit crime to obtain drugs because the drugs are so expensive, and they are expensive because they are illegal. Lower the price, and they won't commit crime so much. Methadone maintenance patients display the pattern: Off methadone, they commit a great deal of crime; on methadone, in comparison, their crime rate drops to half to one-third of its former level. And dealers, too, will commit a lot less crime. Right now, they kill one another (and, occasionally, an innocent bystander), often in business-related altercations. Legalization will bring this mayhem to a virtual halt.

A close inspection of the evidence leads us to some not quite so optimistic conclusions. Right now, there are a great many arrests related specifically to illegal alcohol sale and consumption (in fact, more than all drug arrests combined), and alcohol is a legal drug. Second, most experts now reject the "enslavement" model on which the legalizer's argument is based. They are pretty much agreed that—while drug use, addiction, and abuse intensify the crime rate—drugs do not generate crime. In fact, most heavy users are already well into a criminal way of life before they become involved with drugs, and, legalization or no legalization, their lives are saturated with criminal activity. Legalization cannot change this picture. Third, under several less-than-full legalization programs (such as partial decriminalization in the Netherlands), there are as many imprisonments for drug violations (almost exclusively the sale of large quantities of hard drugs) as there are in the United States. And fourth, there is a painful dilemma in "fine tuning" any legalization plan. It goes something like this: To wipe out crime, increase availability; but if availability is increased, use will increase and, along with it, a variety of harms including, in all probability, criminal activities associated with heavy use. But decrease availability, and all the ills associated with the present system will return. It is possible that this dilemma is insurmountable. No intelligent gambler is likely to place much of a bet on a drastic decline in the crime rate under legalization.

A major point in the legalizer's argument is the fact that many of the harms that the currently illegal drugs inflict are secondary or indirect harms, while all the harms of alcohol and tobacco, being legal drugs, are primary or direct harms. Even if the use of heroin and cocaine were to rise, we could not experience the damage that alcohol and tobacco inflict on the society, because these legal drugs are intrinsically more harmful. After all, the legalizers say, over 400,000 Americans die prematurely as a result of smoking cigarettes, and some 100,000 to 150,000 die from the consumption of alcohol. In comparison, the deaths from the illegal drugs represent a fraction of that number. Hence, we have nothing to fear from legalization. The argument is appealing. It is difficult to imagine a drug that contaminates the lungs the way tobacco smoke does, or one that ravages the liver as alcohol does. The problem is, we don't know whether the differential in deaths results from the extent and volume of the legal drugs or from their inherently damaging qualities. Some sources of death from heroin and cocaine would decline under legalization, such as the rate of new HIV infections. (Although, even under our current system, we could institute needle exchange and condom distribution programs, which should have the same impact.) It is entirely possible that an increase in the use of these two dangerous drugs would render the legalizer's argument questionable. Certainly the fact that 2 percent of all heroin addicts a year in the United Kingdom, where a more liberal and less punitive drug policy reigns, die, mainly from overdoses—the same figure as in the United States (Goldstein, 1994, p.241)—should make us wonder about whether anything resembling legalization would bring about the public health benefits that its advocates claim. And, at bottom, the fact that the illegal drugs are safer—or more dangerous—on a dose-by-dose, episode-by-episode basis than the legal drugs is really quite irrelevant. The fact is, of all drug programs we could institute, in all likelihood, the one that would save the greatest number of lives would be to restrict access to tobacco and alcohol. This would include huge increases in taxes, banning all vending machines, enforcing laws against the sale and use of cigarettes to minors, further restrictions on public smoking, a vigorous enforcement of the drunk driving laws, and a variety of restrictions on the sale of alcoholic beverages.

Scrutiny of legalization proposals and the criticisms that have greeted them reveals that there is much more to the debate than meets the eye. More specifically, adopting one or another side in the debate is not a simple question of weighing the relevant empirical evidence and reaching a reasoned, informed conclusion. Indeed, moral, political, and ideological considerations come into play in the debate in a major way. Where one stands on the legalization issue depends on where one stands more generally. A spectrum of ideological positions arrays itself along the legalization-prohibition continuum. Cultural conservatives see drug abuse as yet another manifestation of moral decay; they see legalization as a cowardly surrender to that decay. Free-market libertarians see drugs as property and believe that citizens should have the right of access to them, free of any government meddling or restriction. Radical constructionists see the "war on drugs" as a smoke screen; in reality, it is a war on the poor, designed to divert attention away from society's most serious problems. The solution? A redistribution of society's resources and the empowerment of the the poor and the powerless. Progressive legalizers and progressive prohibitionists agree that many reforms are necessary; where they part company is on the question of the relative importance of human rights versus public health.

Given the dense entanglement of the issue of legalization in ideological and political considerations, it is unlikely that it will be decided on empirical or consequentialist grounds alone. It is unlikely that any of the more radical proposals laid out by the legalizers will be adopted any time in the foreseeable future. However, what the debate has done is introduce some crucial issues to the public arena. The debate has been healthy. It will force a reconsideration of our current and very harmful strategy of criminalizing the addict and user. However, legitimate criticism of the present system is not the same thing as devising a viable alternative strategy. Still, perhaps when the current wave of conservatism has subsided, some of the legalizer's more moderate proposals will be given a fair hearing. It is entirely likely that a number of them will be adopted within a generation. While some of them are, in my view, seductively appealing but do not hold up under scrutiny, some others make a great deal of sense. Perhaps a detailed and systematic study will manage to sort out the productive from the harmful. I remain, on the basis of very little evidence, optimistic about the odds that at least several of the best of the legalizer's proposals will be in place in some jurisdictions during my lifetime. We live in dynamic times, and I look forward to progressive changes in our current system with great anticipation.

Appendix: A Brief Guide to Drug Effects

For the purposes of this book, the definition of drugs that pivots on psychoactivity makes the most sense, since drugs that influence the mind are often used for the purpose of intoxication or getting high, and, in turn, many users who seek intoxication use substances that achieve that intoxicating effect frequently, compulsively, chronically, and in an abusive manner. To take the process a step further, publics have become concerned, and legislatures have attempted to curtail, such abuse. Legislation which attempts to control such abuse, and whether it represents a workable and wise approach, are the subjects of this book. Hence, my focus on psychoactivity.

Different psychoactive drugs have very different sorts of effects on the human mind. Drugs are classified according to type, that is, according to the *nature* of their effects. Drugs are placed together in the same category, or put into different categories, because of the similarities and differences in these effects. To be more specific, since all drugs have multiple effects, a drug is classified according to the nature of its "main" or "principle" effect. (Side effects are those the classifier is less interested in than the "main" effect.) Below, I will summarize the effects of the most important of the psychoactive drugs, according to a commonly agreed-upon classification scheme. Following common practice, I capitalize trade or brand names (examples: Seconal, Dexedrine, Prozac) and use the lowercase letter for generic, general, or chemical names (barbiturate, amphetamine, morphine). For a more detailed, book-length, discussion of the effects of the drugs and drug types discussed here, see Goldstein (1994), Julien (1995), and Ray and Ksir (1993).

Some drugs energize, speed up, or "stimulate" signals passing through the central nervous system (the CNS), that is, the brain and spinal column. They are called *stimulants,* and they include amphetamine, methamphetamine, and cocaine. A second category retards, slows down, or "depresses" signals passing through the CNS; they are referred to as *depressants,* and they include the sedatives (such as barbiturates) and alcohol. Tranquilizers or "antianxiety agents," such as Valium and Halcion, are closely related to the sedatives. A third category of drugs comprises those whose principal action is "obtunding" or suppressing pain; they are referred to as *narcotics* or *analgesics,* and they include the opiates, or the natural derivatives of opium (principally, opium, morphine, heroin, and codeine) and the opioids, or artificial narcotics. A fourth category includes drugs which induce profound alterations in perceptions of reality; they are referred to as *hallucinogens* or *psychedelics;* they include LSD, peyote and mescaline, and psilocybin. Marijuana's effects are so different from the others that it is usually placed in a category of its own. In addition, there are several other psychoactive drugs whose use is limited to psychiatry and medicine, that is, which are very rarely used recreationally, for the purpose of intoxication, and whose use almost never leads to abuse. They include the antipsychotics (Thorazine, Stelazine, Haldol) and the antidepressants (Prozac, Elavil, Nardil); they will not be discussed here, since hardly anyone is concerned with their legal status.

STIMULANTS

Someone taking low to moderate doses of stimulants will be more alert, aroused, and mentally acute; he or she will be able to focus on a given task with greater concentration than normally. In addition, stimulants generate a feeling of confidence, competence, and well-being, even a voluptuous sense of mastery. Stimulants generate the need to engage in physical activity. As we saw earlier, of all drugs, stimulants possess the greatest *immediate sensual appeal.* This means that when experimental subjects who are unaware of what they are taking are administered stimulants, they are more likely to say they enjoyed the effects of these drugs, and want to take them again, than any other drug or drug type. Amphetamine and cocaine are stimulants; methamphetamine ("crank," "crystal," "speed," or "ice") is closely related to, but somewhat more powerful than, amphetamine. "Crack" is a crystalline but impure form of cocaine. (Technically, nicotine is also a stimulant, except that it has too many side effects to fit comfortably into this category; caffeine is a stimulant, too, but its effects are mild and subeuphoric.) Stimulants, especially cocaine, are highly reinforcing, and a substantial proportion of users end up taking them frequently and abusively; that is, they become dependent on or "addicted" to these drugs. (Most are moderate in their use, however.) At higher, abusive, levels, a substantial proportion of users become irritable, anxious, compulsively focused on activities others regard as trivial, and even paranoid, psychotic, and violent. A very high proportion of persons who commit common street crimes, especially robbery, have cocaine in their system at the time of committing the crime for which they are arrested. Heavy, chronic abuse is accompanied by a strong craving for the drug, and abstinence will bring on withdrawal symptoms, including depression, anxiety, tremors, and even seizure.

The effects of stimulants, as with all drugs, are highly dependent on *route of administration,* that is, *how they are taken,* as well as on *dose,* that is, *how much* of the drug is taken in a single episode of use. Cocaine and amphetamine are taken by four common routes of administration: first, intranasally, that is, by sniffing or "snorting"; second, by smoking or, to be more precise, by heating then inhaling the drug's vapors; and third, by injection; in addition, amphetamine may be taken orally, in the form of a capsule or tablet. Smoking is by far the quickest, most efficient means of using any drug, including the stimulants. With cocaine, including crack, smoking delivers a sudden, intense orgasm-like "rush" or jolt of pleasure directly to the brain within six to eight seconds of administration. Injecting the drug intravenously (IV), that is, directly into a vein, also generates an intense euphoric, ecstatic sensation, usually within 10 to 12 seconds. Typically, users who take stimulants by smoking or IV injecting will take fairly large quantities of the drug through this route, often 50 to 100 milligrams per "hit" or dose. Injecting directly into a muscle rather than a vein ("joy popping") produces a much slower and less intense high or intoxication. Intranasal administration (or "snorting") is an even slower, more inefficient means of getting high; for most users, its effects are voluptuously pleasurable, but less intensely so, slower to take effect, and more protracted, than is true for smoking and IV injection. The slowest, least efficient, and least intense means of getting high is oral administration, that is, by tablet or capsule, or by drinking the substance in liquid solution.

DEPRESSANTS

Depressants retard the activity of a wide range of organs and functions of the body. As a consequence, they reduce anxiety, release inhibition, and bring on sleep. In larger doses, they can induce unconsciousness and coma. An overdose of a sedative drug results from an inhibition of the breathing mechanism and, hence, deprives the brain of oxygen. Depressants also produce ataxia, or discoordination, and a lowering of an awareness of one's surroundings. In addition, they are highly addicting: If enough of any one of the depressants is taken over a long enough period of time and then use is discontinued, painful, life-threatening withdrawal symptoms will ensue—nausea, vomiting, chills, muscular spasms, and intense bodily aches and pains. With alcohol, these are known as "the DTs"—*delirium tremens*. Alcohol and barbiturates are known to cause brain damage if taken in sufficient doses over an extended period of time. Historically, alcohol and, in the first half of the twentieth century, barbiturates were used for a wide range of medical and psychiatric ailments, including insomnia and anxiety; however, as a result of the generality of their action, their addicting properties, the medical damage associated with their use, and their overdose potential, for the most part, this has been discontinued. Today, the number of legitimate medical uses for barbiturates is extremely limited. Methaqualone (Quaalude, or "'ludes"), a popular sedative of the 1970s, is no longer prescribed at all. At one time a popular street drug, in a sufficient dose, barbiturates produce a stuporous, dazed, half-conscious sensation—similar to being drunk—often accompanied by irritability and belligerence. Such use has declined sharply since the 1970s. At sufficiently large doses, antianxiety agents or tranquilizers have effects that are remarkably similar to the sedatives.

NARCOTICS

The narcotic drugs "obtund" or reduce the mind's sensation of pain; hence, they have been used for thousands of years as *analgesics,* or painkillers. (Aspirin, acetaminophen, or Tylenol, and ibuprofen are weak analgesics, but they have none of the other properties of the narcotics, including intoxication.) Narcotics generate an intense, voluptuous, orgasm-like "rush" upon IV administration; produce a strong dependency or addiction; and can precipitate death by overdose in only 10 times the dose that generates a high or intoxication. Opium, which is derived from the opium poppy, has been smoked for millennia for both ecstasy and analgesia. Morphine, first isolated in the early 1800s, is derived from opium; it is even more effective both as an intoxicant and as a painkiller. Heroin, in turn, is derived from morphine, and it produces a quicker and more intense high. The narcotic drugs that are derived from opium are generally referred to as "opiates." There are a number of synthetic or chemically produced narcotics ("opioids") as well, with effects very similar to the natural opiates—methadone, Demerol, fentanyl, and Dilaudid. All are addicting, produce an intense high, and can produce death by overdose. Heroin is the drug of choice among street narcotic addicts and abusers, but any of the other narcotic drugs will be substituted in the absence of a heroin supply. Until the late 1980s, the principal means by which street heroin addicts administered narcotic drugs was IV injection. However, recently, a new generation of abusers is taking heroin by means of smoking and snorting, often in conjunction with cocaine or crack cocaine.

HALLUCINOGENS

A group of drugs produces profound alterations in the user's perceptions of the material world. These drugs are often referred to as "hallucinogens," although this term is not entirely appropriate, since users are typically aware that these alterations are not literally or concretely "real"; in fact, true hallucinations are rare and take place only at very high doses. The term "psychedelic" is often used to refer to these drugs; it means that the mind works best (or is "made manifest") under their influence. Again, this designation is not altogether accurate either, since some perceptions of the world are reduced or distorted, while others are much more intense. There is no single term that is entirely appropriate for this drug type. LSD is the best known of the hallucinogens or psychedelics. Closely related to LSD in its effects are the peyote cactus, mescaline (the psychoactive ingredient in peyote), psilocybin (the so-called magic mushroom, or "'shrooms"), morning-glory seeds, and DMT. Some experts include Sernyl (PCP, or "angel dust") as a hallucinogen. But although some users of PCP experience hallucinations, the drug produces none of the profound alterations of perceptions of reality associated with the true psychedelics. It is best classified as a sedative and an analgesic with contradictory side effects. Likewise, MDMA, or "ecstasy," is often seen as a hallucinogen. Here, too, we observe none of the perceptual alterations associated with the true hallucinogens. Some observers prefer to refer to ecstasy as an "empathogen," or an agent which facilitates closeness with others.

Psychedelic drugs have an extremely long duration of action; with LSD, the effects can last up to eight hours. Different sets of perceptions are likely to take place at different periods or phases of the experience. Perceptual alterations and distortions are extremely common in a psychedelic drug "trip." Colors will seem extremely vivid; solid objects are often seen as unstable, dynamic, in motion; time is said to stand still or lose meaning; the senses will blend or translate into one another, so that one will "hear" color or "taste" sounds (this is referred to as "synesthesia"); boundaries between oneself and the world and between disparate phenomena in the world will seem to dissolve; mental associations will tumble one after the other, seemingly uncontrollably; one will perceive parts of one's body, and the bodies of others, in a profoundly different way—skin will seem to turn green, for instance, or hair will seem to be made of snakes; emotional intensity or exaggeration is common; one will often have the sense that one's thoughts are momentous, extraordinary, profound; great swings in mood, from ecstasy to despair, are typically reported. The "psychotic episode," or extreme panic reaction—an emotional disturbance so serious that it requires professional attention—seems to be quite rare. Likewise, "flashbacks," or the uncontrollable return of psychedelic drug effects in the absence of having taken a drug, have been reported in a significant proportion—a minority—of users. In the 1960s, it was thought that LSD damaged chromosomes and produced birth defects in the children of mothers who took the drug. This proved to be a false alarm; the drug produces no such effects.

MARIJUANA

The effects of marijuana are so different from those of all other types of drugs that it is most often placed in a category of its own. One expert refers to it as "a unique sedative-euphoriant-psychedelic drug" (Julian, 1995, p.330). Very, very few users report the sorts of profound visual and perceptual transformations with marijuana that are common with the psychedelic experience; even then, they occur only at extremely high doses. Marijuana is a natural product of the hemp or *cannabis* plant; its psychoactive ingredient is tetrahydrocannabinol, or THC. Most marijuana contains the flowering tops and some leaves of the *cannabis* plant; hashish contains only the resin of the female plant. Most commercial-grade marijuana sold on the street in the United States is 2 to 5 percent THC; hashish can be as much as 10 to 15 percent. Some specially cultivated marijuana products, such as *sinsemilla* (cultivated "without seeds") contain as much THC as potent hashish, or more. In the United States, marijuana is most often smoked; its effects rarely last longer than three or four hours, and they typically begin to tail off or decrease gradually after a half hour to an hour after smoking. Since THC is not soluble in water, it is stored in the fat or lipid cells of the body, including the liver. Hence, metabolites of THC can be found in the body more than a week after one's last episode of use. This has caused some experts to fear that chronic marijuana use may produce an accumulation of THC over a period of time, which could prove to be harmful.

Marijuana does not produce a "rush," or an intense, orgasm-like sensation, upon administration. Hence, it is not strongly dependency-producing, or "addicting." Users report feeling relaxed, peaceful, pleasant, mildly euphoric, lethargic, and drowsy. Intellectual and motor skills decline under the influence; short-term memory is temporarily impaired. Under the influence, users often report feeling hungry and finding many more things amusing than normally. Many of these effects fit in well with a variety of recreational activities, such as socializing with friends, listening to music, and making love. Most experts believe that death as a result of a marijuana "overdose" is next to impossible. Psychotic reactions seem to be extremely rare, especially considering the huge number of episodes of use. Most of the medical ravages of marijuana that were reported in the 1970s and early 1980s have not been confirmed by later research, with the exception of a decline in the efficiency and effectiveness of the lungs. The use of marijuana is associated with a decline in ambition and the motivation to succeed (the "amotivational syndrome"); it is not clear whether this is a direct effect of the drug or is an accompaniment of the characteristics of the persons who use it.

References

Abadinsky, Howard. 1989. *Drug Abuse: An Introduction.* Chicago: Nelson-Hall.

Akers, Ronald L. 1984. "Delinquent Behavior, Drugs, and Alcohol: What Is the Relationship?" *Today's Delinquent,* 3 (1): 19–47.

Anglin, M. Douglas, and George Speckart. 1988. "Narcotics Use and Crime: A Multisample, Multimethod Analysis." *Criminology,* 26 (May): 197–233.

Anonymous. 1991a. "Death Toll from Smoking Is Worsening." *The New York Times,* February 1, 1991, p.A14.

Anonymous. 1991b. "Secondhand Smoke Assailed in Report." *The New York Times,* May 30, 1991, p.A22.

Anonymous. 1995. "Drug Crackdown Is Believed to Sap Colombia's Economy." *The New York Times,* November 24, p.A7.

Anonymous. 1996. "Boston to Give Victim's Widow $1 Million in Wrongful Death Suit." *The New York Times,* April 15, p.A17.

Ball, John C., and John C. Urbaitis. 1970. "Absence of Major Medical Complications Among Chronic Opiate Addicts." In John C. Ball and Carl D. Chambers (eds.), *Epidemiology of Opiate Addiction in the United States.* Springfield, Ill.: Charles C Thomas, pp.119–142.

Beck, Jerome, and Marsha Rosenbaum. 1994. *Pursuit of Ecstasy: The MDMA Experience.* Albany: State University Press.

Beers, David. 1991. "Just Say Whoa!" *Mother Jones,* July/August 1991, pp.36–43, 52–56.

Benedict, Ruth. 1934. *Patterns of Culture.* Boston: Houghton Mifflin.

Bennett, William J. 1994. *The Index of Leading Cultural Indicators.* New York: Touchstone/Simon & Schuster.

Best, Susan. 1990. "We Can't Do Worse by Legalizing Drugs." *The New York Times,* October 3, p.A32.

Blum, Richard, et al. 1969. *Society and Drugs.* San Francisco: Jossey-Bass.

Bonner, Raymond. 1995. "Drug Smuggling Growing in Ex-Communist Lands." *The New York Times,* June 5, p.A2.

Bourgois, Philippe. 1995. *In Search of Respect: Selling Crack in El Barrio.* Cambridge, United Kingdom: Cambridge University Press.

Bozarth, Michael A., and Roy A. Wise. 1985. "Toxicity Associated with Long-Term Intravenous Heroin and Cocaine Self-Administration in the Rat." *Journal of the American Medical Association,* 254 (July 5): 81–83.

Brinkley, Joel. 1984. "The War on Drugs: Can It Be Won?" *The New York Times,* September 14, pp.A1, A12.

Brooke, James. 1995a. "Colombia Marvels at Drug Kingpin: A Chain-Saw Killer, Too." *The New York Times,* June 21, p.A8.

Brooke, James. 1995b. "Crackdown Has Cali Drug Cartel on the Run." *The New York Times,* June 27, pp.A1, A8.

Brookes, Stephen. 1990. "The Perilous Swim in Heroin's Stream." *Insight,* February 5, pp.8–17.

Brownstein, Henry J. 1993. "What Does 'Drug-Related' Mean? Reflections on the Problem of Objectification." *The Criminologist,* vol.18 (March/April): 1, 5–7.

Butterfield. Fox. 1995. "More in U.S. Are in Prisons, Report Says." *The New York Times,* August 10, p.A14.

Carter, Hodding, III. 1989. "We're Losing the Drug War Because Prohibition Never Works." *Wall Street Journal,* July 13, p.A15.

Cassidy, John. 1995. "Who Killed America's Middle Class?" *The New Yorker,* October 16, pp.113–124.

Caulkins, Jonathan P., Patricia A. Ebener, and Daniel F. McCaffrey. 1995. "Describing DAWN's Dominion." *Contemporary Drug Problems,* 22 (Fall): 547–567.

Chaiken, Jan M., and Marcia R. Chaiken. 1982. *Varieties of Criminal Behavior.* Santa Monica, Calif.: Rand.

Clouet, Doris, Khursheed Asghar, and Roger Brown (eds.). 1988. *Mechanisms of Cocaine Abuse and Toxicity.* Rockville, Md.: National Institute on Drug Abuse.

Cotts, Cynthia. 1992. "Hard Sell in the Drug War." *The Nation,* March 9, pp.300–302.

Courtwright, David T. 1982. *Dark Paradise: Opiate Addiction in America Before 1940.* Cambridge, Mass.: Harvard University Press.

Currie, Elliott. 1993. *Reckoning: Drugs, the Cities, and the American Future.* Farrar, Straus & Giroux.

Cuskey, Walter R., Lisa H. Berger, and Arthur H. Richardson. 1978. "The Effects of Marijuana Decriminalization on Drug Use Patterns." *Contemporary Drug Problems,* 7 (Winter): 491–532.

Dennis, Richard J. 1990. "The Economics of Legalizing Drugs." *The Atlantic Monthly,* November, pp.126–132.

DiFranza, Joseph, et al. 1987. "Legislative Efforts to Protect Children from Tobacco." *Journal of the American Medical Association,* 257 (24 June): 3387–3389.

Duster, Troy. 1995. "The New Crisis of Legitimacy in Controls, Prisons, and Legal Structures." *The American Sociologist,* 26 (Spring): 20–29.

Eckholm, Erik. 1986. "Cocaine's Vicious Spirals: Highs, Lows, Desperation." *The New York Times,* August 17, p.2E.

Epstein, Roberta, and Eugene E. Eubanks. 1984. "Drug Use Among Medical Students." *New England Journal of Medicine,* 311 (October 4): 923.

Falco, Mathea. 1992. "Foreign Drugs, Foreign Wars," *Daedalus,* 121 (Summer): 1–14.

Farah, Douglas, and Steve Coll. 1993. "The Cocaine Money Market." *Washington Post National Weekly Edition,* November 8–14, pp.6–8.

Feder, Barnaby J. 1996. "A Study Finds Minors Buying More Cigarettes." *The New York Times,* February 16, p.A24.

Flynn, Stephen. 1993. "Worldwide Drug Scourge: The Expanding
    Trade in Illicit Drugs." *The Brookings Review,* Winter 1993, pp.6–11.
Friedman, Milton, and Thomas Szasz. 1992. *On Liberty and Drugs: Essays on
    Prohibition and the Free Market.* Washington, D.C.: Drug Policy Foundation
    Press.
Gazzaniga, Michael S. 1990. "The Federal Drugstore." *National Review,* February 5,
    pp.34–41.
Goldstein, Avram. 1994. *Addiction: From Biology to Drug Policy.* New York: W.H.
    Freeman.
Goldstein, Avram, and Harold Kalant. 1990. "Drug Policy: Striking the Right
    Balance." *Science,* vol.249 (28 September): 1513–1521.
Goldstein, Paul J. 1985. "The Drugs/Violence Nexus: A Tripartite Conceptual
    Framework." *Journal of Drug Issues,* 15 (Fall): 493–506.
Goldstein, Paul J., Patricia A. Bellucci, Barry J. Spunt, and Thomas Miller. 1991.
    "Volume of Cocaine Use and Violence: A Comparison Between Men and
    Women." *Journal of Drug Issues,* 21 (Spring): 345–367.
Goldstein, Paul J., Henry H. Brownstein, Patrick J. Ryan, and Patricia A. Bellucci.
    1989. "Crack and Homicide in New York City, 1988: A Conceptually Based
    Event Analysis," *Contemporary Drug Problems,* 16 (Winter): 651–687.
Goldstein, Richard. 1986. "Getting Real about Getting High: An Interview with
    Andrew Weil." *The Village Voice,* September 30, pp.21–22, 24.
Gonzales, Jose E. 1992. "Guerrillas and Coca in the Upper Huallaga Valley." In David
    Scott Palmer (ed.), *Shining Path of Peru.* New York: St. Martin's Press, pp.105–125.
Gonzales, Laurence. 1985. "Why Drug Enforcement Doesn't Work." *Playboy,*
    December, pp.104, 108, 238ff.
Gooberman, Lawrence A. 1974. *Operation Intercept: The Multiple Consequences of
    Public Policy.* New York: Pergamon Press.
Goode, Erich. 1993. *Drugs in American Society* (4th ed.). New York: McGraw-Hill.
Gottfredson, Michael R., and Travis Hirschi. 1990. *A General Theory of Crime.*
    Stanford, Calif.: Stanford University Press.
Grasmick, Harold G., Robert J. Bursik, Jr., and Bruce J. Arneklev. 1993. "Reductions
    in Drunk Driving as a Response to Increased Threats of Shame,
    Embarrassment, and Legal Sanctions." *Criminology,* 31 (February): 41–67.
Grasmick, Harold G., Elizabeth Davenport, Mitchell B. Chamlin, and Robert J.
    Bursik, Jr. 1992. "Protestant Fundamentalism and the Retributive Doctrine of
    Punishment." *Criminology,* 30 (February): 21–45.
Gravelle, Jane, and Dennis Zimmerman. 1994. "The Marlboro Math." *Washington
    Post,* June 5, pp.C1, C4.
Grinspoon, Lester, and James B. Bakalar. 1976. *Cocaine: A Drug and Its Social
    Evolution.* New York: Basic Books.
Grinspoon, Lester, and James B. Bakalar. 1993. *Marihuana: The Forbidden Medicine.*
    New Haven, Conn.: Yale University Press.
Hamid, Ansley. 1990. "The Political Economy of Crack-Related Violence."
    Contemporary Drug Problems, 17 (Spring): 31–78.
HHS (U.S. Department of Health and Human Services). 1987a. *Alcohol and Health,*
    Sixth Special Report to the U.S. Congress from the Secretary of Health and
    Human Services. Rockville, Md.: National Institute on Alcohol Abuse and
    Alcoholism.

HHS (U.S. Department of Health and Human Services). 1987b. *Smoking, Tobacco, and Health: A Fact Book.* Washington, D.C.: U.S. Department of Health and Human Services.

HHS (U.S. Department of Health and Human Services). 1990. *Alcohol and Health,* Seventh Special Report to the U.S. Congress from the Secretary of Health and Human Services. Rockville, Md.: National Institute on Alcohol Abuse and Alcoholism.

HHS (U.S. Department of Health and Human Services). 1993. *Alcohol and Health,* Eighth Special Report to the U.S. Congress from the Secretary of Health and Human Services. Rockville, Md.: National Institute on Alcohol Abuse and Alcoholism.

HHS (U.S. Department of Health and Human Services). 1994a. *Annual Emergency Room Data, 1992: Data from the Drug Abuse Warning Network (DAWN).* Rockville, Md.: Substance Abuse and Mental Health Services Administration, Office of Applied Studies.

HHS (U.S. Department of Health and Human Services). 1994b. *Annual Medical Examiner Data, 1992: Data from the Drug Abuse Warning Network (DAWN).* Rockville, Md.: Substance Abuse and Mental Health Services Administration, Office of Applied Studies.

HHS (U.S. Department of Health and Human Services). 1994c. *Annual Emergency Room Data, 1992: Data from the Drug Abuse Warning Network (DAWN).* Rockville, Md.: Substance Abuse and Mental Health Administration, Office of Applied Studies.

HHS (U.S. Department of Health and Human Services). 1994d. *Preliminary Estimates from the Drug Abuse Warning Network: 1993 Preliminary Estimates of Drug-Related Emergency Department Episodes.* Rockville, Md.: Substance Abuse and Mental Health Services Administration, Office of Applied Studies.

HHS (U.S. Department of Health and Human Services). 1995a. *National Household Survey on Drug Abuse: Population Estimates 1994.* Rockville, Md.: Substance Abuse and Mental Health Services Administration.

HHS (U.S. Department of Health and Human Services). 1995b. *Annual Medical Examiner Data, 1993: Data from the Drug Abuse Warning Network (DAWN).* Rockville, Md.: Substance Abuse and Mental Health Services Administration, Office of Applied Studies.

Hilton, Michael E. 1989. "How Many Alcoholics Are There in the United States?" *British Journal of Addiction,* 84 (May): 1083–1101.

Hindelang, Michael J., Travis Hirschi, and Joseph G. Weis. 1981. *Measuring Delinquency.* Newbury Park, Calif.: Sage.

Hubbard, Robert L., et al. 1989. *Drug Abuse Treatment: A National Study of Effectiveness.* Chapel Hill: University of North Carolina Press.

Hyse, Richard. 1994. "Prohibition, for Drugs as for Alcohol, Only Fails." *The New York Times,* February 11, p.A44.

Inciardi, James A. 1992. *The War on Drugs II.* Mountain View, Calif.: Mayfield.

Inciardi, James A. (ed.). 1991. *The Drug Legalization Debate.* Newbury Park, Calif.: Sage.

Inciardi, James A., and Duane C. McBride. 1991. "The Case *Against* Legalization." In James A. Inciardi (ed.), *The Drug Legalization Debate.* Newbury Park, Calif.: Sage, pp.45–79.

Isbell, Harris. 1966. "Medical Aspects of Opiate Addiction." In John A. O'Donnell and John C. Ball (eds.), *Narcotic Addiction.* New York: Harper & Row, pp.62–75.

Jacobs, James B. 1990. "Imagining Drug Legalization." *The Public Interest,* no.101 (Fall): 28–42.

Jansen, A.C.M. 1991. *Cannabis in Amsterdam: A Geography of Hashish and Marijuana.* Muiderberg, The Netherlands: Dick Coutinho.

Johanson, Chris E. 1984. "Assessment of the Abuse Potential of Cocaine in Animals." In John Grabowski (ed.), *Cocaine: Pharmacology, Effects, and Treatment of Abuse.* Rockville, Md.: National Institute on Drug Abuse, pp.54–71.

Johnson, Bruce D., et al. 1985. *Taking Care of Business: The Economics of Crime by Heroin Abusers.* Lexington, Mass.: Lexington Books.

Johnson, Bruce D., et al. 1990. "Drug Abuse in the Inner City: Impact on Hard-Drug Users and the Community." In Michael Tonry and James Q. Wilson (eds.), *Drugs and Crime.* Chicago: University of Chicago press, pp.9–67.

Johnston, Lloyd D. 1980. "Marijuana Use and the Effects of Marijuana Decriminalization." Unpublished testimony delivered at the hearings on the effects of marijuana held by the Subcommittee on Criminal Justice, Judiciary Committee, U.S. Senate, Washington, D.C., January 6.

Johnston, Lloyd D., Patrick M. O'Malley, and Jerald G. Bachman. 1994. *National Survey Results on Drug Use from the Monitoring the Future Study, 1975–1993:* Volume II, College Students and Young Adults. Rockville, Md.: National Institute on Drug Abuse.

Johnston, Lloyd D., Patrick M. O'Malley, and Jerald G. Bachman. 1995. *National Survey Results on Drug Use from the Monitoring the Future Study, 1975–1994:* Volume I, Secondary School Students. Rockville, Md.: National Institute on Drug Abuse.

Julien, Robert M. 1995. *A Primer of Drug Action* (7th ed.). New York: W.H. Freeman.

Kaplan, John. 1970. *Marijuana: The New Prohibition.* New York: World.

Kaplan, John. 1983. *The Hardest Drug: Heroin and Public Policy.* Chicago: University of Chicago Press.

Kaplan, John. 1988. "Taking Drugs Seriously." *The Public Interest,* no.92, Summer, pp.32–50.

Karel, Richard B. 1991. "A Model Legalization Proposal." In James A. Inciardi (ed.), *The Drug Legalization Debate.* Newbury Park, Calif.: Sage, pp.80–102.

Kerr, Peter. 1988. "The Unspeakable Is Debated: Should Drugs Be Legalized?" *The New York Times,* May 15, pp.1, 24.

Kleiman, Mark A.R. 1992a. "Neither Prohibition Nor Legalization: Grudging Toleration in Drug Control Policy." *Daedalus,* 121 (Summer): 53–83.

Kleiman, Mark A.R. 1992b. *Against Excess: Drug Policy for Results.* New York: Basic Books.

Kleiman, Mark A.R., and Aaron J. Sager. 1990. "Drug Legalization: Asking the Right Question." *Hofstra Law Review,* 18 (Spring): 527–565.

Kleiman, Mark A.R., and Kerry D. Smith. 1990. "State and Local Drug Enforcement: In Search of a Strategy." In Michael Tonry and James Q. Wilson (ed.), *Drugs and Crime.* Chicago: University of Chicago Press, pp.69–108.

Kolata, Gina. 1989. "Taxes Fail to Cover Drinking's Costs, Study Finds." *The New York Times,* March 17, p.A13.

Kraar, Louis. 1990. "How to Win the War on Drugs." *Fortune,* March 12, pp.70–71, 74–75, 78–79.

Lasagna, Louis, John M. von Felsinger, and Henry K. Beecher. 1955. "Drug-Induced Changes in Man." *Journal of the American Medical Association,* 157 (March 19): 1006–1020.

Lazare, Daniel. 1990. "The Drug War Is Killing Us." *The Village Voice,* January 23, pp.22–29.

Lee, Felicia R. 1994. "Data Show Needle Exchange Curbs H.I.V. Among Addicts." *The New York Times,* November 26, pp.1, 26.

Lender, Mark Edward, and James Kirby Martin. 1987. *Drinking in America: A History* (rev. & exp. ed.). New York: Free Press.

Lettieri, Dan J., Millie Sayers, and Helen Wallenstein Pearson (eds.). 1980. *Theories on Drug Abuse: Selected Comparative Perspectives.* Rockville, Md.: National Institute on Drug Abuse.

Leuw, Ed., and I. Haen Marshall (eds.). 1994. *Between Prohibition and Legalization: The Dutch Experiment in Drug Policy.* Amsterdam/New York: Kugler Publications.

Levine, Harry G. 1991. "Just Say Poverty: What Causes Crack and Heroin Abuse." Talk presented for a plenary session on Drugs and the Underclass for the Drug Policy Foundation Annual Meeting, Washington, D.C., November.

Levine, Harry G., and Craig Reinarman. 1988. "The Politics of America's Latest Drug Scare." In Richard O. Curry (ed.), *Freedom at Risk: Secrecy, Censorship, and Repression in the 1980s.* Philadelphia: Temple University Press, pp.251–258.

Levine, Michael. 1996. "King Rats." *Utne Reader,* May–June, pp.87–95.

Lindesmith Center, The. 1993. "Drug Prohibition & The U.S. Prison System" (leaflet).

Lusane, Clarence. 1991. *Pipe Dream Blues: Racism and the War on Drugs.* Boston: South End Press.

MacCoun, Robert J. 1993. "Drugs and the Law: A Psychological Analysis of Drug Prohibition." *Psychological Bulletin,* 113 (3): 497–512.

Maier, Thomas, and Timothy Yu. 1995. "AMA Demanding Tobacco Controls." *Newsday,* July 14, pp.A6, A30.

Manning, Willard G., et al. 1989. "The Taxes of Sin: Do Smokers and Drinkers Pay Their Way?" *Journal of the American Medical Association,* 261 (March 17): 1604–1609.

Massing, Michael. 1990. "The Two William Bennetts." *The New York Review of Books,* March 1, pp.29–33.

McAuliffe, William E., and Robert A. Gordon. 1974. "A Test of Lindesmith's Theory of Addiction: The Frequency of Euphoria Among Long-Term Addicts." *American Journal of Sociology,* 79 (January): 795–840.

McAuliffe, William E., et al. 1984. "Psychoactive Drug Use by Young and Future Physicians." *Journal of Health and Social Behavior,* 25 (March): 34–54.

McAuliffe, William E., et al. 1986. "Psychoactive Drug Use Among Practicing Physicians and Medical Students." *The New England Journal of Medicine,* 315 (September 25): 805–810.

McCoy, Clyde B., and James A. Inciardi. 1995. *Sex, Drugs, and the Continuing Spread of AIDS.* Los Angeles: Roxbury.

McWilliams, Peter. 1993. *Ain't Nobody's Business If You Do: The Absurdity of Consensual Crimes in a Free Society.* Los Angeles, Calif.: Prelude Press.

Merton, Robert K. 1957. *Social Theory and Social Structure* (rev. & exp. ed.). New York: Free Press.

Messenger, Ruth W. 1995. "New York Needs to Enforce the Tobacco Act." *The New York Times,* August 10, p.A18.

Michael, Robert T., John H. Gagnon, Edward O. Laumann, and Gina Kolata. 1994. *Sex in America: A Definitive Survey.* Boston: Little, Brown.

Mitchell, Chester Nelson. 1990. *The Drug Solution.* Ottawa, Canada: Carleton University Press.

Molotch, Harvey. 1994. "Going Out." *Sociological Forum,* 9 (June): 221–239.

Moore, Mark H. 1973. "Achieving Discrimination on the Effective Price of Heroin." *American Economic Review,* 63 (2): 270–277.

Moore, Mark H. 1976. *Buy and Bust: The Effective Regulation of an Illicit Market in Heroin.* Lexington, Mass.: D.C. Heath.

Moore, Mark H. 1989. "Actually, Prohibition Was a Success." *The New York Times,* October 16, p.A21.

Moore, Mark H. 1990a. "Drugs: Getting a Fix on the Problem and the Solution." *Yale Law and Policy Review,* 8 (1): 8–35.

Moore, Mark H. 1990b. "Supply Reduction and Drug Law Enforcement." In Michael Tonry and James Q. Wilson (eds.), *Drugs and Crime.* Chicago: University of Chicago Press, pp.109–157.

Morgan, H. Wayne. 1974. *Yesterday's Addicts: American Society and Drug Abuse, 1865–1920.* Norman: University of Oklahoma Press.

Morgan, John P. 1991. "Prohibition Is Perverse Policy: What Was True in 1933 Is True Now." In Melvyn B. Krauss and Edward P. Lazear (eds.), *Searching for Alternatives: Drug-Control Policy in the United States.* Stanford, Calif.: Hoover Institution Press, pp.405–423.

Mugford, Stephen. 1993. "Harm Reduction: Does It Lead Where Its Proponents Imagine?" In Nick Heather et al. (eds.), *Psychoactive Drugs and Harm Reduction: From Faith to Science.* London: Whurr Publishers, pp.21–33.

Musto, David F. 1987. *The American Disease: Origins of Narcotic Control* (exp. ed.). New York: Oxford University Press.

Nadelmann, Ethan A. 1988. "The Case for Legalization," *The Public Interest,* no.92, Summer, pp.3–31.

Nadelmann, Ethan A. 1989. "Drug Prohibition in the United States: Costs, Consequences, and Alternatives." *Science,* 245 (1 September): 939–947.

Nadelmann, Ethan A, 1990. "Should Some Illegal Drugs Be Legalized? Legalization Is the Answer." *Issues in Science and Technology,* 6 (Summer): 43–46.

Nadelmann, Ethan A. 1991. "America's Drug Problem: Alternative Perspectives, Alternative Problems." *Bulletin of the American Academy of Arts and Sciences,* 45 (December): 24–40.

Nadelmann, Ethan A. 1992. "Thinking Seriously About Alternatives to Drug Prohibition." *Daedalus,* 121 (Summer): 85–132.

Nadelmann, Ethan A. 1995. "Europe's Drug Prescription." *Rolling Stone,* January 26, pp.38–39.

Nadelmann, Ethan, and Jann S. Wenner. 1994. "Toward a Sane National Drug Policy." *Rolling Stone,* May 5, pp.24–26.

National Institute on Drug Abuse (NIDA). 1991. *National Household Survey on Drug Abuse: Population Estimates 1991.* Rockville, Md.: National Institute on Drug Abuse.

National Institute on Drug Abuse (NIDA). 1993. *National Household Survey on Drug Abuse: Population Estimates 1992.* Washington, D.C.: U.S. Department of Health and Human Services.

Nurco, David N., Thomas E. Hanlon, Timothy W. Kinlock, and Karen R. Duszynski. 1988. "Differential Criminal Patterns of Narcotic Addicts Over an Addiction Career." *Criminology,* 26 (August): 407-423.

O'Donnell, John A., et al. 1976. *Young Men and Drugs—A Nationwide Survey.* Rockville, Md.: National Institute on Drug Abuse.

Ostrowski, James. 1990. "Has the Time Come to Legalize Drugs?" *USA Today,* July, pp.27–30.

Pileggi, Nicholas. 1982. "There's No Business Like Drug Business." *New York,* December 13, pp.38–43.

Pollan, Michael. 1995. "How Pot Has Grown." *The New York Times Magazine,* February 19, pp.31–35, 44, 50, 56–57.

Priver, David. 1993. "For Drink or Drugs, Prohibition Doesn't Work." *The New York Times,* December 16, p.A28.

Rangel, Charles B. 1988. "Legalize Drugs? Not on Your Life." *The New York Times,* May 17, p.A25.

Rangel, Charles B. 1991a. "USA 1991: One Year After Legalization." *USA Today,* July pp.31–32.

Rangel, Charles B. 1991b. "Legalizing Drugs." *The Atlantic,* March, p.11.

Ravenholt, R.T. 1984. "Addiction Mortality in the United States: Tobacco, Alcohol, and Other Substances," *Population and Developmental Review,* 10 (December): 697–724.

Ray, Oakley, and Charles Ksir. 1996. *Drugs, Society, and Human Behavior* (7th ed.). St. Louis: Times Mirror/Mosby.

Reeves, Jimmie L., and Richard Campbell. 1994. *Cracked Coverage: Television News, the Anti-Cocaine Coverage, and the Reagan Legacy.* Durham, N.C.: Duke University Press.

Reinarman, Craig. 1994. "Unanticipated Consequences of Criminalization: Hypotheses on How Drug Laws Exacerbate Drug Problems." *Perspectives on Social Problems,* 6: 217–232.

Reinarman, Craig, and Harry G. Levine. 1995. "The Crack Attack: America's Latest Drug Scare, 1986-1992." In Joel Best (ed.), *Images of Issues: Typifying Contemporary Social Problems* (2nd ed.). New York: Aldine de Gruyter, pp.147–186.

Reuter, Peter. 1988. "Can the Borders Be Sealed?" *The Public Interest,* no.92 (Summer), pp.51–65.

Reuter, Peter. 1992. "Hawks Ascendant: The Punitive Trend of American Drug Policy." *Daedalus,* 121 (Summer): 15–52.

Reuter, Peter, Gordon Crawford, and Jonathan Cave. 1988. *Sealing the Borders: The Effects of Increased Military Preparation in Drug Interdiction.* Santa Monica: Rand.

Riding, Alan. 1988. "Brazil Now a Vital Crossroad for Latin Cocaine Traffickers." *The New York Times,* August 28, pp.1, 18.

Robins, Lee N. 1973. *The Vietnam Veteran Returns.* Washington, D.C.: U.S. Government Printing Office.

Sandwijk, J.P., P.D.A. Cohen, and S. Musterd. 1991. *Licit and Illicit Drug Use in Amsterdam.* Amsterdam: Instituut voor Sociale Geografie.

Schillinger, Liesl. 1995. "The Drug Peacenick." *New York,* January 23, pp.20–21.

Seelye, Katharine Q. 1995. "Helms Puts the Brakes to a Bill Financing AIDS Treatment." *The New York Times,* July 5, p.A12.

Sethi, B.B., and R. Manchanda. 1980. "Drug Use Among Resident Doctors." *Acta Psychiatrica Scandinavica,* 62 (November): 447–455.

Shenon, Philip. 1996. "Opium Baron's Rule May End With Surrender in Myanmar." *The New York Times,* January 6, p.4.

Single, Eric W. 1981. "The Impact of Marijuana Decriminalization." In Yedy Israel et al. (eds.), *Research Advances in Alcohol and Drug Problems,* vol.6. New York: Plenum Press, pp.405–424.

Skolnick, Jerome H. 1988. "The Social Transformation of Vice." *Law and Contemporary Problems,* 51 (Winter): 9–29.

Speart, Jessica. 1995. "The New Drug Mules." *The New York Times Magazine,* June 11, pp.44–45.

Specter, Michael. 1995. "Opium Finding Its Silk Road in the Chaos of Central Asia." *The New York Times,* May 2, pp.A1, A10.

Steinberg, Neil. 1994. "The Law of Unintended Consequences." *Rolling Stone,* May 5, pp.33–34.

Stout-Wiegand, Nancy, and Roget B. Trent. 1981. "Physician Drug Use: Availability or Occupational Stress?" *The International Journal of the Addictions,* 16 (2): 317–330.

Stuart, Reginald. 1996. "Kemba's Nightmare." *Emerge,* May, pp.28–48.

Szasz, Thomas. 1992. *Our Right to Drugs: The Case for a Free Market.* New York: Praeger.

Thornton, Mark. 1992. "Prohibition's Failure: Lessons for Today." *USA Today,* March, pp.70–73.

Treaster, Joseph B. 1993. "With Supply and Purity Up, Heroin Use Expands." *The New York Times,* August 1, pp.1, 41.

Trebach, Arnold S. 1993. "For Legalization of Drugs." In Arnold S. Trebach and James A. Inciardi, *Legalize It? Debating American Drug Policy.* Washington, D.C.: American University Press, pp.7–138.

Ungerleider, J. Thomas, George D. Lundberg, Irving Sunshine, and Clifford B. Walberg. 1980. "The Drug Abuse Warning Network (DAWN) Program." *Archives of General Psychiatry,* 37 (January): 106–109.

Van Natta, Pearl, Henry Malin, Darryl Bertolucci, and Charles Kaelber. 1984–85. "The Hidden Influence of Alcohol on Mortality." *Alcohol Health and Research World,* 9 (Winter): 56–59.

Viscusi, W. Kip. 1995. "Cigarette Taxation and the Social Consequences of Smoking." In James M. Poterba (ed.), *Tax Policy and the Economy.* Cambridge, Mass.: MIT Press, pp.51–101.

Walker, Samuel. 1994. *Sense and Nonsense about Crime and Drugs* (3rd ed.). Belmont, Calif.: Wadsworth.

Warner, Kenneth E., et al. 1995. "Criteria for Determining an Optimal Cigarette Tax: The Economist's Perspective," *Tobacco Control,* 4 (Winter): 380–386.

Weaver, Mary Anne. 1995. "Children of Jihad." *The New Yorker,* June 12, pp.40–47.

Weiner, Tim. 1994. "Blowback: From the Afghan Battlefield." *The New York Times Magazine,* March 13, pp.52–55.

White, Jason M. 1991. *Drug Dependence.* Englewood Cliffs, N.J.: Prentice-Hall.

Wikler, Abraham. 1968. "Drug Addiction: Organic and Physiological Aspects." *International Encyclopedia of the Social Sciences.* New York: Macmillan, pp.290–298.

Wilbanks, William. 1992. "The Monkey Model of Addiction: A Dangerous Myth." In Erich Goode (ed.), *Drugs, Society, and Behavior.* Guilford, Conn.: Dushkin, pp.63–65.

Williams, Gerald D., David A. Clem, and Mary C. Dufor. 1994. *Apparent Per Capita Consumption: National, State, and Regional Trends, 1977–1992.* Bethesda, Md.: National Institute on Alcohol Abuse and Alcoholism.

Wilson, James Q. 1990a. "Against the Legalization of Drugs." *Commentary,* February, pp.21–28.

Wilson, James Q. 1990b. "Drugs and Crime." In Michael Tonry and James Q. Wilson (eds.), *Drugs and Crime.* Chicago: University of Chicago Press, pp.521–545.

Wilson, William Julius. 1996. "Work." *The New York Times Magazine,* August 18, pp.26–31, 40ff.

Wilson, William Julius. 1987. *The Truly Disadvantaged: The Inner City, the Underclass, and Public Policy.* Chicago: University of Chicago Press.

Wisotsky, Steven. 1990a. *Beyond the War on Drugs.* Buffalo: Prometheus Books.

Wisotsky, Steven. 1990b. "Rethinking the War on Drugs." *Free Inquiry,* Spring, pp.7–12.

Wisotsky, Steven. 1993. "A Society of Suspects: The War on Drugs and Civil Liberties." *USA Today,* July, pp.17–21.

Yett, Andrew. 1990. "All Agree on Failure of Our Drug Strategy." *The New York Times,* January 1, p.24.

Zimring, Franklin E., and Gordon Hawkins. 1992. *The Search for Rational Drug Control.* Cambridge, England: Cambridge University Press.

Name Index

Subject Index